EARTH-FRIENDLY INNS
and Environmental Travel
N O R T H E A S T

A Green Guide
to the Northeastern United States

by Dennis Dahlin

Ŝandbar
willow

Published by
Sandbar Willow Press
an imprint of WPM, Inc.
Sacramento, CA

Distributed by
Chelsea Green Publishing Company
PO Box 428
White River Junction, VT 05001
(800) 639-4099
www.chelseagreen.com

EARTH-FRIENDLY INNS
AND ENVIRONMENTAL TRAVEL NORTHEAST:
A Green Guide to the Northeastern United States
by Dennis Dahlin

Published by
Sandbar Willow Press, an imprint of WPM, Inc.
PO Box 261, Sacramento, CA 95812

Cover design by Hannelore Fischer
Cover photo: Bascom Lodge, Mt. Greylock, Mass. (Dennis Dahlin)

Back cover photo: Oil House at the Keeper's House,
Isle au Haut, Maine (Dennis Dahlin)

Text design by Tamara L. Dever
TLC Graphics, www.TLCGraphics.com

Editor: Mary Rodgers
Research Assistant: Lynn Eder
Maps: Dennis Dahlin
Illustrations: Dennis Dahlin and Lynne Green
Photos: Dennis Dahlin, unless otherwise noted
Index: Carolyn Acheson

Printed in the United States of America
on recycled-content paper using soy-based ink.

Library of Congress Catalog Card Number: 99-85717

ISBN: 0-9677076-0-9

ACKNOWLEDGMENTS

In addition to the professionals listed on the copyright page, I wish to thank Mary Proteau, Pat and Leroy Egenberger, Marge Fletcher, Bill Reinman, Mary Ruggieri, Margaret Dewar, Bill Sehl, Bruce Olson, Rudy and Janiene Platzek, Malcolm Wells and others who provided advice and support in the preparation of this book.

I also wish to express my appreciation to the staff at Chelsea Green, The Ecotourism Society, Green Hotels Association, Professional Association of Innkeepers, the library of the American Hotel & Motel Association, and the many other organizations that provided assistance.

This guide is dedicated to earth-friendly innkeepers everywhere who are providing an example for a more sustainable future.

The following acknowledgments for the use of copyrighted materials are an extension of the copyright page of this book.

- Excerpt from *Lighthouse Inn: A Chronicle*, copyright © 1997 by Jeffrey Burke, published by Pilgrim Press, Cleveland, Ohio.

- Excerpt from *The Sea around Us*, copyright © 1961 by Rachel Carson, renewed 1979 by Roger Christie; special edition published 1989 by Oxford University Press, New York, New York.

- Excerpts from the poems "Consecration by Crow" and "Urania" from *One Another* are copyright © 1999 by Jim Schley. Used with permission of Chapiteau Press, South Strafford, Vermont.

- Excerpt from *The Bottom Line of Green Is Black*, copyright ©1993 by Tedd Saunders and Loretta McGovern, published by Harper Collins, New York, New York.

- Excerpts from *Rural Hours*, by Susan Fenimore Cooper, edited by Rochelle Johnson and Daniel Patterson, copyright © 1998 and published by University of Georgia Press, Athens, Georgia.

- Excerpt from *Raptors in Love: A Wildlife Drama in Central Park*, copyright ©1999 by Marie Winn, published by Pantheon Books, New York, New York.

- Poems from *Sounds of the Land*, copyright © 1985 by William R. Stubbs, published by Sinking Springs Herb Farm, Elkton, Maryland.

MAP LEGEND

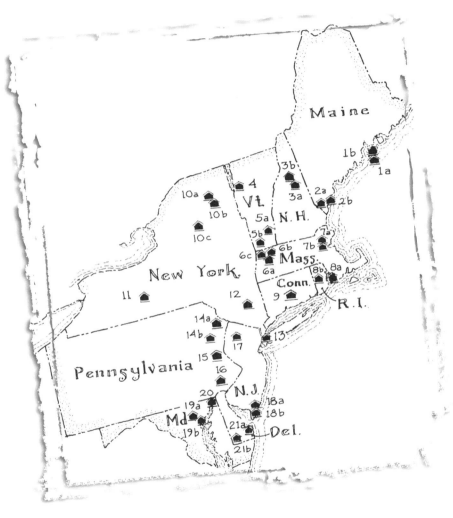

EARTH-FRIENDLY INNS OF THE
NORTHEASTERN UNITED STATES

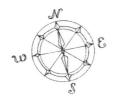

CONTENTS

Bog Laurel

Kalmia polifolia

INTRODUCTION

Across the Northeast, innovative innkeepers are finding imaginative ways to design and operate accommodations in harmony with the earth. This concern for environmental quality is embedded in the construction and operation of these pioneering inns.

Although the specifics vary, these places share a commitment to the conservation of our planet.

Organic gardens provide blackberries for the diners at a solar-heated bed-and-breakfast. On the coast, visitors study ecology at a restored lighthouse. In the mountains, guests hike to a car-free wilderness lodge. In each case, these inns serve as models where guests can learn about living lightly on the land.

This is the first in a series of environmental guides to regions of North America and beyond. Along with the featured inns, each chapter includes information about earth-friendly restaurants, natural food stores, farmers' markets, and destinations for low-impact recreation.

EARTH-FRIENDLY TRAVEL

Ill-advised travel and tourism can wreak havoc on the environment. However, travel is an important part of life for many people, providing new perspectives and an opportunity to learn about other parts of the planet.

This guide provides a way for thoughtful travelers to seek out earth-friendly places to stay overnight. Visitors to these facilities support innkeepers and nonprofit organizations working to protect the environment. In exchange, earth-friendly inns provide a safer, healthier setting for travelers.

Camping probably is the most environmentally sound accommodation, and campground guides are available for this purpose. However, when there's snow on the ground, or when you have an important business meeting in the morning, a roof over your head may be in order.

What is an earth-friendly inn?

The focus on environmental issues varies widely from inn to inn. Some facilities focus particularly on resource conservation and recycling, while others emphasize environmental education.

All of the inns in this guide have distinguished themselves in at least one area of earth-friendly endeavor. In addition, each place has its own unique poetry. Site-sensitive design, cuisine and decor in tune with the region, and idiosyncratic details all combine to provide a unique sense of place.

The term *inn* is used here in a general sense. Accommodations reflect a broad range of prices and preferences. This guide presents luxury hotels along with humble hostels. Owners may be nonprofit foundations or entrepreneurs. Lodging may serve business travelers or provide retreats for personal healing and growth.

Other than demonstrating an interest in environmental issues, these inns generally are not places that push a particular ethical agenda or religious creed. One exception is the Farm Sanctuary Bed and Breakfast, a nonprofit actively involved in animal rights issues.

TYPES OF EARTH-FRIENDLY INNS

Along with more traditional accommodations, this guide showcases unusual places to stay, such as the restored keeper's quarters at Rose Island Lighthouse and the sugarhouse at Blue Heron Farm. Across the United States, guests also can spend the night in grain bins, wine barrels, cabooses, and other recycled accommodations.

Bed and breakfast inns

In recent years, B&Bs have become a popular alternative, and the Northeast has a good selection of these inns. Owners often have rescued historic structures from an untimely demise, putting them to new use for overnight guests. For this reason alone, many B&Bs have environmental value.

Eco-friendly hotels

Owners such as the Saunders Hotel Group and Inter-Continental Hotels have led the way with earth-friendly transformations of their properties. While these highrise buildings may not look that different from conventional hotels, innovative environmental programs are operating behind the scenes. In addition, downtown accommodations usually have convenient access to energy-saving public transportation.

Camps and conference centers

The focus of this guide is on overnight lodging for individuals and families, rather than on group accommodations. However, many camps and conference centers have earth-friendly design and management. Facilities such as the University of Rhode Island's Whispering Pines Conference Center will accept individual travelers on a space-available basis.

Eco-lodges

Particularly oriented to earth-friendly visitors, eco-lodges usually provide a nature-oriented travel experience in a remote location. Environmental considerations have a high priority in the lodge design and operation.

Spas and resorts

With their lap pools and massage tables, spas may have a rigorous fitness regimen or a more laid-back ambience. Environmentally-minded spas and resorts may have organic gardens and high-quality eco-friendly furnishings, helping to promote planetary as well as personal health.

Hostels

In the past hostels were mainly the domain of vagabond students. Today hostels actually cater to a full selection of singles, senior citizens, and families who appreciate their low cost. The AMC Mohican Outdoor Center in New Jersey, an extreme example, actually offers free lodging in exchange for work.

Travelers who assume that hostels have the ambience of forced-labor camps should check the diversity of accommodations available. Although shared bathrooms are typical, many hostels have private rooms for couples and families.

Farm vacations

Agri-tourism is a growing trend, offering a chance for urbanites to spend some time in the country. At earth-friendly accommodations such as Blue Heron Farm in Massachusetts, guests can help with maple syrup production and other farm activities.

Park cabins and lodges

Travelers often assume that parks offer only camping facilities for overnight guests, but a number of state parks in the Northeast include lodges and rental cabins. Of course, a park location does not guarantee an earth-friendly seal of approval. On the contrary, park lodgings may infringe on natural habitat, and cabins may be charmlessly crowded into rural recreation ghettoes. The best of park accommodations, though, quietly nestle into the landscape, with trails and nature programs nearby.

EARTH-FRIENDLY CREDENTIALS

There are several organizations and certification programs that provide guidance in finding an eco-friendly accommodation. These memberships are not infallible screens, but listings are a good indication of earth-friendly accommodations.

An **ECOTEL** must achieve certification through a rigorous technical analysis of its operations. The ECOTEL qualifications were developed by HVS Eco Services in cooperation with the U.S. Environmental Protection Agency. Requirements include superior performance in the areas of waste management, resource conservation and code compliance. ECOTELs typically are large hotels or resorts.

■ *For more information*: www.hvs-intl.com/ecotel

The Ecotourism Society (TES) is an international nonprofit organization dedicated to sharing information about earth-friendly travel. TES has been a leader in establishing standards for responsible ecotourism. The Society serves researchers, conservationists, and businesses, providing reference materials and workshops on topics such as eco-lodge design. Several of the inns featured in this guide are TES members.

■ *For more information*: tel. 802-447- 2121
    www.ecotourism.org

The **Green Hotels Association** promotes environmental awareness in the lodging industry, focusing mainly on operational details. Compliance is voluntary, so the level of environmental commitment may vary widely. The Association's Web site has a list of current member hotels.

■ *For more information*: tel. 713-789-8889
 www.greenhotels.com

Sustainable Living Centers participate in the Hostelling International program for hostels that reduce waste, conserve resources, and use nontoxic products whenever possible. Several of these Sustainable Living Centers are in the Northeast.

■ *For more information*: tel. 202-783-6161, www. hiayh.org

USING THIS GUIDE

Each chapter features a region such as southern Vermont. One or more inn descriptions are followed by other environmental travel information on restaurants, natural food stores, and eco-friendly travel destinations.

Inn-formation

This guide does not describe the more technical aspects of environmentally conscious innkeeping and hotel management. Instead, some key features of environmental interest are highlighted.

Each inn description begins with a summary of the inn's qualities and unique attributes, followed by information on guest rooms and services.

THE FACTS

Inns frequently alter their vital statistics, so consider these facts as a fluid starting point. Web sites are particularly helpful in obtaining current information.

address
This often is a post office box. For location of the inn, check the *access* section.

phone
Inns often have a toll-free number for reservations. Fax numbers are shown in brackets.

E-mail
Handy for ordering brochures and information, these electronic addresses may change without notice.

Web site
Many inns have helpful Internet sites, often with color photos to allow a cyberview of the place. Again, don't be surprised if the Internet address has changed by the time you read this.

lodging
A summary of available rooms. Rooms with disabled access are noted where available.

rates
Since prices change frequently, approximate daily room rates are shown in the range available at press time. Actual prices are likely to vary, but at least this provides some indication of relative cost. Off-season rates or special discounts can bring down the price.

It's advisable to confirm current rates with the inn before arriving at the door. Web sites provide a handy way to check on current rates and specials.

caveats   This section flags some key limitations or unusual conditions. Inns may restrict pets or children, for example. Unless otherwise noted, inns are nonsmoking facilities.

In general, larger lodgings will be open year round. Smaller inns may shut down during holidays and slow seasons. Known closure times are listed under this heading, but it's always prudent to check ahead of time.

Keep in mind that smaller inns may not have the services a traveler would expect in a larger hotel. Some inns may not accept credit cards, and front desk hours may be limited.

credentials   These include environmental awards and memberships, as well as AAA and other general tourism ratings. Local awards often are a good indication that an inn is making a sincere and sustained effort to benefit the environment.

special interest   Key environmental features such as solar heating or organic gardening. Also included are special low-impact recreation amenities such as cross-country skiing.

DINING

For on-site dining, many inns specialize in *green cuisine*, where chefs use organic or pesticide-free products when available. Other earth-friendly culinary practices can include buying locally from quality suppliers, buying in bulk, and cooking from scratch.

Most of the inns in this guide are "vegetarian-friendly." Meatless meals can be an environmental plus, since animal products usually require more resources to produce than plant-based food.

Some places even have their own vegetable and herb gardens. For fortunate diners at these inns, the lettuce in their salad may be freshly harvested instead of shipped from remote climes.

ACCESS

The trip to the inn is an important and often-overlooked part of earth-friendly innkeeping. Guests traveling by public transit can help to reduce fuel use and air pollution. This guide provides information about bus and train access when available, in addition to directions for arrival by private vehicle.

Many innkeepers will pick up guests at nearby bus stations, train stations, or airports, sometimes at no extra charge. New York's Mohonk Mountain House staff will even pick up regional guests at their homes!

Other inns are linked by a network of hiking or bicycle routes. The Appalachian Mountain Club operates a series of huts and hostels providing shelter at the end of a hikeday on the Appalachian Trail. In Delaware, the Biking Inn to Inn program offers a welcome alternative to automobile travel.

A few places such as the Rose Island Lighthouse are reached only by water. This is a particularly fine way to arrive at an inn, allowing time to wind down while watching seagulls wheel overhead.

Each chapter includes a map showing the general location of the featured inns and nearby points of reference. These maps are not intended to provide precise directions to the inn; consult brochures or Web sites for detailed orientation.

CONSERVATION AND WASTE MANAGEMENT

Inn managers have found a multiplicity of methods to reduce waste and conserve resources. Some larger hotels and resorts have spent millions of dollars for energy-efficient equipment and materials. Even simple actions at small inns can add up to significant savings.

All of these accommodations have recycling programs in place. In addition, many inns practice "precycling," cutting down the amount of waste material by using local and bulk products with minimal packaging.

Some inns conserve resources by using solar and other alternative energy sources. Even in the northern latitude of Maine, for example, guests at Tatnic Bed & Breakfast enjoy solar-heated accommodations.

CONSTRUCTION AND RENOVATION

Some new or renovated inns have made use of eco-friendly techniques and materials. At the White Mountain

Hostel in New Hampshire, for example, tiles have been fashioned from recycled windshield glass.

In addition to their cultural value, historic inns have environmental merit, for they have helped to prolong the life of a building. Some inns are examples of *adaptive re-use*, where an old building has a new purpose.

The National Trust for Historic Preservation has designated a number of inns in this book for their historic value. National Historic Landmarks are selected by the Secretary of the Interior for their significance in illustrating or representing American history.

ENVIRONMENTAL PROGRAMS

Inns often serve an important role in providing information about natural history, as well as awareness of environmental issues. Nature walks, evening presentations, and libraries of natural history books all help to raise environmental awareness. Some inns also serve as centers of environmental education and advocacy.

ALMANAC

Each inn occupies a unique niche on the planet, where guests can rediscover subtle natural rhythms, tastes, and aromas. Inn descriptions end with a special moment in the year, a time when blueberries are ripe or the ruddy turnstones return on their yearly migration.

IN THE REGION ...

Along with the featured inns, this guide includes other earth-friendly travel information at the end of each chapter. This is not intended to be a complete guide to environmental points of interest, but a sampling of some noteworthy natural attractions, eco-friendly restaurants and shops. Environmentally-oriented destinations may include a nearby national wildlife refuge or a pedestrian-friendly city center.

other places to stay

In addition to the inns featured in each chapter, other area lodgings may have design features or programs of environmental interest. The guide's brief descriptions are not intended to be a full account of the inn's amenities and features, so phone numbers and Web sites are provided for follow-up information.

green dining

This includes regional cafés and restaurants that are noted for their earth-friendly features. In addition to vegetarian restaurants, this guide also lists eco-friendly establishments that are making positive environmental statements by selecting organic produce, using recycled products, and supporting environmental causes.

Along with their earth-friendly emphasis, most of these places have unique ambience and innovative, sometimes zany food and decor. For example, at the Joy America Cafe in Baltimore, guests can create their own chalk art on the slate bar as they wait for their drinks.

While some earth-friendly restaurants such as Philadelphia's White Dog Café serve world-class cuisine, other places are casual, often with buffet or counter service. Many are associated with natural food stores or bakeries.

provisions and shopping

This section lists stores and co-ops selling natural foods, along with specialty eco-shops. You can find out where to buy organic chokecherry wine in Brookville, Maine, or learn about a Rhode Island gallery specializing in sculpture fashioned from recycled highway signs.

resources

Under this heading are groups working to protect environmental quality in the region, ranging from local land trusts to national organizations.

for more information

Each chapter concludes with suggestions for followup reading about the region's natural history or environmental attributes. Of special interest are cookbooks, poetry, or other books written by the innkeepers.

1

MIDCOAST MAINE

We all need an "island" somewhere.
A private rooftop in Brooklyn may
do, a favorite cafe in L.A., or a
lone old oak in an Iowa cornfield.
The sum total of all our little
cubbyholes makes up the planet
earth, and the earth is no more
or no less than an atoll sanctuary
itself, adrift in a vast sea of island
stars that stretch forever.

~ Jeffrey Burke,
Island Lighthouse Inn:
A Chronicle

MIDCOAST
MAINE

ISLAND LIGHTHOUSE LODGING
The Keeper's House, Isle au Haut, Maine

"Seven hundred ninety-six panes of glass."

Jeff Burke, co-owner of The Keeper's House,
was working in the boathouse, scraping old paint
from the inn's storm windows.

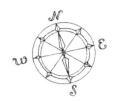

THE FACTS
The Keeper's House

address	P. O. Box 26, Isle Au Haut, ME 04645
phone	Off-island and information number: 207-367-2261.
Web site	**www.keepershouse.com**
lodging	Four rooms and two shared baths in the main house, plus a tiny furnished cottage with private outhouse. No disabled access.
rates	Price is in the $275 range per day, including all meals. Think of it as virtually your whole on-site vacation budget, since there is little opportunity to spend money on this isolated isle.
caveats	Limited communication with mainland. No pets. Often booked far in advance in summer.
credentials	Featured in national magazines and major newspapers.
special interest	Historic lighthouse, remote island setting, self-sufficiency, green cuisine.

"Each pane has wood trim on four sides. That makes three thousand one hundred eighty-four surfaces that I have to scrape, prime, reputty, prime again and then paint. And that's just the outside."

He paused to look out over the bay.

"I could replace them with modern windows," Jeff mused. "But then, a bridge could be built to the island, too."

Sometimes the old ways are best. And The Keeper's House on Isle au Haut is a living museum, a relic of Maine's maritime history. Built in 1907 by the Coast Guard, the building and its isolated island surroundings have changed only slightly. The lighthouse operation is now automated, and the living quarters have metamorphosed into an inn operated by Jeff and Judi Burke.

Isle au Haut (pronounced *eye-la-HOE*) is an ideal sanctuary for regaining your bearings and responding to the natural rhythms of this forested outpost. If you want space, this is the place to be. Even at the peak of summer season, no more than about three hundred people will be found on this twelve-square-mile island.

ACCESS

Isle au Haut is located several miles off the Maine coast. While the island itself is virtually car-free, private transportation or rental cars are needed to reach this isolated part of Maine. Or, if you're arriving by air, local residents can provide shuttle service from the Bangor or Bar Harbor airports to the mailboat.

From Highway 1, follow sinuous Route 15 through about thirty-six miles of coastal scenery. Along the way, you'll pass through Blue Hill, one of Maine's most picturesque villages.

The road ends at the water's edge in Stonington. Other than charter craft, the only way to reach the island is via mailboat. Check on schedules when you make inn reservations, and plan to arrive early. Secure parking is available near the Seabreeze Avenue dock.

While you're waiting for departure, Stonington's picturesque streets offer architectural surprises ranging from weathered dockside warehouses to an improbable opera house. If you have time, stop in at the eccentric antique and junk shop just up the hill from the ferry dock, where you can buy "experienced" golf balls for twenty-five cents.

The forty-five-minute mailboat ride to the island is a minor adventure in itself. The craft handles freight as well as passengers, so you may share space with lumber and crates of produce. Even on a sunny summer day the mailboat will pitch around a bit, so the trip in rough weather is not for timid landlubbers.

The route to Isle au Haut wends through an ellipsis of islets and wave-sculpted granite rocks. Channels around the island bear quaint names such as The Turnip Yard, while two peninsulas are labeled Eastern and Western Ear. Observant passengers may spot porpoises, harbor seals, guillemots, and a wide variety of other wildlife.

Arriving by boat, with its measured pace, allows a transition from journey to destination. While timetables are of the utmost importance in beginning the ferry ride, time seems suspended once you're on the water.

The mailboat docks a short distance from the inn. A vehicle is available to help with luggage. Once you're on the island, though, bicycles and footpower are the preferred transportation modes. The inn provides bikes for guests.

THE INN

The gambrel-roofed Keeper's House rises from the island's bedrock. Sharing the forested shoreline are the light tower (not accessible to guests) and the Oil House, an outbuilding formerly used for storing fuel.

Facing the light tower, *The Keeper's Room* allowed the lighthouse keeper to maintain a close vigil over the beacon. Furnishings include an iron bed, sea chest, painted antiques, and potbelly stove. *The Garret* is an eccentric space on the top floor, with water views, angled ceilings, and a generous sitting area. *The Horizon Room* features the innkeepers' favorite water view, while the spacious *Sunrise Room* has a sunny exposure and a trundle bed.

A few hundred feet up the shore, *The Oil House* is a tiny masonry building with slate roof and private deck. The adjacent outhouse has an open-air solar shower. Tucked among the trees, the Oil House is a favorite of honeymooners, notwithstanding the outdoor plumbing.

THE
OIL
HOUSE

Keep in mind that this is an isolated, get-away-from-it-all place. No TV, no fax, no video games, no in-room phones. In fact, there is no phone at the inn, *period*, although a telephone is located at the general store on the island. A VHF radio is on hand for emergency communication.

CONSERVATION

Out of necessity, the isolated inn is largely self-sufficient. Photovoltaic panels provide solar power for the lighthouse beacon. Wood stoves rage constantly in cold weather, providing heat for the inn. A small amount of propane is used to run a generator, which primarily is used to pump water. After sunset, the night horizon is punctuated only by solar-powered lighthouse beacons, while candles and kerosene lanterns illuminate the inn's quaint rooms.

In spite of the abundant rainfall, water is scarce on the island, and conservation is essential. Even at full capacity, The Keeper's House uses less than 500 gallons of water per day.

The island has a model recycling program, with virtually every resident participating. The inn's owners strive to generate as little trash as possible, by buying in bulk and using returnable bottles. Recycling bins are provided for guests.

LOBSTER WITH PASTA

meat from two steamed lobsters, cut into chunks

1 tsp. fresh or ¼ tsp. dried dill

1 tsp. fresh or ¼ tsp. dried tarragon

juice of one lemon and one lime

2 tbsp. olive oil	2 cloves garlic, minced
2 tbsp. dark rum	½ cup heavy cream
4 chopped scallions	½ tsp. pepper

Heat oil in large skillet, and brown garlic over high heat. Add lobster meat and cook for one minute. Add all ingredients except cream. Stir in cream and heat gently. Serve over homemade pasta.

—Judi Burke, from *Kitchen with a View*

DINING

The Burkes have published a cookbook, *Kitchen with a View*, featuring Ida's Sea Clam Pie and other popular recipes. Other recipes are included in *Island Lighthouse Inn: A Chronicle*, Jeff's account of innkeeping adventures. Candlelight dinners featuring fresh local seafood are a highlight, as well as the Finnish pancakes that frequently appear at breakfast. Sunday night is lobster night.

The innkeepers have zero tolerance for processed food. Even pasta is made fresh. With most cooking from scratch, there is little packaging to discard. Plenty of fresh Maine seafood is provided, as well as chicken, but no red meat is served. Vegetarians are welcome, and nonmeat options are available. Picnic lunches can be packed for day hikers.

An organic kitchen garden contributes lettuce, tomatoes, peppers, herbs, and flowers for the table. Seaweed provides phosphate for the garden, while a six-foot fence deters deer.

ACTIVITIES

Here is one of Maine's best kept secrets: an outlying portion of Acadia National Park is located on the island. Intrepid visitors can experience Acadia without the crowds and cars. The Isle au Haut park unit is limited to fifty visitors per day, so hikers wanting solitude can find it here.

With the dearth of automobiles, the entire island is a great place for hiking and bicycling. For those intimidated by the frigid ocean water, Long Pond offers somewhat more temperate temperatures for swimming.

*A*n early autumn stroll on
Isle au Haut is framed by
russet ferns, lichens, and mosses.
White puffs of Alaska cotton dot
the marshes. Along the trail are
numerous blowdowns; these felled
trees are testaments to gales from
winters past.

To the Canadian north, cirrus
commas scrawl across the sky.
These high clouds hint at the coming
season of legendary winter storms
that sweep through these parts.
But for the present, the bay's waves
still reflect the September sun,
and gulls wheel easily on the
breeze around The
Keeper's House.

Tides and Tombolos on Penobscot Bay

Goose Cove Lodge, Sunset, Maine

From your vantage point on Barred Island,
you watch as the tide rises almost imperceptibly,
narrowing the tombolo of sand that links the
offshore islet with the Goose Cove Lodge property.
The swirling coastal currents have created this
ephemeral land bridge, building up two sandy cusps
that have created a sandbar — at low tide.

But the width of the peninsula shrinks with each wave.
Finally, as the bar is about to close, you stride back
to Deer Isle and the waiting lodge.

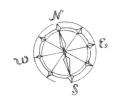

THE FACTS
Goose Cove Lodge

address	Deer Isle, PO Box 40 Sunset, ME 04683
phone	207-348-2508, reservations 800-728-1963 [Fax 207-348-2508]
e-mail	goosecove@goosecovelodge.com
Web site	**www.goosecovelodge.com**
lodging	Twenty-three private cabins, rooms, and suites, all with private baths. One disabled-accessible unit.
rates	From $120 single or double per day in low season to about $450 for cabins in high season.
caveats	Restaurant and most rooms closed mid-October to mid-May. No televisions, telephones, or radios in rooms.
special interest	astronomy, guided nature walks

Earth-Friendly Inns: Northeast

Barred Island is a diminutive nature preserve, just a few minutes' walk from your room at Goose Cove Lodge. This is just one of the many special features that accent a stay at this inn.

The Lodge was built in the 1940s by Dr. Ralph Waldon, a naturalist and university professor who would offer botany and other nature courses. This tradition has been continued by the current owners, Dom and Joann Parisi.

THE INN

Guests can choose from seven secluded cottages or rooms in the main lodge. The *Lookout Room* in the main lodge is a suite with a splendid ocean view.

Most rooms have living rooms with fireplaces. Cottages include kitchenette facilities and sleep four to six persons, while attached cottages sleep two to four persons. All cottages and attached cottages have an ocean view, while rooms in the main lodge have ocean or woodland views.

DINING

Locally grown food is featured here, from fresh Maine blueberries to shiitake mushrooms. Breakfast is served buffet style, and guests gather around large tables for family-style dinners. Penobscot Bay fisherman's stew with *aioli* is a specialty, and fish-shaped pastries provide a whimsical touch. On Friday nights, guests are treated to a lobster bake on the beach.

The dining room ambience combines classical music with the coastline view. During the peak season, children dine separately in the recreation hall.

The owners buy locally from organic purveyors of produce, chickens, and eggs. Two kitchen gardens provide herbs and vegetables for the table. The garden is fertilized with seaweed and manure. The surrounding woods and

meadows contribute wild raspberries, blackberries, and blueberries. Vegetarian menu options are provided daily.

Modified American Plan is required during peak season, including a full breakfast, hors d'oeuvres, and a four-course dinner. Optional bed and breakfast rates are available in the off season. Meal service is limited to breakfast mid-May to mid-June and mid-September to mid-October.

CONSERVATION

Recycling is incorporated into the lodge operation. For starters, kitchen scraps are fed to a neighbor's pig. For a small but significant touch, glass stemware is provided in rooms, instead of plastic glasses.

The property is heavily wooded, mostly with red spruce and balsam fir. At last count, 169 bird species have been identified on the site. Native rugosa roses form a solid stand along the beach in front of the lodge. No pesticides or commercial fertilizers are used on the property.

The Lodge provides a wealth of information about the local environment, including nature walks and presentations by local craftspeople. The inn's library includes natural history guides, Maine literature, and old astronomy magazines. After dinner, guests or locals often provide music, a movie, or a slide show.

ACTIVITIES

Naturalists, hikers and artists seek out Goose Cove Lodge. Many migratory birders return year after year. Guests can paddle the inn's kayaks and canoes past seals and porpoises.

A former science teacher, Dom shares his knowledge on guided nature walks. Hikes on the site are a delight, with networks of narrow trails winding through the forest.

Dom has a special interest in astronomy. On clear nights, he may set up his 550-power telescope for guests to explore the sky. A Peruvian guest once arrived armed with computer printouts and spent several nights gazing through the telescope at the unfamiliar Northern Hemisphere heavens.

ACCESS

Goose Cove Lodge is reached by Highway 15. After crossing the causeway southbound onto Deer Isle, turn right at the village. Continue for three miles to Goose Cove Road; turn right and follow for 1.5 miles to the Lodge at the end of the road. No public transit is available.

I n late summer, dried seaweed and mussel shells crunch underfoot as you stroll along the beach. Waves mark the sand with subtle strands of sea foam, and wind fills the sails of an offshore windjammer.

Red spruce and balsam fir provide a backdrop for the first New York asters, an incipient sign of autumn. The wild roses along the shore combine their scent with the salt air to produce the essence of Goose Cove Lodge.

In the region ...
MIDCOAST MAINE

The corrugated coastline of **Acadia National Park** has been a popular tourist destination since the mid-nineteenth century, when Frederic Church and other landscape painters popularized the scenery. Although parts of the park are overrun at times with many, many, many tourists, Acadia offers opportunities for quality low-impact recreation away from the publicized attractions.

In addition to the seldom-visited park segment on Isle au Haut, Acadia includes most of Mount Desert Island, as well as the Schoodic Peninsula on the mainland. In summer, the crowds concentrate in the Bar Harbor area and along the Park Loop Road.

Sand Beach, along the loop road, is the exception to the typical stony shoreline in the park. Tiny fragments of clam, mussel, and sea urchin shells add a distinct texture to the beach sand. In contrast, smooth cobblestones pave **Little Hunter's Beach,** a seldom-visited stretch of coast accessible by wood stairs.

Ironically, none other than John D. Rockefeller (and his fossil-fuel fortune) was instrumental in providing for nonmotorized transportation in the park. Rockefeller first donated more than ten thousand acres of parkland. Then, concerned about the impact of automobiles, he funded the construction of one-lane carriage roads winding for fifty miles through the park. Seventeen stone bridges along these routes are noteworthy for their fine craftsmanship. Today, these paths are appreciated by bicyclists, hikers, and equestrians, as well as cross-country skiiers in winter.

OTHER PLACES TO STAY

On Penobscot Bay's western shore, **The Craignair Inn** was originally built in the 1930s as a boardinghouse for stonecutters. This gambrel-roofed building, as well as a former church and general store, have been recycled as an inn, with a dining room open to the public. Located on the edge of a quiet village, the inn has an organic garden. A nearby 300-acre island is accessible at low tide, featuring spruce forests and abandoned apple orchards. Open mid-May to mid-October.

- *Clark Island Road, Spruce Head, ME 04859, tel. 207-594-7644,* **www.craignair.com**

GREEN DINING

The time-honored way to partake of fresh local fare is at one of the lobster shacks along the coast. A genuine Down-East establishment will provide an ocean-view picnic table — and a rock for cracking your steamed lobster.

Since the 1970s, this part of the state also has sprouted a good selection of environmentally oriented restaurants. In particular, the port town of Belfast is a haven for organic produce and vegetarian cuisine. Sauteed fiddleneck ferns are a regional delicacy in late spring.

A durable Maine institution, **Darby's** has operated continuously since 1865. The pressed tin ceiling and antique bar add to the atmosphere. A favorite hangout of local artists, Darby's features creative cuisine using natural ingredients. Pad Thai is a menu standout, along with the Mahogany Duck marinated in honey and soy sauce. The menu has plenty of vegetarian options. Open seven days a week for lunch and dinner; lunch in the $5 to $8 range, with dinner running about $10 to $16.

- *155 High Street, Belfast, ME, tel. 207-338-2339*

PROVISIONS AND SHOPPING

The village of Blue Hill is noted for its artists and antiques. The **Blue Hill Co-op** offers a variety of natural foods, including organic cheeses, baked goods, and seasonal organic produce. Open seven days a week in summer.

- *Greene's Hill Place, Main Street, Blue Hill, ME 14614 tel. 207-374-2165*

Belfast Co-op is a diverse place with cafe, deli, and bakery as well as whole natural foods, flowers, seafood, and organic produce. Open seven days a week.

- *123 High Street, Belfast, ME, tel. 207-338-2532*

The **Sow's Ear Winery** sells English-style hard cider produced from organic apples, as well as fruit from the winery's orchard. The Sow's Ear also produces organic rhubarb, blueberry, and chokecherry wines. A tasting and sales room is seasonally open Tuesday through Saturday. Watch for the copper sign of the sow at the corner of Route 176 and Herrick Road.

- *Brooksville, ME 04617, tel. 207-326-4649*

RESOURCES

Friends of Acadia is a nonprofit organization dedicated to preserving the park and its surroundings. The group works with park visitors, area businesses, and government agencies to create a local conservation ethic.

- *P.O. Box 725, Bar Harbor ME 04609*
  www.foacadia.org

FOR MORE INFORMATION

Jeff Burke has written *Island Lighthouse Inn: A Chronicle,* recounting his experiences as an innkeeper on the Maine coast. This award-winning book includes accounts of everyday adventures and simple pleasures of life in this remote setting. *Cleveland, Ohio: The Pilgrim Press. Hardback, 182 pages, $21.95.*

2

SOUTHERN MAINE

*... the continents themselves dissolve
and pass to the sea, in grain after
grain of eroded land. So the rains
that rose from it return again
in rivers. In its mysterious past it
encompasses all the dim origins of
life and receives in the end, after,
it may be, many transmutations, the
dead husks of that same life.
For all at last return to the sea —
to Oceanus, the ocean river, like the
ever-flowing stream of time,
the beginning and the end.*

— Rachel Carson, *The Sea around Us*

MAINE

Portland

295

95

Biddeford

1

Tatnic
B & B

9A

9

the Colony Hotel

Kennebunkport

Wells

9

North
Berwick

95

Ogunquit

Cape Neddick

Mt.
Agamenticus

N

to
Boston

ATLANTIC

OCEAN

SOUTHERN
MAINE

QUILTING AT A SOLAR INN
Tatnic Bed & Breakfast, Wells, Maine

Long before recycling bins were in vogue,
quilting was a resourceful way to re-use fabric scraps.
This tradition is updated at Tatnic B&B, where co-owner
Jane Smith is nationally known for her quilting
workshops. Jane sews and sells custom quilts, totebags,
quilted sweatshirts, and mail- order quilting supplies.
In addition, she organizes an annual Amish bus trip,
travels to quilting seminars on weekends,
and offers weekly quilting classes.

Guests arriving at Tatnic know that they are in for
something different when they walk across the
long boardwalk from the road to the house,
crossing a frog-filled bog. A quilted banner
by the door gives the first hint of what is ahead.
Inside this solar home, quilts are everywhere.

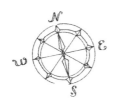

THE FACTS
Tatnic Bed & Breakfast

address	62 Tufts Road, Wells, ME 04090-7427
phone	207-676-2209
e-mail	tjsmith@gwi.net
lodging	Two rooms with shared bath.
rates	About $42 to $65. Rates for single travelers are particularly reasonable. Breakfast is included in the price.
caveats	No disabled access to guest rooms. The winding staircase may be a concern for some visitors.
credentials	The inn and its quilting programs have been featured in national magazines.
special interest	Solar heating, organic farming, quilting, land conservation.

Complimenti al maestro! Grazie.
— *an Italian guest at Tatnic*

Accommodations

In the tradition of barnraising, friends helped the Smiths build the rustic, passive solar home in the late 1970s. Additions have come along in each succeeding decade. Jane now has a two-story studio for private quilting lessons, complete with a Gammill quilting machine.

The two "treetop" rooms on the second floor (complete with quilts, of course) are reached via an open curved oak staircase. One room has an extra-long queen bed and space for three cots, while the other has a twin-king option. A sleeping playpen is available for infants. The bath on the first level is shared with the owners.

Access

The inn is located a short drive from Route 1 or I-95, at the end of a rural road. Check with the innkeepers for directions. With advance arrangements, the owners will pick up guests arriving by public transportation.

The Land

While Jane quilts, her husband Tin is working in the fields or forest with Sparky and Chrissy, the draft horses. Tin farms organically, and he's an active member of the Maine Organic Farmers and Gardeners Association.

Tin practices sustainable logging in the third-growth forest, selectively thinning trees. Most of the construction lumber for the inn was sustainably harvested, using draft horses to reduce forest damage. Logs then were milled on the property.

With the assistance of the horses, Tin farms eight acres of Maine potatoes and other crops. The farm also includes an apple orchard, beehives, and assorted turkeys.

Tin seeks out alternatives to commercial fertilizer. For example, he collects seaweed that washes up on the road in Wells. The seaweed, as well as compost and manure, have helped to rejuvenate the Maine soil.

DINING

Breakfast is served after Tin feeds the horses. A typical breakfast at Tatnic includes fresh-baked blueberry muffins or breads, granola, and honey from the farm's beehives. Corn pancakes are served with real maple syrup, and homemade applesauce is another breakfast highlight. Vegetarian, vegan, and other special diets are cheerfully accommodated.

The garden, apple orchard, and woodland supply fresh fruit and vegetables in season. And after the first frost arrives, there is an abundance of home-canned goods and apple cider in the pantry.

Factoring in produce from neighbors, in fact, the Smiths are largely self-sufficient. The inn's owners have gone for a month or more in winter without venturing out to the grocery store.

CONSERVATION

This is a rare example of a solar home with no need for fossil-fuel backup heating. In winter, at this northern latitude, solar heating is supplemented with wood heat, using firewood from the property.

Domestic hot water is solar-heated in two thirty-gallon tanks. To take full advantage of the sun's heat, evening showers are suggested, although auxiliary backup heat is available. Water is heated by the wood stove in winter.

The surrounding forest keeps the home cool on warm summer days, for the house is designed to be cooled with natural ventilation.

ENVIRONMENTAL INFORMATION

Many visitors come to the inn because of their interest in land conservation. Tin is an active member of the Great

Works Regional Land Trust, and is glad to share his knowledge with guests. In addition, Tin works on special projects with the Wells National Estuarine Research Reserve, such as measuring mummichogs (small fish) and installing a computerized weather station.

An orientation booklet includes information on local environmental groups and programs. Tin also will prepare a local map, customized for each visitor's special interests.

ACTIVITIES

This is a low-key place for relaxing rambles along the miles of trails that wend through the woods. Visitors also can use these disused lanes for cross-country skiing in winter. Guests are invited to come along with Tin for the morning feeding of the horses and other farm activities.

TIN WORKING THE FIELDS WITH SPARKY AND CHRISSY.

The tree swing is a great place to listen to the wind singing in the pines. A screened porch offers a place to enjoy the outdoors minus mosquitoes.

It's just six miles to the oceanfront at Ogunquit. Tin reports that there is great surfing at the nearby beaches. By the way, in case you think that the Maine coastal waters are too cold, Tin can tell you stories about the iceberg-infested water on his six-week kayaking trip in Greenland.

*T*he inn is open all year,
so guests have the opportunity
to enjoy the changes of the seasons
here. The apple orchards burst into
bloom in mid-May, highlighting
the spring season.

As midsummer day approaches,
hummingbirds visit the abundant
flower gardens. Visitors can pick
wild blueberries in July and August.

The first frost arrives in
mid-September, and the apple
harvest extends from about the tenth
of September to the tenth of October.
And at the close of the calendar
year, winter is a time for hardy
visitors to enjoy walks on the
nearby uncrowded beaches.

SEASIDE CONSERVATION
The Colony Hotel, Kennebunkport, Maine

Perched on a promontory, the Colony Hotel
is a great mass of Georgian architecture gone to sea,
with shutters and verandas and white-painted
dormers overlooking the Atlantic. One of the last
grand oceanfront resorts still in business in
New England, the Colony also is one of the
best examples of eco-friendly hotel
management in America.

Owner Jestena Boughton's family has owned
and operated the Colony since 1948. Jestena,
a landscape architect, took on full responsibility
for hotel management in 1986. Building on the
hotel's tradition of conservation, Jestena has
worked with the staff to begin a complete
environmental program at the hotel.

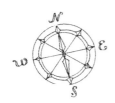

THE FACTS
The Colony Hotel

address PO Box 511
Kennebunkport, ME 04046

phone 800-552-2363 (reservations)

207-967-3331 (fax 207-967-8738)

e-mail reservations@thecolonyhotel.com

Web site **www.thecolonyhotel.com/maine**

lodging 123 rooms, with breakfast included.

rates $175 to $425 per day. High-end peak season rates from early July to early September. Group rates available. Reduced off-season rates.

caveats Closed November to mid-May.

credentials Member, Green Hotels Association and The Ecotourism Society. Winner of the Maine Chamber & Business Alliance Environmental Excellence Award and other environmental awards.

special interest Historic preservation, oceanfront location, comprehensive environmental programs.

THE HOTEL

With 123 rooms in three buildings, the hotel offers a variety of ocean-view or garden-view rooms. The Ocean Grand Rooms are particularly spacious, with king-size beds and hand-hooked wool rugs on hardwood floors. The Ocean Rooms command a premium for their ocean view, while the Gardenside Hotel and Garden House Rooms are lower on the price ladder. Rooms in the original building are preferred to quarters in a modern addition.

Breakfast is included in all room rates. Guests receive a 25% discount on other meals.

DINING

The hotel supports Maine fishermen and the regional economy through its policy of purchasing locally whenever possible. The hotel's gardens provide organic herbs for the kitchen, as well as table bouquets and edible flowers for desserts and garnish.

During summer months, the award-winning Sunday brunch is a highlight of the week. Throughout the week, local seafood is a specialty, and vegetarian options are available. Typical entrees include crab and shrimp Newburg, lobster and maple-cured ham, while English trifles are a standout on the dessert list. In summer, guests enjoy poolside lunches. Weekday afternoon tea is served throughout the season.

The hotel's lobster buffet includes New England clam chowder, Maine potatoes, fresh corn on the cob, fresh local steamed mussels, and steamed lobster with drawn butter and lemon. Colony-baked cornbread and blueberry pie top off this traditional feast.

CONSERVATION

The Colony Hotel Environmental Responsibility Program focuses on solid waste reduction, material reuse, recycling, and resource conservation. To translate the program into action, the staff includes a recycling chief, a director and manager of environmental programs, and an on-site naturalist.

Hotel workers have played a central role in the Colony's environmental efforts. Representatives from each department of the hotel meet monthly to discuss environmental issues, and to share information about new products and program changes. There are "Eco-Tip" bulletin boards for employees and guests. Staff members participate in an Employee Suggestion Program for ways to improve the resort's environment.

Staff members are active in environmental and green business organizations. The hotel's memberships include the Green Hotels Association, The Maine Buy Recycled Alliance, National Audubon Society, Sierra Club, the Ecotourism Society, and other groups.

Organic and mechanical pest control techniques are used in buildings. Nontoxic cleaning materials are selected for kitchen and housekeeping use. In the laundry, environmentally safe detergents are put to use. The administrative offices and purchasing department support community businesses by purchasing as many locally made products as possible, reducing the need to ship goods from distant sources.

To save energy, the hotel is replacing incandescent lighting with more energy-efficient fixtures. Whenever possible, new machinery is Energy Star Compliant.

Signs in the rooms give guests the option to skip having sheets and towels changed every day. About one-third of the guests choose this option, which saves substantial energy and water.

The hotel's operations have been analyzed down to minute details to maximize recycling. For example, old sheets are trimmed and used to line cribs. Even the lint from laundry dryers is made available to birds for nesting material.

Buying in bulk eliminates excessive packaging. Soda and food cans, paper, glass, and plastics are recycled, with bins placed in all work areas, dormitories, and hotel floors. Each guest room has a recycling bin.

The Colony's gift shop takes recycling in a whimsical direction. Remnants of the hotel's old comforters, bed skirts, and curtains are stitched together to make balsam-filled frogs and pillows. Worn-out bedspreads are metamorphosed into mannequins. Wine corks, spools, and other debris from the Colony's beach become holiday ornaments. These gifts can be placed in crafted boxes produced from discarded cardboard and calendars.

Recycling applies to the office as well. The hotel buys recycled paper products for office use. Newsletters and promotional materials are printed on recycled paper. For additional paper savings, all photocopying is double-sided.

When the Colony is ready to close in autumn, leftover food and supplies are donated to area churches and shelters. The hotel also works with a local waste management entrepreneur to donate materials that local recycling centers do not accept.

As a result, the Colony diverts massive amounts of material from the local landfill. Over a period of several years, some sixty tons of potential trash have been recycled and re-used.

THE SITE

Surrounding the hotel are eleven acres of wetlands, meadow, woodland, orchard, and ocean beach. Formal herb and flower gardens flank the building, including roses planted by the current owner's grandmother.

As might be expected with a landscape architect at the helm, the site is treated in a resource-conscious manner. Kitchen waste is composted and applied to herb and flower gardens. Composted sludge is used for fertilizer. Prunings are chipped and placed as mulch around landscape plants to control weeds and to retain moisture.

Rather than pesticides, the hotel relies on biological controls to treat fungus and insect problems. Maintenance workers pull weeds by hand rather than spraying herbicides.

In renovating the site, Jestena Boughton selected native plants that are accustomed to the coastal climate and soil. Left in remote parts of the site, logs and brush piles serve as shelter for wildlife. To reduce the need for lawn mowers, some areas of turf have been replaced with natural vegetation. As a result, the National Wildlife Federation has certified the hotel as a U.S. Backyard Wildlife Habitat.

GREEN CONSTRUCTION

Each year, about twenty to twenty-five rooms are renovated at the Colony. The hotel emphasizes the use of environmentally conscious construction materials and methods such as the use of cellulose insulation made of recycled newspapers.

To enhance natural lighting in guest rooms, the hotel re-uses antique transom glass. Furniture is restored rather than replaced when possible, and latex paints are selected to minimize paint fumes.

For a finishing touch, birdhouses and bathouses on the hotel grounds are built from wood scraps and other left-over construction materials. Their diminutive designs evoke local traditional architecture.

ENVIRONMENTAL INFORMATION

The in-room guest services directory includes a summary of the hotel's Environmental Responsibility Policy, a pamphlet for a self-guided Eco Visit, and information on current events and programs of environmental interest. The hotel also makes a bird and animal sighting list available. The Colony also sponsors presentations by local experts on history, fishing, and the natural environment of the area.

Use of recycled building materials has an honorable tradition at the Colony Hotel. When an earlier resort was destroyed by fire, the cupola was rescued from the ruins and placed atop the hotel. Since 1914, the hotel cupola has served as a nautical landmark for mariners entering the Kennebunk River.

ACTIVITIES

Hotel guests can choose from a variety of recreation programs, including bocce, horseshoes, putting green, croquet, badminton and shuffleboard. A heated Olympic-sized saltwater pool is popular on warm days, and hardy swimmers also can head for the hotel's sandy beach.

Bicycles are available for rent. With its pedestrian-friendly location, the Colony is well-situated for summer strolls on the streets of Kennebunkport.

On summer Saturdays, the hotel's naturalist conducts guided walks geared to children and adults. With a focus on coastal ecology, the groups visit tidepools and other natural habitats. On rainy days, visitors can inspect the original oil paintings of Maine artists on display throughout the hotel.

Nearby maritime recreation options include interpretive sea kayak trips, sailing, kayaking, lobster-boat cruising, and whale watching. Inland, there's a choice of horseback riding, canoeing on the Mousam River, tennis, golf, antiquing, and architectural walking tours. Birders can visit nearby Mt. Agamenticus, a premier hawk-watching lookout. For transit history enthusiasts, the Seashore Trolley Museum in Kennebunkport features rides on restored trolleys.

After a day exploring the coast, the hotel's verandas are a welcome place to relax. The view from the Colony takes in a panorama stretching from Gooch's Beach to Nubble Light.

S ummer is the season at the Colony. With the changing of the tides comes a sea turn, an onshore breeze in the summer afternoons, cooling the rooms at the Colony Hotel. The breeze stirs the spectacular summer show of cleome blossoms in the hotel's half-moon garden, appreciated by generations of hotel guests.

In the region ...
SOUTHERN MAINE

Wells National Estuarine Research Reserve protects 1600 acres of natural habitat and a historic saltwater farm, with marsh, upland, and four miles of coastal barrier beaches. Within the preserve are Rachel Carson National Wildlife Refuge lands, as well as state property and land owned by the town of Wells. There's a visitor center, guided tours, and seven miles of trails for recreational hiking.

■ *342 Laudholm Farm Road, Wells, ME 04090*
   tel 207-646-1555

Portland, Maine's largest city, has achieved recognition for its efforts to improve urban ecology. The city is noted for its parks, pedestrian-friendly streets and traffic-calming plans. In downtown Portland, the **Maine College of Art** has successfully recycled a neglected department store building. Eco-friendly construction materials and methods were incorporated into the renovation, and the completed building has been designated as a noteworthy recycling project by the federal government.

■ *522 Congress Street, Portland, ME 04101*
   tel. 207-775-3052

OTHER PLACES TO STAY

Rocky Meadow Farm Bed & Breakfast is a recently-constructed log cabin with a stone foundation and fireplace. The two guest rooms have a separate entry. Energy-conserving features include a solar greenhouse and solar domestic water heating.

■ *607 Emery's Bridge Rd., South Berwick, ME 03908*
   tel. 207-676-9264

GREEN DINING

Frankie and Johnny's Natural Foods is recommended by the Tatnic Innkeepers. A local artist has provided exuberant decor. Potato pancakes are served with smoked tomato chutney and sour cream. *Crustolis* are a specialty here, with their ten-inch diameter crust; the Zaatar incorporates capers, olives, red onions, and feta cheese. The menu is plentifully sprinkled with vegetarian items. *Inexpensive. No credit cards.*

- *1594 Route 1, North Cape Meddick, ME 03902
  tel. 207-363-1909*

Located in an industrial area of Portland, **Silly's** is a small but energetic restaurant with an eclectic menu selection and retro fifties decor. Many meals are served on large pita rounds. Locals recommend the Jamaican rice and beans. Vegan options are offered. All menu items are made from scratch. The owners make special efforts to recycle and to compost food waste. Open daily for lunch and dinner. *Inexpensive.*

- *40 Washington Avenue, Portland, ME 04101
  tel. 207-772-0360*

Voted best vegetarian restaurant in a recent poll of area diners, **Pepperclub** divides its menu between innovative seafood and vegetarian items such as crabmeat-and-asparagus quesadillas and vegetarian moussaka. Organic wines and coffee are served, and local organic produce is used whenever possible. *Moderate.*

- *78 Middle Street, Portland, ME 04101, tel. 207-772-0531*

PROVISIONS AND SHOPPING

In a convenient town location, **New Morning Natural Food Market**, supplies the area with organic produce. This new shop's shelves are packed with healthy items.

- *6774 York Street, Kennebunk, ME 04043
  tel. 207-985-6774*

The Whole Grocer offers seasonal organic produce and dairy products as well as a large selection of bulk foods. The store has a large offering of vitamins and eco-friendly household products. The small natural foods deli sells soups by the pound, sandwiches and salads. The store is active in recycling efforts and gives food waste to a local farmer for composting.

- *127 Marginal Way, Portland, ME 04101, tel. 207-774-7711*

RESOURCES

The **Great Works Regional Land Trust** is a conservation organization serving southern Maine. The trust works with landowners to encourage the protection of natural, agricultural, historic, and other resources. So far, the Trust has protected sites ranging from working farms to woodland and stream corridors, through the use of conservation easements, land donations, and acquisitions. The Trust's zany fundraising auctions feature everything from face-painting to handpainted mailboxes and hand-carved canoe paddles. Tatnic innkeeper Tin Smith is a former president of the trust.

- *P.O. Box 151, South Berwick, ME 03908, tel. 207-676-2209*

The **Laudholm Trust** is a supporting organization for the Wells National Estuarine Research Reserve. The trust works in partnership with the private sector and government agencies in the areas of land preservation, environmental research, education, and restoration of Laudholm Farm.

- *P.O. Box 1007, Wells ME 04090, tel. 207-646-4521*

FOR MORE INFORMATION

The Maine coastline offers some of the best birding in the United States, and the Maine Audubon Society maintains an excellent Web site for the latest information on rare bird alerts, a Puffin Page, an online birding bookstore, and a Maine Bird Checklist.

- Check it out on the Society's Web site:
  www.mainebirding.net

Lowbush blueberry

3

NEW HAMPSHIRE

After the sun set to us, the bare summits were of a delicate rosaceous color, passing through violet into the deep dark blue or purple of the night which already invested their lower parts, for this night-shadow was wonderfully blue, reminding me of the blue shadows on snow. There was an afterglow in which these tints and variations were repeated. ... In the meantime, white clouds were gathering again about the summits, first about the highest, appearing to form there, but sometimes to send off an emissary to initiate a cloud upon a neighboring peak ...

— Description of White Mountains,
Journal of Henry David Thoreau, July 13, 1858

NEW
HAMPSHIRE

Green Construction in the White Mountains

Hostelling International – White Mountains, Conway, New Hampshire

Bathroom tiles made from smashed airplane windshields.

Carpet fabricated from recycled plastic bottles.

Drywall produced from construction scraps.

This is not your ordinary building.

Architect Richard Moore has incorporated recycled and eco-friendly materials everywhere in this award-winning retrofit of a New Hampshire farmhouse. And the day-to-day management of the hostel carries out the environmental theme, from colorful recycling chutes in the kitchen and rain barrels to capture roof runoff.

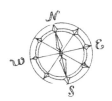

THE FACTS

Hostelling International – White Mountains

address	36 Washington Street, Conway NH 03818
phone	603-447-1001
e-mail	hiconway@nxi.com
Web site	**www.angel.net/~hostel** A detailed and well-designed site, with a virtual tour of the hostel and its eco-features.
lodging	Total of 43 beds, including dorm rooms and four private rooms. The recently renovated building is designed for disabled access.
rates	Inexpensive. At last report, $16.00 buys IYH members overnight lodging and linens *plus* a continental breakfast. For nonmembers, the cost is just $3.00 more.
caveats	Closed in November. During the day, closed from 10:00 am to 5:00 pm. Hostel doors are locked at 10:00 pm. Reservations are advised, especially during busy winter weekends and holidays.
credentials	Earth-friendly design features have been featured in many publications.
special interest	Sustainable construction and operation, bicycling

THE INN

Guests arriving at the hostel can put on headsets and take a self-guided sustainable tour that explains the inn's various eco-features. The tour highlights environmental aspects of the interior and exterior and concludes with a description of plans for a straw-bale amphitheater, wood-chip heater, and solar hot tub. A virtual tour is available on the hostel's Web site.

White Mountain Hostel has a total of 43 beds. Rather than the military-sized dormitories of many hostels, the smaller dorm rooms here have four to six beds each. In addition, three private rooms hold up to two adults and two children.

ACCESS

Conway is located on Routes 16 and 302 in northern New Hampshire, just a short distance from Maine. Detailed driving directions are available from the hostel, or on their Web site.

Concord Trailways has service from Boston to Conway. There's also a private shuttle service from Boston. Consult the hostel's Web site or call them for details.

Many visitors arrive by bicycle, since the hostel is a stop on a national bike route. The hostel has a new bike repair room, with full truing stands and all necessary tools.

DINING

Guests have a complimentary continental breakfast of juice, coffee or tea, and bagels. For other meals, guests can make use of a full kitchen as well as a backyard barbecue. Visitors are welcome to pick seasonal vegetables, blueberries, and blackberries from the hostel's garden.

CONSTRUCTION

The building's numerous green features begin with the front steps and access ramps. These are constructed of

TREX, a product which blends recycled plastic and saw-dust.

Underfoot, the carpet is made from recycled soda bottles, and bathroom floor tiles were produced from recycled airplane windshields. The hostel's linoleum floors are made with renewable-source oils. The underlayment for the flooring is produced from recycled newspaper.

Overhead is a traditional pressed-tin ceiling, supported by a composite beam made of wood chips assembled with a nontoxic glue. The drywall was produced from recycled construction scraps.

Special care was taken to use VOC-free paints that don't release toxic chemicals into the air. A water-based ure-thane was selected for the wood floors.

Wood furnishings also have an environmental focus. Most furniture was purchased from a New Hampshire company known for its recycling of wood waste. Many tables and chairs are made of local ash surfaced with water-based cat-alyzed finishes and lacquers. Rather than the formalde-hyde furniture glues in common use, the hostel's furniture is joined with a low-toxic multi-bond glue.

CONSERVATION

Recycling is most visible in the kitchen, where three chutes for recycled materials have been decorated by local artist Anne McCoy. These chutes zip recyclables to the basement for convenient sorting and removal. A compost bucket collects kitchen scraps that eventually become a rich soil amendment for the garden.

The office operates on the Three Rs of "Recycle, Re-Use, and Reduce." Office staff members use recycled products, right down to the paper clips.

To save energy, many light switches have been replaced by motion detectors. These sensors automatically acti-vate the lights when someone is in the room, then turn them off when people leave. The elegant old light fixtures were retrofitted with efficient compact fluorescent bulbs. Since older buildings often leak a lot of heat, the structure was weatherized and thoroughly insulated. A hyper-efficient Swedish washing machine saves water, energy, and detergent.

For water conservation, faucets are metered, shutting off the flow after a predetermined amount of water is delivered. Low-flow shower heads have been installed in the bathrooms. Outside, roof runoff is collected in rain barrels.

MAINTENANCE

The hostel management selects non-toxic cleaning products to protect the health of visitors as well as the planet. They avoid phosphates and chlorine bleach. Paper goods are produced from post-consumer recycled paper. The hostel's citrus-based cleaner comes in handy for everything from kitchen grease removal to cleaning bicycle chains.

THE SITE

The hostel has an organic garden and compost facilities. Any leftover produce is donated to the local soup kitchen.

Trees have been planted around the hostel to reduce stormwater runoff and to help with natural cooling in summer. The exterior deck is made from wood treated with a low-toxic preservative.

ACTIVITIES

The main attraction here, of course, is the White Mountains. With over 750,000 acres of forest, there's plenty of room to hike, ski, and canoe. During the summer, bikes, canoes, and kayaks can be rented at nearby Kayak Jack's, where hostel guests receive a discount. Volleyball is a popular activity on the hostel's spacious grounds.

For winter guests lacking ski equipment, there are free loaner cross-country skis (check first before leaving yours at home, though). The hostel provides free lockers for guests.

Winter options range from downhill and cross-country skiing to snowshoeing, sledding, and snow tubing. Ice climbing is big in these parts, and local instructors are available for novices.

*A*lthough winter is the most popular time to visit, don't count out other times of the year. From spring windflowers to the fall foliage display, there are eleven months of variety (the hostel is closed in November). Guided or self-directed hiking, moose watching, birdwatching, and porcupine watching all are popular. Ripe blueberries are an added attraction in early autumn.

Hiker-friendly Huts

AMC Huts and Lodges, White Mountain Region, New Hampshire

Crawford Hostel

For more than a century, the Appalachian Mountain Club has operated an innovative system of hiker-friendly facilities in New Hampshire and elsewhere in the Northeast. Spaced along the Appalachian Trail, huts provide shelter for distance hikers who don't want to lug around a tent. AMC lodges provide another option for hikers.

The AMC manages these accommodations in cooperation with the U.S. Forest Service. This partnership is known internationally as a model of cooperative stewardship.

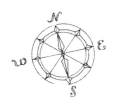

THE FACTS

AMC Huts and Lodges, White Mountains

address	Pinkham Notch Visitor Center Route 16, Box 298, Gorham NH 03581
phone	Reservations 603-466-2727
e-mail	Access through Web site
Web site	**www.outdoors.org** is the AMC's master Web site, with detailed and current information about lodging, membership, publications, trip planning, and "Hut Flash" reports.
lodging	Lodges have shared bunkrooms of two to five beds. Double-bed rooms are available. Huts have bunkrooms.
rates	For adult nonmembers, overnight lodging cost ranges from $18 to $62, depending on service and season. Reduced prices for children; discounts for AMC members. Lodging packages are available.
caveats	Shared bathrooms. No pets.
special interest	Hiking, environmental programs.

THE LODGES

Nestled at the eastern base of Mt. Washington, *Joe Dodge Lodge at Pinkham Notch* provides a dramatic setting for guests. The lodge accommodates 108 guests in shared bunkrooms for two to five people. Double-bed rooms also are available. Guests share large bathrooms with hot showers.

Crawford Hostel offers convenient access to the southern Presidential Range and Willey Range. The hostel has bunkroom accommodations and a self-service kitchen available for a nominal charge. Guests can browse through a natural history library or attend scheduled programs.

BACK COUNTRY HUTS

Set back at least two miles from a road, the huts offer educational displays, backcountry supplies, and basic sleeping accommodations. Lights and appliances run on solar electricity or propane. Don't expect any linens, heat, or showers. Conservation is emphasized; guests help by shlepping out whatever they brought in.

The AMC huts have two levels of service. During the full-service season from early June to early September, a cooking crew serves two hot meals a day. For the rest of the year, one AMC staffer is on hand, and guests bring their own food. Check with the AMC for details on each hut.

At 4,200 ft. elevation, *Greenleaf Hut* offers lofty views of sunsets

AMC's CARTER NOTCH HUT

and autumn foliage. Located near the treeline, this hut holds 46 guests in two bunkrooms.

Galehead Hut is the most remote hut in the entire AMC chain. Strenuous hiking is required to reach this shelter. At 3,800 ft. elevation, guests are greeted with great views of the Pemigewasset Wilderness. The hut holds 36 guests in two bunkrooms.

Lonesome Lake Hut is the most popular family destination. Located in Franconia Notch State Park, next to the National Forest, the hut is reached by an easy hike to the lakeside setting. Two separate bunkhouses hold 44 guests with rooms for four, six, or eight.

... and there are several other huts. Check with the AMC for details. The club also operates camping facilities with earth-friendly features such as the Clivus Multrum composting toilets at the Pinkham Notch campground.

ACCESS

Located on Route 16 between Gorham and Jackson, Joe Dodge Lodge at Pinkham Notch serves as a convenient staging area for the AMC trail network in the White Mountains. Concord Trailways provides service to the lodge from Boston's Park Street bus station and Logan Airport.

A hiker shuttle operates daily from early June to early October. Vans stop at the Crawford Hostel and the Pinkham Notch Visitor Center. Hikers can ride these shuttles to various trailheads near the huts. For reservations and more information on the shuttle, phone 603-466-2727.

DINING

At Joe Dodge Lodge, guests have the option of lodging only, or a bed-breakfast-and-supper package. The hearty evening meals include fresh-baked breads, soups, and entrees. A snack bar is seasonally available to alleviate midday hunger. Diners have views of Wildcat Ridge.

ENVIRONMENTAL INFORMATION

At Pinkham Notch, disoriented guests can consult a mammoth relief map of the Presidential Range. Clerks at the information desk can answer questions about backcountry travel, and the Trading Post sells books, maps, and mountain gear.

With views of Wildcat Ridge, the lodge's library provides a suitable setting for learning about the White Mountains. Educational displays explain the natural setting. Free programs and lectures are offered in the evenings, and AMC workshops are available.

I n the White Mountains, mid-June is a favored time for visiting the krummholz at the tree line. These low-spreading balsam fir and black spruce normally would tower overhead, but here they stay close to the ground in deference to the demanding climate. Kneeling is an appropriate position to view the tiny alpine flowers near the summit, where species are more typical of Labrador than of New England.

ALMANAC

In the region ...
WHITE MOUNTAINS

Mount Washington, the highest mountain in the Northeast, is a biological island of subarctic plants and wildlife. The mountain's legendary weather statistics include gusts of 231 miles per hour, the highest recorded wind velocity on earth. Hurricane-force winds howl over the summit on about one hundred days per year.

At an elevation exceeding six thousand feet, the peak is notorious for treacherous weather that can trap unwary travelers. Snow is possible any month of the year. Visitors who are fortunate to arrive on a clear day can gain a view of five states, the Atlantic Ocean, and Canada.

Cathedral Ledge, famous among rock climbers, is an impressive sheer-sided outcropping. Hikers on Crawford Path, on the southwest slope, pass **Lake of the Woods**, the highest Alpine lake east of the Rockies. **Tuckerman Ravine**, a glacier-carved amphitheater, is about two and one-half miles from Pinkham Notch. Wind-blown snow from the mountain summit settles here to a depth of seventy-five feet or more.

GREEN DINING

The word *fresh* acquires new meaning at **Café Chimes,** where bread is baked from wheat berries ground in the café's mill. Other menu items such as hummus also are made from scratch. Soups are a welcome menu item on snowy New Hampshire days, and hikers can stock up on homemade granola bars. Café Chimes is a patron of a local community-supported agriculture program. This inexpensive deli is open for breakfast and lunch only.

■ *Norcross Place, Main Street, North Conway, NH 03860 tel. 603-356-5500*

PROVISIONS AND SHOPPING

Fresh seasonal produce is available at New Hampshire's network of farmers' markets. A list of these markets and maple sugar producers is included in the *New Hampshire Guidebook*, published by the state's Office of Travel and Tourism Development, Box 1856, Concord, NH 03302, tel. 603-271-2343. The guide can be ordered online at **www.visitnh.gov**.

The **League of New Hampshire Craftsmen** is a non-profit organization dedicated to preserving and inspiring the state's living craft tradition. The League operates seven stores, including a shop in the White Mountains.

- *Route 16, 2526 Main Street, North Conway, NH 03860 tel. 603-356-2441*

Peppercorn Natural Foods in Plymouth carries seasonal produce. The store's own maple syrup is worth a stop.

- *43 Main Street, Plymouth, NH 03264, tel. 603-536-3395*

RESOURCES

The **Appalachian Mountain Club** offers memberships to people who share the AMC's commitment to preserving the region's natural beauty for future generations. Members receive a subscription to *AMC Outdoors*. In addition, they have access to scheduled workshops, clinics, expeditions, and family programs from Maine to Washington, D.C.

- *AMC, 5 Joy Street, Boston, MA 02108, tel. 617-523-0636* **www.outdoors.org**

On his 1858 visit to Mt. Washington, Henry David Thoreau complained in his journal that he tore up his fingernails trying to cross the packed snow in Tuckerman Ravine. On the same trip, he sprained his ankle, and his inept guide started a forest fire.

Founded in 1901, the **Society for Protection of New Hampshire Forests** played a key role in the creation of the White Mountain National Forest and the protection of Mt. Monadnock. The group holds more than 25,000 acres of land in trust. The Society headquarters building (designed by the architectural firm of Banwell White and Arnold of Hanover, New Hampshire) has solar heating and other resource-conserving design features.

- *54 Portsmouth Street, Concord, NH 03301*
  tel. 603-224-9945, **www.spnhf.org**

FOR MORE INFORMATION

The *AMC White Mountain Guide* and the *AMC Guide to Mt. Washington and the Presidential Range* provide complete trail descriptions and digital maps for these areas. Other publications for New Hampshire hikers include *Fifty Hikes in the White Mountains, High Huts of the White Mountains, Fifty Hikes in New Hampshire, Waterfalls of New Hampshire,* and *Walks and Rambles in the Upper Connecticut Valley*.

- *Call 800-262-4455 to order.*

AMC Outdoors is the organization's member magazine. **Appalachia Journal,** also published by the AMC, is a more literary periodical, with essays, poetry, and conservation news.

More than thirty New Hampshire wildlife sanctuaries are maintained by the **Audubon Society of New Hampshire**. A pamphlet, "Guide to ASNH Wildlife Sanctuaries," is available from the Society.

- *ASNH, 3 Silk Farm Road, Concord, NH 03301*
  tel. 603-224-9909, **www.nhaudubon.org**

4

NORTHERN VERMONT

*We are committed to the principle of
stewardship, to managing the Farms'
natural and agricultural resources well,
and to sharing our knowledge and
experience with others. Through our
programs we're striving to set an example
on a local and regional scale for land
conservation, agricultural production and
marketing, and innovative education.
We hope that you will join us in these
critical endeavors — both here at
the Farms and in trying to make a
difference across the country.*

—Louis Borie, "Shelburne Farms:
Stewardship in Practice"

NORTHERN
VERMONT

PROTECTING OPEN SPACE ON VERMONT'S WEST COAST

The Inn at Shelburne Farms
Shelburne, Vermont

Late afternoon sun highlights the handsome
old buildings on the shore of Lake Champlain.
As an orchestra tunes up for a summer concert,
cattle graze in forest-framed pastures, and clusters
of children learn about the lake's ecology.

For guests gazing at this bucolic scene, it's difficult to
imagine what might have been. Several decades ago,
the thousand-acre site was about to be sliced into
lots and lost to public access. But, thanks to a visionary
idea and waves of local support, Shelburne Farms
is now one of the world's preeminent models
for environmental education and
sustainable agriculture.

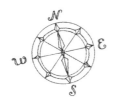

THE FACTS
The Inn at Shelburne Farms

address	1611 Harbor Road Shelburne, VT 05482
phone	Inn and restaurant: 802-985-8498 Shelburne Farms: 802-985-8686 (fax: 802-985-8123)
Web site	**www.shelburnefarms.org**
lodging	Twenty-four rooms (seventeen with private baths), plus two cottages. Two-night stay required on weekends.
rates	$95 to $350 per day. Rates vary according to season and room size.
caveats	No heat or air conditioning in the Inn. No pets allowed. Closed mid-October to mid-May.
special interest	Historic buildings, open space preservation, sustainable agriculture, Lake Champlain setting

THE INN

The Queen Anne Revival building now serving as the inn originally was constructed as a country manor. Built in 1887 by Dr. William Seward Webb and Lila Vanderbilt Webb as part of their model farm and agricultural estate, the building has been completely restored.

Most of the inn's furnishings are original. The combination of Colonial and Renaissance Revival with Empire styles reflect late nineteenth-century tastes. Other historic structures on the site include the Farm Barn, the Coach Barn, the Breeding Barn, and the original Dairy Barn.

ACCESS

The inn is located about seven miles south of Burlington, at the intersection of Bay and Harbor Roads on Shelburne Point. Amtrak trains stop at Essex Junction, near Burlington.

CONSERVATION

The 1,400-acre landscape as well as the buildings on the property are listed on the National Register of Historic Places. The Farm Barn is one of several structures designed by architect Robert H. Robertson. The site was planned with the assistance of Frederick Law Olmsted, landscape architect of New York's Central Park, and Gifford Pinchot, a prominent conservationist of the early twentieth century.

Rather than being cooped up in feedlots, cows at Shelburne Farms roam across the estate's pastures, dining on pasture grass and clover. Dispersing the cattle on the site reduces water pollution.

DINING

Breakfast and dinner at the inn feature contemporary regional cuisine and fresh, local products. Vegetarian options are available. No lunches are served at the inn, but the kitchen staff can pack picnic lunches for inn guests upon request. Day visitors can enjoy breakfast or dinner at the inn by reservation.

Cheese naturally has a prominent place on the Inn's menu.

The Cheddar and Vermont Ale Soup with caramelized onion crostino is a standout. The house salad also has a Vermont theme: local greens with maple ginger vinaigrette dressing. Entrees include pasta, seafood, beef, lamb, and free-range chicken.

Shelburne Farms' award-winning cheddar is produced by hand in the restored Farm Barn. The resident Brown Swiss cows produce high-protein milk that is ideal for cheese-making. Cheese sales help to support the farm.

Visitors also may purchase sourdough bread baked at Shelburne Farms. The bread is produced from organically grown grain leavened with natural sourdough.

ENVIRONMENTAL INFORMATION

The historic buildings and landscape at Shelburne Farms serve as a living laboratory for teaching and demonstrating the conservation of natural and agricultural resources.

SHELBURNE FARMS

The Stewardship Institute at Shelburne Farms offers school field trips for Vermont children, hands-on science training for teachers throughout the Northeast, year-around preschool programs, and Project Seasons, a national elementary science curriculum.

At the Welcome Center, visitors can watch a short slide show describing the Farms' metamorphosis from a private agricultural estate to a nonprofit educational organization. Visitors then can take guided tours in an open-air wagon.

At the Farm Barn, visitors can milk a cow, collect eggs, and learn about a wide variety of farm animals in the Children's Farmyard. At the cheesemaking facility, guests can see cheddar cheese being produced from the milk of the Farms' herd of Brown Swiss cows.

Our purpose is to develop a conservation ethic in students, teachers and the general public by teaching and demonstrating the stewardship of natural and agricultural resources.

Shelburne Farms brochure

Archives at the Farms are open by appointment. The Stewardship Institute has several full-time educators, and school programs and public tours are conducted with the help of numerous volunteers and college interns.

A three-day natural history course for adults includes geology of the Champlain Basin, bird and wildflower identification, literary readings and astronomy, with accommodations at the Inn.

ACTIVITIES

Each year, more than one hundred thousand visitors come to Shelburne Farms. Day visitor passes are available.

From May to October, Shelburne Farms has a packed calendar of events and festivals. The Vermont Mozart

Festival Orchestra performs several summer concerts on the inn's south porch.

Eight miles of trails start at the Welcome Center, traversing the Farms' meadows and forests. From the top of Lone Tree Hill, hikers can enjoy views of Lake Champlain, the Adirondacks, and the Green Mountains. Day visitors can use the walking trails free of charge from November through April, and hikers pay a day-use fee during the rest of the year.

Other summer recreation options for inn guests at Shelburne Farms include tennis, canoeing, croquet, hiking, and lake swimming.

The inn is open mid-May through mid-October. Guided tours are conducted five times a day in season. The Children's Farmyard is open daily mid-May through mid-October, and weekends only during late spring and early fall. Walking trails are open daily, weather permitting. The Welcome Center is open daily all year.

E*arly October is a fine time to stay at the Inn, away from the tour buses on the highways. The weather may start out mild and misty, before a Canadian cold front sweeps through during the night. Then, in the morning, there's a crisp blue sky, a perfect time for a walk along the lake.*

ALMANAC

In the region ...
NORTHERN VERMONT

Nearby Burlington is well-known as an environmentally-minded city. A bike path follows Lake Champlain along the entire nine miles of the city's lakefront. Burlington's highly walkable downtown district offers views of the lake at the foot of each east-west street.

OTHER PLACES TO STAY

The Inn at Long Trail is located on Sherburne Pass in the Green Mountains. Strategically situated where the Long Trail and Appalachian Trail cross Highway 4, the inn serves as a way station for hikers. At the front desk, "care packages" mailed to the inn await the arrival of trail users. Another hiker-friendly feature is the Hikers Grab Box, where transients on the trail take or leave teabags or other supplies. Amenities include a well-stocked library, TV room, and a ski tuning bench, along with a hot tub for soaking after a day on the trail.

The inn's rather ordinary exterior does not prepare you for the cozy ambience inside, especially in the wood-paneled Fireside Room with its immense fireplace. Much of the inn's furniture was built by the original owner, including some truly eccentric lamp stands fashioned from branches. Rooms range from basic quarters to the more elaborate fireplace suites.

It's worth a visit to the inn just for a thick slice of the McGrath's famed Irish soda bread, served hot from the oven. The cheerful dining room has a close-up view of huge boulders, framed by ferns. Photos of the Inn's history line the walls. Dinner is served Thursday through Sunday.

McGrath's Irish Pub is a great place for Irish, bluegrass, and other folk music, performed every weekend with billion-year-old boulders as a backdrop. The pub, heated with a wood stove, serves Irish beers along with Long Trail Ale on tap.

■ *The Inn at Long Trail, Rt. 4, P.O. Box 267*
Killington, VT 05751, tel. 802-775-7181, 800-325-2540
Hikers receive preferential rates.
www.innatlongtrail.com

PROVISIONS — NORTHERN VERMONT

Well-known for environmental and social activism, **Ben and Jerry's** produces ice cream just north of Waterbury. This factory visit has been rated by one national magazine as one of the top ten tour experiences in the country. A variety of flavors are available for sampling and sale. The gift shop also sells Rainforest Crunch and other socially-responsible gifts. To reach the plant, take exit 10 on I-89 and follow Route 100 north to the north side of Waterbury.

■ *P.O. Box 240, Waterbury, VT 05676, tel. 802- 244-TOUR*
www.benjerry.com

Watch cider being pressed throughout the year at **Cold Hollow Cider Mill**. A bakery showcases the mill's renowned apple cider doughnuts. Other Cider Mill products include raspberry apple butter, cider jelly, and applesauce. Abner Apple explains the cider-making process on the Mill's Web site.

■ *Route 100, P.O. Box 420, Waterbury, VT, tel. 800-327-7537*
802-244-8771, **www.coldhollow.com**

The member-owned **Onion River Food Co-op** is situated on the north side of downtown Burlington. The co-op is a community-run business with organic produce, bulk grains, herbs, spices, and (of course) Vermont maple syrup. Open seven days a week, with reduced hours on Sunday.

■ *274 North Winooski Avenue,*
Burlington VT, tel. 802-863-3659

At Burlington's core is **Church Street Marketplace,** a thriving pedestrian shopping area. **Frog Hollow on the Marketplace** sells Vermontalia such as baroque walking sticks crafted by a local bus driver.

■ *30 Church Street, Burlington, VT*
tel. 802-863-6458

Billed as the East's number one wildflower seed center, the **Vermont Wildflower Farm** has acres of flowers on display in season. Pathways through the natural gardens wind past plaques that explain herbal histories, romantic legends, and other plant lore. Wildflower seeds, nature jewelry, and pressed flowers are for sale at the attractive gift shop, along with a wide selection of books on nature and the environment. The farm is located a few miles south of Shelburne Farms.

■ *Route 7, Charlotte, VT 05445*, tel. *802-425-3500*

GREEN DINING

Rustic expressionist decor provides atmosphere at **Muddy Waters** in downtown Burlington. This coffee house and juice bar serves vegetarian lasagna and hummus, as well as vegan muffins to go with your coffee.

■ *184 Main Street, Burlington, VT 05401*
tel. 802-658-0466

Located in Vermont's diminutive capital, the **Horn of the Moon Cafe** is reputedly the oldest vegetarian restaurant in New England. Local organic produce and ingredients are used whenever possible. Vegan and heart-healthy selections are noted on the menu, and area artists have their work displayed on the walls.

■ *8 Langdon Street, Montpelier, VT 05602*
tel. 802-223-2895

RESOURCES

The **Green Mountain Club**'s 7,500+ members share a love of hiking and a commitment to protecting the Long Trail system for future generations. The main purpose of the GMC is to maintain the Long Trail, but the club's advocacy and educational efforts also help to safeguard Vermont's other hiking trails. Through its land protection program in northern Vermont, the Club has protected more than fifty-five miles of the Long Trail system and sixteen thousand acres of backcountry land. The club maintains the trail in cooperation with the Vermont Department of Forests, Parks and Recreation, U.S. Forest Service, National Park Service, Appalachian Trail Conference, and private landowners.

The Marvin B. Gameroff Hiker Center, headquarters of the GMC, is housed in a red barn midway between Stowe and Waterbury. At the center are educational displays, a bookstore, outdoor gear, and friendly staff to help plan a hike. From I-89 in Waterbury, take Exit 10 and follow Route 100 north four miles to Waterbury Center.

- *GMC, Route 100, P.O. Box 650, Waterbury Center, VT 05677, tel. 802-244-7037.*
  www.greenmountainclub.org

FOR MORE INFORMATION

The Green Mountain Club offers *Trailmaster* for dedicated cyber-hikers. This desktop mapping software allows high-tech hike planning, with maps and trail descriptions from various New England hiking guides.

- *CD-ROM or 3.5-inch diskette, available from the Green Mountain Club order center, 802-244-7037, or online at the GMC Web site.*

Southern Vermont

Land conservation is good for our communities and good for businesses in general. It enhances the rural character, making Vermont one of the most livable environments in the country. This helps to attract a skilled work force, and it encourages businesses to locate and expand here.

Lyman Orton, President,
Vermont Country Store,
quoted in Vermont Land
Trust brochure.

81

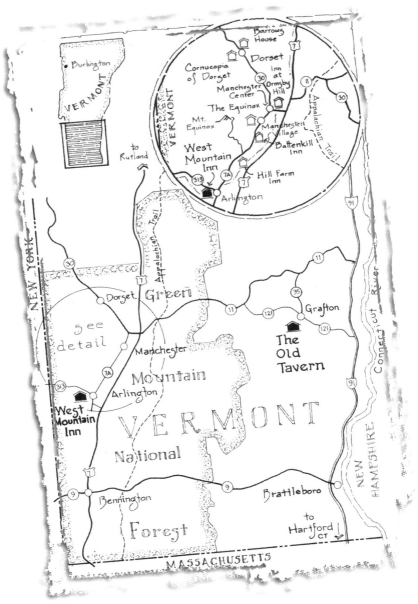

SOUTHERN
VERMONT

RESTORATION OF A VILLAGE INN
The Old Tavern, Grafton, Vermont

Like many small towns in the American landscape, the fortunes of Grafton have waxed and waned with changing economic times. In the early 1800s, the Vermont village was thriving, and the local tavern was a key stop on the post road from Boston to Montreal. Thoreau, Emerson, Kipling, President Grant, and many other notables were guests.

As the years progressed, though, Grafton and its tavern began to decline. By the early 1960s, the tavern was faltering, on the brink of ruin. Just in time, philanthropist Dean Mathey stepped in. He set up the Windham Foundation to restore buildings and economic vitality in the village of Grafton.

Now, several decades later, the Foundation serves as a model for rural sustainable development. The inn and virtually the entire village's architectural heritage have been restored. The various community enterprises employ about one hundred people. Foundation profits are plowed back into ongoing community restoration.

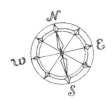

THE FACTS
The Old Tavern

address	Grafton, Vermont 05146
phone	802-843-2231 Reservations: 800-843-1801
e-mail	Tavern@sover.net
Web site	**www.old-tavern.com** An outstanding site with copious information about the inn and the village.
lodging	25 guest rooms and six suites in main building and adjacent cottages, plus seven guest houses and cottages.
rates	$135 to $260 daily for rooms, $620 to $850 daily for cottages and guest houses. Check out the midweek specials, and remember that profits go to good causes.
caveats	No public transit service. Closed during the month of April. Some restrictions on young children.
credentials	Member, Historic Hotels of America, founding member, Original Historic Inns of New England.
special interest	Historic preservation, rural sustainable development, low-impact recreation.

THE LAND AND THE VILLAGE

The Foundation owns nearly two thousand acres in and around the village. Dairy cattle and sheep graze in peaceful meadows worthy of a Constable painting, while the hills have reverted to forest.

Working with the University of Vermont, the Foundation has reintroduced wild turkeys and ruffed grouse to the woodland near the village. Wandering in from points north, moose occasionally visit Grafton Ponds.

The Foundation has restored forty-six structures in the village. Representative native trees and other plants have been placed in the pleasure garden near the Tavern. Walking around town, you'll notice bluebird houses installed as part of the Foundation's bluebird project.

THE INN

Built at the turn of the nineteenth century, the Tavern has seen a succession of owners and additions. The inn's original qualities were restored in the 1960s, under the direction of architects Wyckoff & Coles. Many rooms have hand-hewn beams and wide pine flooring. Antiques include a number of Chippendale pieces, along with appointments of pewter and brass. The Tavern is noted for its fine collection of prints and paintings, including a number of Audubon works and a large portrait of Daniel Webster in the lobby.

The Tavern's accommodations include a number of Grafton's historic buildings. There are twenty-five rooms and six suites in the main building, and in the Windham and Homestead cottages. In addition, a number of nineteenth-century homes in the village have been restored as guest houses. In keeping with Grafton's historic ambiance, there are no phones or televisions in most rooms.

Guest houses accommodating eight to fourteen people can be an excellent option for families and small groups. Visitors can choose from various historic homes located

VILLAGE GARDENS AT GRAFTON

near the Tavern on Grafton's quiet streets. All have antique furnishings, kitchen facilities, living rooms (usually with fireplaces), and other comforts of home. While the antiques in many of the Tavern's rooms are incompatible with young children, three of the guest houses have been specifically furnished with young families in mind.

The gambrel-roofed *White Gates* is particularly picturesque. Just around the corner from the Old Tavern, this large Colonial home has four bedrooms, as well as a spacious front porch, bay window, and an antique-stuffed living room. For musically inclined guests, the four-bedroom *Woodard House* has a piano in the living room, as well as a screened porch. Across the street from the Tavern is the four-bedroom *Barrett House*, featuring two rooms with queen canopy beds. The first and second floors of the five-bedroom *Tuttle House* may be rented separately.

One-half mile from the village on a country lane, the secluded *Hillside Cottage* has a living room and bedroom with full bath. The cottage is particularly popular during fall foliage season, with its panoramic views across the meadows to the hills beyond.

ACCESS

Grafton is located at the intersections of Routes 35 and 121, twelve miles west of Bellows Falls. From northbound Interstate 91, take Exit 5, follow Route 5 north to 121, and take 121 west to the village. No public transit is available.

DINING

The *Dining Room at the Old Tavern* features New England fare with a focus on Vermont products. Decor includes antique-laden sideboards and Chippendale furniture. The Dining Room is open for breakfast, lunch, and dinner, as well as Sunday brunch. Former jacket-and-tie rules no longer apply, but t-shirts would seem out of place in the elegant dining room.

Menu items may include mushroom stew, chicken with cornbread dumplings, native field-green salad, and (of course) cheese from the Foundation's supply. The current menu is posted on the Tavern's Web site.

In season, most of the Tavern's vegetables, herbs, and flowers are garnered from local organic gardens. The cook's helper often can be seen in the Tavern's herb garden, snipping fresh greens for use in the kitchen. A greenhouse addition to the restaurant looks onto the gardens.

Down the street, the *Phelps Barn Lounge* is a more casual setting, with the bar specializing in Vermont microbrewery ales (McNeill's Ale is highly recommended). Also on hand is light fare such as chili with Grafton cheddar cheese. The lounge often offers live entertainment on weekends.

ENVIRONMENTAL PROGRAMS

Each year, the Foundation sponsors the Grafton Conference Project, a series of forums to discuss important issues facing Vermont. At these forums, held at the Old Tavern, topics range from environmental protection to health care, education, and the arts. Regional performers are featured at monthly classical and jazz concerts.

The Grafton Museum of Natural History has collections and interpretive displays of the local environment. The museum also organizes field trips, lectures, and workshops for children and adults. The Museum has limited hours; call 802-843-2347 for information.

The **Grafton Information Center** is a good place to begin exploring the village. The center provides visitor literature, exhibits, and a video. The adjacent **Windham Foundation Exhibits** are open daily, with carriages, old tools, and photo exhibits of Grafton history.

ACTIVITIES

For a Yankee stay, plant yourself on the front porch and practice laconic sayings. Take a leisurely saunter through the woods. Or, to appreciate the historic architecture at close range, take a walking tour through the village. Bucolically inclined visitors can check out the barn; the Tavern posts a note to announce the arrival of newborn lambs.

Ten-speed and mountain bikes are available for exploring the back roads around Grafton. The area is regionally known as an outstanding area for bicycle tours. An annual bike race, the Cheddar Cheese Challenge, is sponsored by the Grafton Village Cheese Company.

The Grafton Ponds Cross-Country Ski Center also is operated by the Windham Foundation. First established as an informal amenity for Tavern guests, the Center now sports more than thirty kilometers of groomed trails, along with a 600-ft. tubing hill and a skating rink. Rental skis, snowshoes and ice skates are available at the log cabin warming hut, along with instruction and refreshments. Each winter, the Grafton International Criterium attracts top-ranked cross-country competitors. Up-to-date snow conditions and events are posted on the Tavern's Web site.

Equestrian enthusiasts can bring their own horses to the Old Tavern. The inn's stable has six box stalls and an adjacent carriage shed for the exclusive use of Tavern guests.

Tennis courts are popular in summer, and in winter, guests can shift to short-paddled platform tennis on an elevated court. On hot summer days, guests can enjoy a brisk swim in the spring-fed, sand-bottomed pond near the Tavern. Shuffleboard, billiards, and ping pong round out the inn's recreation options.

I n early September, before the influx of foliage-seeking tourists, red and gold leaves appear as accents on a green backdrop. Butterflies visit the herbs in the Tavern's garden, or alight on rock walls in the village. While this pre-season setting may not have the high drama of the full fall color show, it's a choice time to visit Grafton and to enjoy the splendor of a single leaf illuminated by the afternoon sun.

The crow appeared
        suddenly, as if hatched
by inadvertent
        incantation.
Pinion feathers
        jagged as a fakir's
        tasseled vest.

Cinder-black shadow,
        not cast but embodied:
heard coming in fast
        before seen, then seen
askance at an eye's edge
        reversing direction
from a downward plunge
        to exact placement
of talons on the 2-by-6.

– *Jim Schley, from "Consecration by Crow"*

INNS, FOOD, AND FARMLAND
West Mountain Inn, Arlington, Vermont

Vermont's landscape of farms and forest, church steeples and barns is embedded deep in the American psyche. Concerned about the possible loss of the state's special qualities, several innkeepers have formed the Conservation Inns of Southwestern Vermont to help protect their region's productive farmland.

The West Mountain Inn has been a leader in linking tourism with a healthy environment and rural economy. Through special events and programs, guests have the opportunity to find out about the values of open space. Inn visitors have toured area farms on harvest weekends, followed by gourmet meals featuring local foods. Other seasonal events have focused on winter woodlots and wildlife.

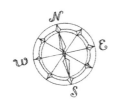

THE FACTS
West Mountain Inn

address	River Road, Arlington, VT 05250
phone	802-375-6516 [fax 802-375-6553]
e-mail	info@WestMountainInn.com
Web site	**www.westmountaininn.com** (winner of Vermont Travel Industry Council award for best Web site)
lodging	18 rooms and suites in a variety of sizes and configurations, located in three buildings, all with private baths. One room offers barrier-free access. Modified American Plan, with B&B rates available for some rooms.
rates	$105-194 single, $145-$244 double per day, Modified American Plan. Lower midweek rates.
caveats	Not accessible by public transit
credentials	Member, Independent Innkeepers Association and the Ecotourism Society.
special interest	Land conservation, llamas.

The inn's owners and manager have a harmonious blend of earth-friendly attitudes and skills. Co-owner Mary Ann Carlson, a former Vermont state senator, is active in promoting organic gardening and agriculture as one way to preserve the state's farms. Her husband Wes Carlson is the "resident visionary, llama breeder, architect, and hug giver," who focuses on raising the inn's herd of llamas. Meanwhile, manager Paula Maynard takes an active role in the Conservation Inn program and other environmental efforts.

THE INN

Set on a forested hillside, the inn overlooks the village of Arlington and the Battenkill River Valley. The inn's commitment to the local economy is evident in the sitting areas, with pine and oak furniture along with paintings by local artists. Tiled in Vermont marble, the sunroom is a place for book-browsing guests. Super-sized chess and backgammon boards share the game room with jigsaw puzzles, and a cheerful children's playroom is bright with murals and primary colors.

In their rooms, guests are welcomed with fresh fruit in a locally crafted pottery bowl and a trail map of the Inn's 150 acres. In addition, the innkeepers have written and provided a guide to southern Vermont that includes various self-guided hiking or bike trips in the area.

The main building has thirteen rooms and suites. Disabled guests have convenient access to *Gwendolyn's Room*. The *Grandma Moses Suite* is particularly inviting, with a cozy sitting room, fireplace, a queen bed and pull-out, and views across the valley to the mountains beyond. For families, the three wall nooks of Room 11 provide cozy space for children.

The two suites in the *Cottage in the Pines* each have two bedrooms. These two accommodations share a living room with wood stove and also share a small kitchen.

The historic *Millhouse* has three suites, each with two bedrooms, private bath, living room, and a kitchen. The

Dorothy Thompson and Remember Baker suites have open hearth woodburning stoves and decks with river views.

DINING

The inn is a member of the Vermont Fresh Network, a "farm and chef partnership" that links area agriculturalists with restaurants seeking fresh local produce. In this way, the inn supports local farms while gaining access to high-quality vegetables, cheese, and other Vermont products. For an even more localized food source, an herb garden outside the dining room supplies fresh seasonings in season.

The Inn's pine-paneled dining room is open to outside guests as well as overnight patrons. Green checked gingham tablecloths, a fireplace, and candlelight combine to create a cozy ambience. Window tables have a fine view.

Breakfast choices extend from the Inn's popular sticky buns to Belgian waffles, buttermilk pancakes, and elegantly prepared eggs. In keeping with Vermont tradition, the inn also offers pie for breakfast.

For dinner, guests might begin with rope-grown mussels steamed in Vermont microbrewed beer. Wild mushroom and fresh spinach soup could be followed by portobello mushrooms sauteed with roasted red peppers and seasonal vegetables over a five-rice blend. Dessert selections may include Vermont apple crisp, chocolate bread pudding, or cheesecake made by the nearby Nuns of New Skete.

The inn participates in a Creative Cuisine Program of the Vermont Department of Health and the Vermont Heart Association. Vegetarian entrees are offered daily.

ACTIVITIES

The Inn's 150 acres include many woodland trails of various lengths and destinations. Guests also can venture

CHOCOLATE BREAD PUDDING

½ cup + one tablespoon sugar

1 cup heavy cream

8 oz. sweet or bittersweet chocolate, coarsely chopped

5 eggs

1 stick butter

1 tablespoon vanilla

2 cups bread crumbs from firm bread

Simmer cream and add butter. Chop chocolate in food processor to fine stage. With machine on, pour hot cream in and add ⅓ cup sugar, vanilla and egg yolks, one at a time. Beat til smooth. Transfer to large bowl, then add the bread crumbs.

In another bowl, beat egg whites til form soft peaks. Gradually add rest of sugar. Beat til whites are glossy and stiff. Stir ⅓ egg whites into chocolate and egg mixture. Fold in remaining whites. Turn into greased baking dish. Place baking dish in warm water until ½ way up side of pan. Bake 40-45 minutes in 350° oven. Let cool 10 minutes and serve.

— Folk and Fare *cookbook,*
West Mountain Inn

beyond the property for a walk down River Road. This quiet, level lane begins at the inn and extends for ten miles along the Battenkill River. En route, the road passes both of Norman Rockwell's homes and one of the most beautiful covered bridges in Vermont.

Further afield, the Green Mountain National Forest has an abundance of hiking trails for all levels of hiker. In addition, the Appalachian Trail/Long Trail crosses Kelly Stand Road east of Arlington, providing an entry point for longer hikes.

When winter snows arrive, the Inn's trails are used for cross- country skiing or snowshoeing. The trails are not groomed, so skiers can face the challenge of pristine snow. Or guests can build a snowman or take a toboggan run down the llama pasture.

For committed canoeists, the Battenkill is a favored destination. The innkeepers can direct you to several companies that rent canoes and provide portage services. Guests can cool off by tubing down the river on a hot summer day.

Nearby villages have an abundance of antique shops and special events. Manchester provides the opportunity to stroll on elegant sidewalks paved with slabs of Vermont marble.

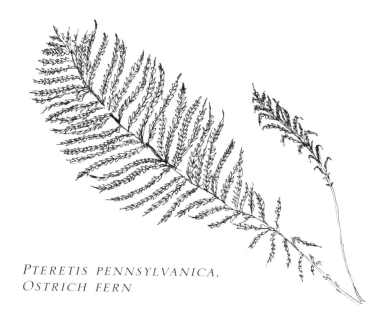

PTERETIS PENNSYLVANICA,
OSTRICH FERN

*E*ach May, the inn hosts a Leek and Fiddlehead Weekend to celebrate Vermont's spring flora and fauna. Guests venture into the woodland to seek out and collect these wild delicacies.

Fiddleheads are the tender emerging fronds of the ostrich fern, Pteretis pennsylvanica, or certain other edible ferns. Fiddleheads are harvested in late April or early May, just as the frondlets are beginning to unroll.

Large colonies of ostrich ferns often are found on riverbanks and low-lying areas. They spread by underground runners, and a light pruning of fiddleheads can stimulate the growth of a fern colony. To assure that the ferns are not harmed, no more than half of the unrolling fronds should be picked from each plant.

Fiddleheads can be prepared in a similar manner to asparagus. The West Mountain Inn cookbook includes fiddlehead recipes such as fritto misto, where the ferns are coated with a mixture of eggs, flour, butter and beer, then deep-fried.

In the region ...
SOUTHERN VERMONT

Home to moose, black bears, and peregrine falcons, **Green Mountain National Forest** covers over 350,000 acres of south and central Vermont. Visitors have abundant opportunities for hiking and canoeing.

■ *Green Mountain National Forest, 231 North Main Street Rutland, VT 05701, tel. 802-747-6700*

GREEN DINING

Several decades ago, hundreds of local people donated cash and a lot of labor to open **The Common Ground** in Brattleboro. This grassroots effort has survived by serving healthy food at a reasonable price. The restaurant is worker-owned and operated in an eco-friendly manner, and serves as a center for music, poetry readings, dances, and presentations.

■ *25 Elliott Street, Brattleboro, VT 05301 tel. 802-257-0855*

A group of South Strafford residents operate The **Full Moon Café**, a grassroots nonprofit enterprise dedicated to promoting local farms and businesses. Paintings and photography by area artists adorn the walls. Diners can enjoy salads with organic vegetables and sandwiches in the $4 to $5 range. Hungarian mushroom soup is a menu highlight. Homemade ice cream and organic coffee are added attractions. Open Monday through Friday, 7 am to 4 pm, 8 am to 3 pm on weekends. With two computers available for Internet access, the Café slogan is "Come in for a bite or a byte."

■ *Route 132, South Strafford, VT 05070 tel. 802-765-4480,* **www.straffordvt.net**

PROVISIONS

An environmental variety store, **Earth Advocate** stocks organic cotton and hemp clothing, natural household cleaners, and such. Products also can be ordered online. Closed Wednesdays.

- *Route 7A, Sunderland, VT 05250, tel. 802-362-2766*
  www.mainstreetvt.com/earthstore

Village Cheese Company, down the street from the Old Tavern, also is operated by the Windham Foundation. The mainstay of the Cheese Company is its premium, 100% natural, aged cheddar. Local Jersey cows supply the milk for the cheese; no preservatives, additives, or synthetic hormones are used in milk or cheese production. All profits are returned to the Foundation, to be used for charitable purposes. Visitors can sample maple smoked cheddar, garlic cheddar, or sage cheddar. Other regional products for sale include maple syrup, honey, cider jelly, and Vermont apple wine summer sausage.

- *Townshend Road, Grafton, VT 05146*
  tel. 800-472-3866 **www.graftonvillage.com**

Located about 30 miles south of Grafton, Brattleboro is noted for its music festivals and artist community. The **Brattleboro Food Co-op** includes a deli and cafe. Open seven days a week. Near I-91 Exit 1, the co-op is in the Brookside Shopping Plaza.

- *2 Main Street, Brattleboro, VT 05301, tel. 802-257-1841*

On warm-season Saturdays, a grove of trees along Whetstone Brook serves as the venue for **the Brattleboro Area Farmers Market**, said to be one of the most popular in New England. Along with fresh-picked fruits and vegetables, the market has an array of ethnic food, baked goods, and crafts. Local groups provide music during the lunch hour. The market is open Saturdays, May through October, on Route 9 west of Exit 2,

Interstate 91. Another market operates at Brattleboro Common on Wednesdays, mid-June through mid-September.

- *tel. 802-257-1272 Updated information is included in the town's homepage:* **www.sover.net/~bratchmb**.

OTHER PLACES TO STAY

Six other establishments are members of the Conservation Inns of Southwest Vermont

The Equinox is a prestigious hotel and resort on its namesake mountain near Manchester. The hotel owners have created the 850-acre Equinox Preservation Trust, dedicated to the protection and wise use of the wild lands on the mountain. The Snicket and other trails traverse the mountain, where hikers can learn about the fragile alpine habitats protected in the preserve. The hotel also supports Vermont Institute of Natural Science programs. Depending on season and room type, rates begin in the $160 range for an off-season single room and climb to $600 or more nightly for a suite.

- *The Equinox Hotel, Route 7A, Manchester Village, VT 05254, tel. 800-362-4747* **www.equinoxresort.com**

The **Barrows House Inn and Restaurant** occupies eight historic buildings on twelve acres in Dorset Village. Daily rates range from about $140 to $265, including full breakfast and a four-course dinner. Lower rates are available for bed-and-breakfast stays, as well as off-season and midweek visits. Each year the inn sponsors and hosts the Littlest Music Festival, a benefit for the local Community Food Cupboard.

- *Dorset, VT 05251, tel. 802-867-4455 or 800-639-1620* **www.barrowshouse.com**

Billed as a romantic hideaway, **Cornucopia of Dorset** offers an elegant nineteenth-century setting. Overnight lodging ranges from about $125 for rooms in the main inn to $255 for the Owl's Head Cottage, including in-room champagne and a candlelit gourmet breakfast. Guests can stroll around the village on marble sidewalks.

- *Dorset, VT 05251, tel. 802-867-5751 or 800-566-5751* **www.CORNUCOPIAofDORSET.com**

One of Vermont's first country inns, **Hill Farm Inn** is set on fifty acres of farmland with a mile of frontage on the Battenkill River. Soups, breads, and desserts are made from scratch, using seasonal produce from the inn's garden; the rhubarb crisp is a special treat. Rooms in the restored 1830 main inn or the 1790 guest house range from about $75 to $150, double occupancy, while the seasonal cabins go for $65 and up per day.

- *RR2, Arlington, VT 05250, tel. 802- 375-2269 or 800-882-2545* **www.hillfarminn.com**

The ten-room **Inn at Ormsby Hill** is noted for its gourmet cuisine and ornate woodwork. The building dates back to the 1700s. Multi-course breakfasts are served in the Conservatory, with views of the Green Mountains. In addition to membership in the Conservation Inns of Southwest Vermont, the inn participates in the Vermont Fresh Network, where produce is purchased directly from local farmers. Rates generally are in the $125-240 range.

- *Manchester Center, VT 05255, tel. 802-362-1163 or 800-670- 2841* **www.ormsbyhill.com**

Set on seven acres along the Battenkill River, the **Battenkill Inn** features high ceilings, marble fireplaces, and eleven guest rooms with private baths in a restored Victorian farmhouse. Room rates, in the $90-$165 range, include full breakfast and evening hors d'oeuvres.

- *P.O. Box 948, Manchester Village, VT 05254 tel. 800-441-1628* **www.battenkillinn.com**

RESOURCES

The **Vermont Land Trust** is a private, nonprofit organization working to protect the state's open space. The

Trust's programs assist farm families and communities to conserve productive agricultural land, woods, and shoreline. More than three hundred thousand acres, over six percent of privately-owned land in Vermont, now is conserved under the Trust's stewardship.

- *8 Bailey Avenue, Montpelier, VT 05602*
  tel. 802-223-5234 **www.vlt.org**

The **Vermont Institute of Natural Science** is a non-profit organization dedicated to environmental education and natural history research. Visit the three-ounce saw-whet owl at the **Vermont Raptor Center,** part of the Vermont Institute of Natural Science headquarters in Woodstock. The Center introduces visitors to hawks, owls, and other local birds of prey. All of the birds at the Center have permanent injuries that prevent their being released to the wild. On Church Hill Road, about 1.5 miles southwest of the Woodstock village green, the Center is open all year.

- *Woodstock, VT, tel. 802-457-2779*

FOR MORE INFORMATION

The history of Grafton and the work of the Windham Foundation is documented in *A Vermont Renaissance*. Illustrated with sixty-five color photographs, the book includes many before-and-after comparisons.

- *Available from the Old Tavern, Grafton, VT 05146*

West Mountain Inn manager Paula Maynard has collected recipes and history lore in *Folk and Fare*, a cookbook sprinkled with stories about the inn's owners and local notables. Cookbook sales fund a local high school scholarship for a student who fosters peace globally by actions in his or her school and community. Copies are available at the inn.

6

THE BERKSHIRES

*All around beneath me was spread for a
hundred miles on every side, as far as the eye
could reach, an undulating country of clouds,
answering in the varied swell of its surface to
the terrestrial world it veiled. It was such a
country as we might see in dreams, with all
the delights of paradise. There were immense
snowy pastures, apparently smooth-shaven
and firm, and shady vales between the
vaporous mountains, and far in the horizon
I could see where some luxurious misty timber
jutted into the prairie, and trace the windings
of a water course, some imagined Amazon
or Orinoko, by the misty trees on its brink ...*

—Henry David Thoreau,
Mt. Greylock summit, 1844.

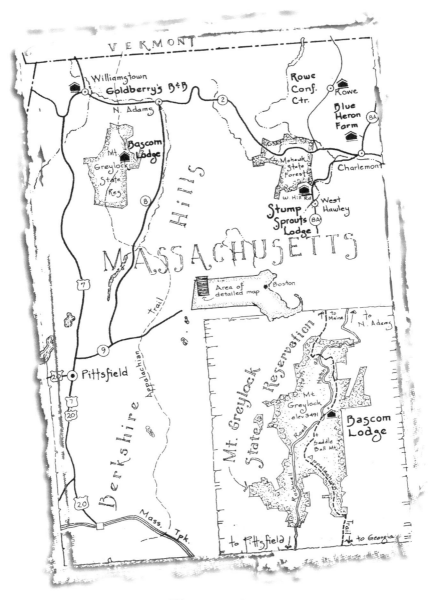

THE NORTHERN
BERKSHIRES

A View from Mt. Greylock
Bascom Lodge, Lanesboro, Massachusetts

Mt. Greylock has long been an inspiration for writers. In addition to Thoreau's description of sunrise on the summit, Nathaniel Hawthorne wrote about the mountain's mist-shrouded mass. And from his study window in Pittsfield, Herman Melville pondered Greylock's wintry silhouette, envisioning the shape of a whale.

On a clear day, Mt. Greylock provides a Tolkienesque view of farms and villages far below, with Berkshire ridges stretching to the horizon. And Bascom Lodge, built of native stone and timbers, stands near the summit among the birches and balsam firs.

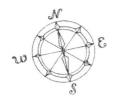

THE FACTS
Bascom Lodge

address	P.O. Box 1800, Lanesboro, MA 01237
phone	AMC: 413-443-0011 for advance reservations, 413-743-1591 for current week reservations.
Web site	**www.outdoors.org** Detailed information on AMC lodging and current programs at Bascom Lodge and throughout the Northeast.
lodging	Four private rooms (shared baths). Co-ed bunk bed rooms. Blankets, sheets and towels provided.
rates	$22 members, $27 non-members per day. Meals are extra.
caveats	No public transit. Not a place for night owls: the lodge doors are locked before midnight. Cold showers. Closed November to mid-May.
special interest	Hiking, low-impact construction, naturalist programs.

THE INN

Civilian Conservation Corps workers built the lodge of native stone, timbers, and shingles. The structure must be one of the best bargains ever procured by the Commonwealth of Massachusetts, since the cost to the state in 1937 totaled just $11,000. Rough stone for the walls and red spruce for the interiors were by-products of trail construction. Logs for the lodge were drawn out of the woods with a team of horses.

Overhead are hand-hewn oak rafters. The handsomely detailed stone fireplace is built of the quartzite that forms the foundation of Mt. Greylock.

The simply furnished rooms provide a basic place to sleep. Patience may be needed for bathroom lines in the morning, although the wait is rewarded with a stupendous vista from the bathroom windows. Don't expect hot showers.

Operated by the Appalachian Mountain Club, the lodge has four private rooms that sleep two each. In addition, four dormitory bunkrooms hold a total of twenty-eight overnight guests. Sheets and towels are provided.

The spartan accommodations mean that guest expenses are kept to a minimum. To cut costs even further, visitors can put in two hours of work in the kitchen and stay for just ten dollars, which includes dinner, lodging and breakfast.

ACCESS

The preferred method of access (and one actually used by many Bascom Lodge visitors) is to arrive on foot via the Appalachian Trail. Other than footpower, private vehicles are your only option. It's regrettable that there isn't an electric shuttle bus to transport visitors up the narrow, winding road to the summit.

If you're arriving from the east on Route 2, watch for an unobtrusive brown "Mt. Greylock Reservation" sign a few hundred yards west of the old cemetery on the west side of North Adams. Take the road south to the reservation. The ascent to the summit requires an alert driver to watch for mountain bikers whizzing down the hill, periodic potholes, chipmunks, sharp curves, errant hikers, deer, and other obstacles.

From the south, follow Route 9 through Lanesboro and watch for the Mt. Greylock signs. The Visitor Center at the southern base of the mountain precedes the climb to the summit.

DINING

The lodge serves family-style breakfasts and dinners. Counter-service lunch is available, or hikers can have a lunch packed for the trail. The cooks buy fresh seasonal produce at nearby farmers' markets. In late summer, diners may be treated to fresh sweet corn.

Vegetarians will feel at home here. Recent lunch options included six or seven salads, spinach calzone, and vegan carrot cake. Fresh-baked breads are another culinary attraction.

From the picnic tables on the porch, diners have a commanding view of the Housatonic Valley, the Taconic Range, and even the Catskills beyond the Hudson River.

ENVIRONMENTAL INFORMATION

The Bascom Lodge facilities are supplemented by a Visitor Center at the southern base of Mt. Greylock. The Visitor Center offers interpretive programs and displays. Trail guides and hiking supplies are for sale at the gift shop.

AMC naturalists at the Lodge and Visitor Center provide guided walks, educational displays, evening campfires, and group hikes. Workshops such as *Tai Chi on the Mountain* are offered.

ACTIVITIES

Bascom Lodge is near the center of Mt. Greylock State Reservation. This forested park, dating back to 1898, currently covers nearly twelve thousand acres. Fifty miles of trails lead directly from the Lodge and thread through the reservation.

The Appalachian Trail is a feature attraction here. Hikers can leave the Lodge and trek all the way to New Hampshire's huts and hostels — or follow the trail south to Georgia, for that matter.

At the lodge, long-distance walkers can trade surplus goods at the thru-hiker exchange box. Hiker bulletins are regularly posted. The howling winters and high elevation have one benefit; according to locals, Mt. Greylock is tick-free.

Other summer activities at the Lodge include Tuesday night barbecues and music night on Friday. Visitors also can join a Volunteer Trail Crew and learn the techniques of trail maintenance. In spite of the long trek to the mountaintop, the Lodge is popular with summer concertgoers attending the Tanglewood Music Festival.

Visitors also can just stay put and enjoy the view from the lodge. At 3,491 feet, Mt. Greylock easily is the highest mountain in Massachusetts. For a full-circle perspective, guests can climb the ninety steps to the top of the War Memorial tower. On a clear day, sharp-eyed visitors may be able to see Mt. Monadnock in New Hampshire.

Bascom Lodge shuts down in October, when heavy snows close the road to the summit. However, the Visitor Center at Mt. Greylock's base is open throughout the year, with a variety of winter skiing and snowshoeing programs and activities.

By the time the Lodge opens for the season in mid-May, violets are appearing on the mountain slopes. The summit is blanketed by the white flower clusters of mountain ash in June. Throughout the summer, birders can enjoy the sight and sound of warblers, white-throated sparrows, and numerous other species.

The Berkshires' legendary autumn leaves provide a dramatic finale to the year. Each Columbus Day, thousands of locals and visitors hike up the Cheshire Harbor Trail as part of the Greylock Ramble. The Adams Chamber of Commerce provides prizes to the participant who has come the longest distance, as well as the oldest and youngest hikers to reach the top.

One of the best choices for a visit to Mt. Greylock would be the autumn equinox. After a day of hiking through crimson and golden leaves, there's time to relax by the fireplace in the main room, as reflections of the setting sun glint off the quartzite walls of Bascom Lodge.

ALMANAC

A Solar Ski Retreat

Stump Sprouts Guest Lodge, West Hawley, Massachusetts

SUZANNE CRAWFORD TENDS THE ORGANIC GARDEN AT STUMP SPROUTS GUEST LODGE

The name suggests new life from old roots, and that's what Lloyd and Suzanne Crawford have achieved with their mountain property in the Berkshires. The Crawfords have adapted an abandoned farm to new use as a cross-country ski lodge, while respecting the land and environment.

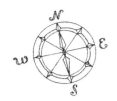

THE FACTS

Stump Sprouts Guest Lodge and Cross-Country Ski Center

address	West Hill Rd, West Hawley, MA 01339
phone	413-339-4265
e-mail	stumpsprouts@stumpsprouts.com
web site	**www.stumpsprouts.com**
lodging	Guest lodge with several bunk rooms that sleep two to eight people. Shared bathrooms.
rates	Reasonable rates, starting at $24 per night (midweek non-ski-season). A winter non-holiday weekend (two nights and six meals) is $129.
caveats	No pets. No transit access. Guests need to bring their own bedding and toilet articles.
special interest	Cross-country skiing, organic gardening, "green" construction.

THE INN

After acquiring the property in 1977, the owners converted the original 1917 barn and silo to a multipurpose space, where a staircase spirals up the silo's interior to reach the upper level.

The Crawfords carefully selected and harvested trees to build a guest lodge. To disturb the land as little as possible, they hitched up a team of horses and pulled individual logs from their forest for use in the new building.

ACCESS

Tucked away in the northwest corner of Massachusetts, this remote part of the Berkshires looks the way that Vermont used to. Along the way to Stump Sprouts, you'll pass weathered barns, stone walls, and vintage tractors in the fields.

There is no public transit in the area, so you'll need a private vehicle to reach the lodge. From the New York City metro area, it's about a four-hour trip. A map provided by the owners is needed for successful negotiation of the back roads to the lodge.

ACCOMMODATIONS

Visitors to Stump Sprouts can bring their own food or can choose to have meals provided. The guest lodge, added circa 1980, includes a kitchen, dining room, shared living area, guest rooms that sleep two to eight people, and shared bathrooms.

From late December to mid-March, Stump Sprouts offers an affordable weekend ski package, including six meals, accommodations, and cross-country skiing right outside the door. Special rates are available for midweek and group visits.

CONSERVATION

The recycled buildings and use of sustainably harvested timber make a hands-on conservation statement at Stump Sprouts. The results appear underfoot at the guest lodge, with its mix of beech, birch, and maple flooring. Lloyd also has crafted furniture from downed trees on the property.

CONVERTED SILO AT STUMP SPROUTS LODGE

Snow actually helps to heat the barn, especially in March, as solar heat gain from the south-facing windows is supplemented by reflected rays bouncing off the snowpack.

The barn and lodge are heated primarily with wood from the property. On hot summer days, open windows provide natural ventilation. In addition to the standard plumbing, an improvised solar shower provides hot water when sun shines on an array of recycled pipes.

KITCHEN AND GARDEN

Home-grown food is provided to visitors whenever possible. Lunch is available for day visitors.

In summer, the owners often can be found tending an assortment of organic flowers, vegetables, and herbs on the sunny slope above the barn. The orchard and berry vines provide apples, blackberries, and raspberries. Succession plantings help to extend the season, and Lloyd has harvested lettuce in December.

ACTIVITIES

The recreational highlight of the Lodge is cross-country skiing for guests and day visitors. Stump Sprouts offers rental equipment, instruction, and access to miles of maintained trails, rental equipment, and instruction. The relatively high elevation results in some of the best natural snow conditions in southern New England.

For novices, there are wide trails on gentle slopes with track-set and skating lanes. More challenging trails also are marked on the Stump Sprouts ski map.

If there is a dearth of snow, winter guests can switch to ice skating in the nearby state forest, or visit one of the nearby cross-country or downhill ski resorts with snow-making equipment. Snowshoes also are available for rent.

After a day on the trails, a wood-fired sauna is waiting.

ICE CROQUET

For a mutation of conventional croquet adapted to the Berkshire winters, the Crawfords have devised croquet-on-ice. Holes are drilled in the ice to hold the wickets, and recycled steel truss rings are substituted for croquet balls. Ice croquet players at Stump Sprouts report precise control of their shots, compared with the vagaries of lawn croquet.

During the long winter evenings, guests can play ping pong and shoot pool in the multi-purpose space. A variety of hand-made wooden games are on hand for children and adults.

In the warmer months the Lodge is used primarily for retreats, workshops, and weddings. Dance groups, meditation sessions, and yoga classes are scheduled periodically.

Guests can hike or ski up Lone Boulder Hill to see a glacial erratic rock some ten feet in diameter, and a three-state view from the nearby summit. The Stump Sprouts property borders the Mohawk Trail State Forest, providing more extensive hiking options.

Lloyd has stacks of books to share. Drawing on his background in biology, he periodically takes guests on birding walks.

January through March is ski season, with weekend packages available at bargain rates. In addition to New England's renowned autumn color, the Berkshires provide a great display of spring foliage. For a quiet stay, early December and April are the slowest times at Stump Sprouts. The Lodge occasionally closes, so call in advance before making the trip.

S pring in the Berkshires
begins in the valleys.
As the weeks progress, a lime-green
line of emerging leaves then
advances steadily up the mountain
slopes, supplanting the sober tones
of winter. Buds opening at the
summit of Lone Boulder Hill finally
announce the new season at
Stump Sprouts Lodge.

SHARING A SUGARHOUSE

Blue Heron Farm,
Charlemont, Massachusetts

SUGARHOUSE, BLUE HERON FARM

Guests at Blue Heron Farm's Sugarhouse share
the structure with maple sugaring equipment.
This mixed-use arrangement has a precedent in
traditional "sugar cabbins" and sugar shacks.
Boiling took place around the clock, and bunks
were needed for off-duty tenders.

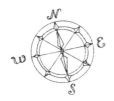

THE FACTS
Blue Heron Farm

address	Warner Hill Road, Charlemont, MA 01339
phone	413-339-4045
lodging	Three fully furnished housekeeping units: the Sugarhouse (up to four guests), The Log Cabin (up to four guests), and the Cottage (up to six guests).
rates	$85 to $180 per night; weekly and monthly rates available.
caveats	Two-night minimum stay. No access by public transportation. Housekeeping units with no meals provided.
special interest	Organic farm, maple syrup production.

FARM BUILDINGS AT BLUE HERON FARM

THE INN

The farm's accommodations are fully-furnished and equipped housekeeping units, not bed-and-breakfast rooms. As co-owner Norma Coli says, "You can get breakfast here, but only if you eat hay or grain." However, guests are welcome to stop at the house for goats' milk with blueberries.

With its self-contained cabin and cottages in a quiet rural setting, the farm is ideal for long-term visitors, such as a brother-sister composer team who recently spent several months working on a musical score. Units are widely spaced for plenty of privacy. Private phone hookups are available for extended stays.

The two-floor **Sugarhouse** unit accommodates one to four guests. A wall separates the maple sugaring equipment from the guest quarters. An upper-level deck is tucked among maple trees.

Passing beneath some maples this afternoon, we observed several with small icicles hanging from their lower branches, although there was neither ice nor snow on the adjoining trees; we broke one off, and it proved to be congealed sap, which had exuded from the branch and frozen there during the night — natural sugar candy, as it were, growing on the tree.

— Susan Fenimore Cooper, *Rural Hours*

The Log Cabin sleeps up to four guests. The winterized cabin is fully equipped, including a full kitchen with utensils and tableware, as well as a washer and dryer. Decor includes vintage toys such as an old sled and metal cars.

With its three floors, *The Cottage* accommodates up to six people. Amenities include two baths, fireplace, a sunporch and a large deck off the main floor.

ACCESS

The farm is nestled in the northwest corner of Massachusetts, just a few miles from the Vermont state line. Visitors arriving from the east can take Route 2 to Charlemont, then follow detailed directions provided by the owners to the end of a gravel road. No public transit is available to this remote location.

THE FARM

The property has been farmed continuously since 1797. By the mid-1800s, most of the land had been cleared for sheep grazing. Now, however, forest has reclaimed much of the site.

The quiet seeped into us, and we are reluctant to leave.

entry in guest book, *Blue Heron Farm*

Each year, the woodland at Blue Heron Farm produces about five hundred gallons of premium organic maple syrup. About thirty to fifty gallons of sap are needed to make one gallon of syrup. Although dependent on the weather, maple sugaring setup typically begins in late January, with boiling through March.

In addition to the maple sugar operation, the owners raise high-bush blueberries and apples. Compost from a long mound goes to the fields to supplement the stony New England soil.

About a dozen horses and fifty goats graze in pastures on the property. Bill and Norma Coli take particular pride in their Fjord horses. As one of the oldest recognized breeds, dating back to the early Viking era, Fjords are noted for being surefooted, easygoing, and people-oriented.

Bill works as a Cooperative Extension Specialist for the University of Massachusetts, and applies his knowledge of nontoxic pest control on the farm. No pesticide sprays are needed in the barn. Instead, parasite wasps and fly strips keep bugs under control.

ACTIVITIES

Guests are encouraged to help with farm activities, from picking blueberries and milking goats to making maple syrup. Depending on the season, guests may have a tour in a horse-drawn wagon, sled, or sleigh.

Along with the farm's namesake blue herons, there is an abundance of avian species for birdwatchers to enjoy. The pineapple weed along the driveway attracts goldfinches. Bluebirds and cardinals nest in the area. Woodcocks are common. Dozens of wild turkeys live in the woods, and downy woodpeckers have a nest next to the cabin. Great gray owls are on hand to announce the moonrise. Also, Bill reports that a group of local grouse often gathers to dine on plump, ripe blueberries.

There are plenty of cultural activities nearby in the Berkshires. Blue Heron Farm is a place to relax and regain an appreciation for nature's rhythms.

S now still coats the Berkshires, but the sun is climbing higher in the sky. As winter wanes, sap begins to rise in the sugar maples at Blue Heron Farm.

It's time for Norma and Bill Coli to start the maple sap harvest. Venturing into their woodland, they set several thousand taps. Two or three holes are drilled in each maple tree. Sap oozing from these orifices is collected and stored in tanks at the sugarhouse. Guests can watch as the sap is boiled down in shallow pans set over a fire.

When the sap has been condensed, the sticky liquid is drawn off, filtered, and put into containers. Each visitor to Blue Heron Farm is rewarded with a container of this pure, certified organic maple syrup.

In the region ...
BERKSHIRES

Shelburne Falls is an old mill town with brawny stone storefronts and industrial architecture, now experiencing a renaissance with candlemakers, glassblowers, and other artisans in residence. For geologists, the key attraction is "The World's Largest Pothole"— some thirty-nine feet in diameter — along with numerous smaller depressions. Eons ago, rushing waters carved these voluptuous swirls of stone below the milldam on the Deerfield River.

The only natural marble bridge in North America is protected in **Natural Bridge State Park** north of Mount Adams. Open from about Memorial Day to Columbus Day; admission fee.

- *Route 8, Mount Adams, MA, tel. 413-663-6392*

The round stone barn is a highlight of **Hancock Shaker Village**, one of a number of restored Shaker villages in the East. Traditional crafts demonstrations, garden tours, and special-event dinners are part of this living history site. Located five miles west of Pittsfield on Highway 20, the Village is open April through November.

- *Rt. 20, West Housatonic Street, Pittsfield, MA 01202 tel. 413-443-0188*

OTHER PLACES TO STAY

In Williamstown, **Goldberry's Bed and Breakfast** is conveniently located within walking distance of the Williamstown Theatre Festival, the Williams College campus, and the Clark Art Institute. The home, which dates to 1830, is featured on the Williamstown historic walking tour. All rooms have private baths.

The owner supports local agriculture by purchasing food at Caretaker Farm (a nearby community-supported organic agricultural operation) and the local Wild Oats food co-op. Pancakes and waffles are made from a combination of organic flours and fruit.

- *Goldberry's, 39 Cold Spring Road, Williamstown, MA 01267, tel. 413-458-3935*

The **Rowe Conference Center** provides a wooded setting for summer camp sessions and retreat workshops. Operated by the Unitarian-Universalist Church, the Center occupies 1,400 acres of forest and wilderness preserve about six miles north of Route 2. Accommodations generally are dorm-style, although a limited number of private rooms are available. The Sun Room is a favorite, with windows on all sides. The moderate cost of workshops includes meals and housing expenses. Work exchange and bartering arrangements are available. Gourmet vegetarian food is the mainstay at the Center.

In addition to sessions on personal growth and social issues, the Center offers workshops on environmental topics, such as "Wilderness and the Defense of the Wild," led by Dave Foreman.

- *Rowe Camp and Conference Center, Kings Highway Road, Rowe, MA 01367, tel. 413-339-4216*
  e-mail: roweccc@javanet.com

PROVISIONS AND SHOPPING

Located by the Bridge of Flowers in Shelburne Falls, **McCusker's Market** carries local organic produce and dairy products. A sit-down deli has fresh organic carrot juice, bagels, and vegetarian sandwiches. The smoked turkey roll-up combines Muenster cheese melted on mountain bread with honeysuckle mustard, while the vegan BLT sandwich is made with tempeh "bacon." For dessert, try the tasty wild cherry "oatscream."

- *McCusker's Market, 3 State Street, Shelburne Falls, MA tel. 413-625-9411*

Along with locally produced goat cheese, the **Berkshire Co-op Market** offers a large selection of organic produce, herbs, and spices, as well as organic and free-range poultry and eggs. Also on hand are sugar-free and wheat-free products, natural personal-care products, and eco-friendly cleaning supplies. The deli offers soups made with organic ingredients, desserts free of refined sugar, and macrobiotic sushi rolls.

- *37 Rosseter Street, Great Barrington, MA 01230*
  tel. 413-528-9697

A consumer-owned market on the east edge of Williamstown, the **Wild Oats Cooperative** has a full line of natural foods, including lots of local organic produce, whole-grain breads and preserves. Specialty items include no-salt snack foods, nitrite-free meats, free-range poultry, natural cosmetics, and locally-made buckwheat pillows.

- *Colonial Shopping Center, 248 Main Street (Route 2)*
  Williamstown, MA, tel. 413-458-8060

GREEN DINING

Comfortably situated in a row of stone-walled shops by the flower-festooned Trolley Bridge, **The Copper Angel** has predominantly vegetarian cuisine with some poultry and seafood. From a table in the back room, projecting out over the water, diners can enjoy an almost European view of the Deerfield River and forested mountains beyond. The friendly, informal interior features hardwood floors and an angel theme in muted, crisp decor. Even the stone-walled bathroom is picturesque. Diners can sit out on the recently added deck in warm weather.

The handsomely designed menu includes items such as grilled chicken breast with peach chili salsa, aduki bean broccoli, roasted vegetables and hummus, and lentil cutlets with vegetarian gravy. Organic coffee is served, along with a variety of teas and fresh organic carrot juice. Local organic produce is available in season. For dessert, try the tasty blackberry mousse made with local berries, and watch the reflection of the Trolley Bridge as dusk settles over the river. Inexpensive to moderate. Lunch and dinner hours Monday and Wednesday through Saturday. Sunday brunch and dinner. Closed Tuesdays.

■ *The Copper Angel, 2 State Street, Shelburne Falls, MA 01370, tel. 413-625-2727*

FOR MORE INFORMATION

Authors Deborah E. Burns and Lauren R. Stevens provide a detailed and entertaining account of Mt. Greylock in *Most Excellent Majesty: A History of Mount Greylock.* Chapters are devoted to geology, climate, biology, and human history. Published in 1988 by the Berkshire Natural Resources Council, the book is for sale at the Bascom Lodge gift shop.

RESOURCES

One of the world's oldest conservation groups, the **Massachusetts Audubon Society** has protected thousands of acres of natural habitat. More than thirty of the Society's sanctuaries are open to the public. The Society serves as an advocate for the environment, and several hundred thousand children have participated in the Society's education programs.

■ *Tel. 800-AUDUBON,* **www.massaudubon.org**

_7_

BOSTON HARBOR

**_Whether a hotel is located
in a bustling urban center like
Boston or on the idyllic islands
of Hawaii, every property has a
shared responsibility to lessen
its impact on the earth's
limited resources._**

—Tedd Saunders,
Director of
Environmental Affairs,
Saunders Hotel Group,
_The Bottom Line of
Green Is Black_

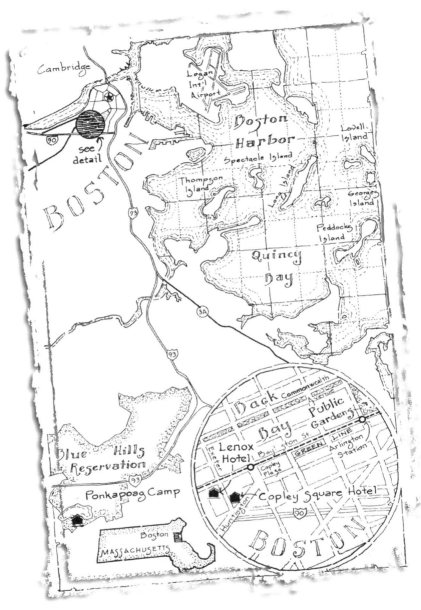

BOSTON
HARBOR

ECO-FRIENDLY ELEGANCE
The Lenox Hotel, Boston, Mass.

As onlookers cheer, contestants commence their competition to hurl recycled cans the greatest distance. This is no ordinary employee picnic, but the S.H.I.N.E. Bowl, an eco-event organized by the owners of The Lenox and Copley Square Hotels in Boston. S.H.I.N.E. stands for Saunders Hotels Initiative to Nurture the Environment.

Each year, Lenox Hotel employees compete with their Copley Square counterparts in Eco-Jeopardy, the Recycled Can Toss and other environmental events. Winners receive recycled plastic mugs, natural cotton tote bags, pencils made of reclaimed denim and other eco-friendly incentive gifts. This event is a whimsical symbol of the hotels' environmental commitment.

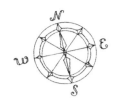

THE FACTS
Lenox Hotel

address	710 Boylston Street, at Exeter Street Boston, MA 02116
phone	617-536-5300, 800-225-7676 (reservations) (fax 617-267-1237)
Web site	**www.lenoxhotel.com** The site includes an environmental page.
lodging	212 guest rooms and suites, including some disabled-accessible rooms
rates	$300-$500 range per day. Check for specials on the hotel's Web site.
caveats	This is an urban hotel, so don't expect a lot of rustic ambience and greenery.
credentials	Numerous environmental and hospitality awards, including recognition for historic lobby renovation (Boston Preservation Alliance, 1994) and Presidential Gold Medal for Conservation. AAA Four-Diamond rating.
special interest	Comprehensive environmental programs, employee involvement.

SHINE stands for Saunders Hotel Initiative to Nurture the Environment. The Saunders Group, owner of the two hotels, is recognized internationally for environmental efforts, with numerous conservation programs in place at the two properties. Over the last decade, the owners have spent millions of dollars on new windows, toilets, and equipment to save water and energy.

While these technical improvements are important, the Saunders Group recognizes that a highly motivated hotel staff is the key to lasting environmental successes. Many small and seemingly mundane actions can add up to big resource and dollar savings, but only if hotel workers understand and follow through. For example, an energy-efficient washing machine becomes inefficient if the housekeepers consistently run it half-full.

"The key to employee awareness is education," says Tedd Saunders, Director of Environmental Affairs for the Saunders Group. "How can we apply environmental principles in everyday life."

The S.H.I.N.E. program begins with orientation for new employees, followed by frequent staff "eco-briefings". In this way, housekeepers learn why new maintenance techniques will result in specific benefits, such as reducing trash volume and improving water quality. Room attendants and maintenance workers are encouraged to think of new resource-conserving techniques.

THE HOTEL

The Lenox provides a stylish option to larger commercial hotels in Boston. Along with typical business travelers and tourists, The Lenox attracts a loyal following of guests in the media and entertainment industry.

Built in 1900, The Lenox Hotel hosted luminaries of the time such as Enrico Caruso, who arrived on his own private train. The distinctive red-and-white terra cotta brick exterior has survived, thanks to the owners' commitment to restoration rather than demolition.

A rocking chair, brass chandelier, and newly renovated marble bathroom are standard features of each high-ceilinged room. The elegant executive corner rooms also have working fireplaces. Many windows look out on the Charles River and Boston's Back Bay neighborhood.

TOILETS TO TARMAC

As part of extensive room renovation, the Saunders Hotel Group recently replaced century-old toilets, thereby saving five gallons of water for every flush. Faced with a small mountain of discarded commodes, the owners located a paving contractor who pulverized the porcelain for use as road fill.

In-room fax machines and dual-line speaker phones with modem ports are available for business travelers. Along with plush terry bathrobes, guests will discover an environmental brochure and discreet conservation reminders in each room.

The hotel's framed environmental mission statement is placed front and center on the reception desk. The wall behind the clerk bears an impressive array of environmental awards received by the hotel.

ACCESS

Driving in downtown Boston's crowded labyrinth of streets is to be avoided if at all possible. Boston's subway system provides convenient links to the airport and the Amtrak station; The Lenox is just a block from the Copley station on the Green Line. Check the hotel's Web site for details.

DINING

The Lenox is home to **Anago,** specializing in contemporary American cuisine and committed to using quality New England ingredients whenever possible. Also on-site is the original **Samuel Adams Brew House**, where a dozen brands of beer are kept on draft. Guests can indulge in room service as well, with breakfast, lunch, dinner, and light snacks provided by Anago's catering service.

To reduce restaurant and bar waste, the staff has eliminated paper placemats and plastic cups from the restaurants at The Lenox. Leftover food is donated to shelters.

CONSERVATION

As a result of the environmental programs at The Lenox and Copley Square Hotels, four million gallons of drinking water are saved annually, and more than one hundred tons of trash are diverted from the dump each year. Cans and bottles are donated to Mass Can, a nonprofit group that trains homeless people to provide recycling services.

The environmental commitment at The Lenox extends to the fine details of housekeeping. Seamstresses recycle damaged tablecloths into chef's aprons. Room attendants clean carpets using a nontoxic process and wield refillable pump-spray bottles filled with biodegradable cleansers.

Vendor education also is an important part of the hotel's environmental efforts. As a member of the Buy Recycled Business Alliance, the hotel uses its substantial buying power as leverage to support eco-friendly products.

ACTIVITIES

A fitness room is located on the property, along with a currency exchange and other services. The Lenox is just one block from the sidewalk cafes, boutiques, and art galleries lining Newbury Street. Guests also are within walking distance of Symphony Hall. The New England Aquarium and the Museum of Fine Arts are just a short subway ride away.

E ach April, the streets fill with panting runners participating in the Boston Marathon. For a few hours, people (rather than motor vehicles) are the dominant species on the race route. The Lenox sits squarely at the finish line of this sweaty New England rite of spring, affording a fine vantage point to watch the race's conclusion.

Rain was forecast for the race, but so far the event has been spared. In the harbor, though, fresh winds are glancing off the waves, creating whitecaps. A light curtain of raindrops is beginning to fall on the Harbor Islands, washing the rock outcrops as beachcombers seek cover.

ALMANAC

Tradition and Eco-Innovation
Copley Square Hotel, Boston, Mass.

The hotel's hundredth anniversary was approaching, and workers were preparing to place a time capsule in the cornerstone of the building. Staff members pondered which items would tell a future generation about the Copley Square in 1991. Along with other memorabilia, they decided to include the hotel's written commitment to protect and preserve the environment.

This was no token gesture. The Copley Square Hotel has undertaken more than one hundred environmental actions, from energy-efficient lighting to recycling. Each year, these efforts have eliminated thirty-seven tons of trash, saved more than 100,000 kilowatt-hours of electricity, and reduced the use of water by nearly two million gallons.

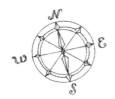

THE FACTS
Copley Square Hotel

address	47 Huntington Avenue, at corner of Exeter Street, Boston, MA 02116
phone	617-536-9000, reservations 800-225-7062 (fax 617-267-3547)
Web site	**www.copleysquarehotel.com** The site includes a description of the hotel's environmental policies and programs.
lodging	143 guest rooms, including five two-bedroom family suites and one parlor suite.
rates	Single rooms start at about $225, with suites in the $299 range. Check for specials on the hotel's Web site.
caveats	While this is definitely eco-friendly lodging, the hotel is in an urban location, so don't expect a leafy setting.
credentials	At the White House, the Saunders Group received the President's Gold Medal for Environmental Achievement. The Group's two hotels have received numerous other national environmental awards. AAA 3-Diamond rating.
special interest	Comprehensive conservation programs.

THE HOTEL

Built in 1891, the Copley Square is the city's oldest continuously-operated hotel. Small, as downtown hotels go, it has a casual European ambience, especially when complimentary afternoon tea is served in the hotel lobby. The hotel's 143 rooms include five two-bedroom suites and one parlor suite.

CONSERVATION

Photo: Saunders Hotel Group

As at The Lenox, each room contains brass "eco-plaques" placed by light switches and faucets. These small signs share facts about the need for conservation, along with a gentle reminder for guests to switch off lighting when leaving the room. In contrast to the sealed windows in many modern hotels, guests at the Copley Square are free to open windows for fresh air.

An unusual eco-feature in some rooms is the use of recycled upholstery for chairs and sofas. The attractive Polartek™ fabric is made from recycled plastic soft drink bottles.

Along with The Lenox, this hotel was one of the first in the country to institute a laundry-saving program. Guests have the choice of having their sheets and towels changed or left on for an additional night.

ACCESS

The hotel is located in Boston's Back Bay district. As with The Lenox, the Copley Square Hotel is easily accessible via Boston's subway system. The Copley Square T Station on the Green Line is only a few hundred feet away.

The hotel's Web site provides detailed directions and a map.

DINING

Three full-service restaurants and Tennessee's takeout restaurant are located on the premises. As at The Lenox, paper placemats and plastic cups have been eliminated from the restaurants. The recycling program further reduces waste, and surplus food is donated to shelters.

RECREATION AND DIVERSIONS

Hotel guests have complimentary use of a nearby health and fitness facility. Nearby Copley Square is a welcome opening in the cityscape. For additional open space, the Public Garden and Boston Commons are just a few blocks away on Boylston Street. Many of Boston's major attractions are within convenient walking distance or a short T-ride.

Fans of historic architecture can walk a short distance from the hotel's entry to visit Trinity Church, a standout in a city of architectural treasures. Fronting on Copley Square, this massive nineteenth-century Romanesque Revival monument is a lavish combination of frescoes, stained glass windows, and intricate Moorish detailing.

T *he Boston metropolitan area has sprawled out to Walden Pond State Reservation, the site of Henry David Thoreau's experiment in resourceful living. If you're planning a pilgrimage to Walden, it's preferable to stay away during summer weekends and holidays, when the pond's shoreline has the ambience of a congested beach. Instead, try to arrive on a rainy weekday, when mist is rising from the water, to get a better sense of how Walden looked in Thoreau's time.*

ALMANAC

In the region ...
BOSTON AREA

The recently created **Boston Harbor Islands National Recreation Area** includes thirty islands managed by a partnership of public agencies and private organizations. The islands are a drumlin field sculpted by retreating glaciers. Peddocks Island, a 113-acre preserve, includes a wildlife sanctuary, rocky beaches, woodlands, salt marsh, and a former fort. Less-developed Lovell Island features beaches and sand dunes. Free inter-island water taxis run in summer from Georges Island, and boats also leave from Long Wharf in Boston. Wildlife cruises, including winter events, are sponsored by the Metropolitan District Commission.

■ *tel. 617-727-7676,* **www.nps.gov/boha**

In addition to its aqueous exhibits, the **New England Aquarium** takes an active role in protecting and saving marine life. In particular, when strandings of cetaceans are reported in the area, Aquarium staff members assist in helping the marine mammals back to sea. A twenty-four hour hot line, (617) 973-5247, is available for reporting strandings. The Aquarium has its own stop on the Blue Line.

■ *Central Wharf, Boston MA 02110*
  tel. 617-973-5200, **www.neaq.org**

Many locations in the Concord area are associated with Henry David Thoreau. The **Great Meadows** near Concord still is a prime birding site. A replica of Thoreau's cabin has been constructed at the **Concord Museum**. The Thoreau Room at the Museum holds the original spartan furniture that Thoreau used in his cabin, along with other artifacts.

- *200 Lexington Road, Concord, MA,*
  tel. 617-369-9609, **www.concordmuseum.org**

Not far from Walden Pond, **Drumlin Farm Education Center and Wildlife Sanctuary** is operated by the Massachusetts Audubon Society. The 232-acre farm provides a setting for children and adults to learn about farm animals, sustainable and organic agriculture, and natural history. The Center is a ten-minute walk from the Fitchburg/Gardner trainlink from Boston's North Station; call for detailed directions.

- *Route 117, South Great Road, Lincoln, MA 01773*
  tel. 781-259-9807, **www.massaudubon.org**

Landscape plans, memorabilia and photos are on display at the **Frederick Law Olmsted National Historic Site**. Olmsted, considered the father of modern landscape architecture, was the designer of New York's Central Park, and was responsible for many visionary open space and recreation plans across the country.

- *99 Warren Street, Brookline, MA, tel. 617-566-1689*

Located just beyond Boston's southern suburbs, the 7,000-acre **Blue Hills Reservation** is the largest dedicated open space in the region. These hills are *monadnocks*, granite domes created by volcanism, then exposed by erosion. The reservation is laced with 150 miles of trails for hikers, skiiers, and equestrians. Great Blue Hill offers a commanding view of the Boston area, as hawks and turkey vultures circle overhead. The Massachusetts Audubon Society operates the Blue Hills Trailside Museum; one indoor exhibit offers a mouse-eye view of the reservation.

- *695 Hillside Street, Milton, MA 02186*
  tel. 617-698-1802, **www.state.ma.us/MDC**

OTHER PLACES TO STAY

For an outstanding bargain just fifteen miles from Boston, try **Ponkapoag Camp**, a group of twenty well-maintained cabins on Ponkapoag Pond. Operated by the Appalachian Mountain Club, the cabins include cots with mattresses (bring your own linens), wood stove, and folk art. Open all year, the inexpensive cabins do not have running water or electricity. The nearby quaking peat bog is well-equipped with species such as pitcher plant and sundew. Advance reservations are required.

■ *AMC Ponkapoag Camp, P.O. Box 582, Randolph, MA tel. 617-523-0636*

GREEN DINING

In Cambridge, **Christopher's Restaurant and Bar** is a popular place for bargain-priced, high-quality meals using natural ingredients. Vegetarian and nonvegetarian meals are given equal emphasis. For starters, there are Buenos Nachos, Yuppie Nachos, and numerous other appetizers. "Burgahs" and other meat dishes are made with Coleman naturally raised beef, free of antibiotics, hormones, artificial additives, and nitrites. Chuck's Veggie Peace Burgahs are a standout; profits from this item support community organizations. Specially filtered water is used, even for ice. Located in a cluster of neighborhood shops, Christopher's is close to the Porter Square T-stop on the Red Line. A fireplace adds to the pubby ambience. Open daily for lunch and dinner.

■ *1920 Massachusetts Avenue, Cambridge MA 02140 tel. 617-876-9180*

Featuring cuisine from Italy's Abruzzi region, **Ristorante Marino** uses fresh organic products, including chemical-free meats from the restaurant's own farms.

■ *2465 Massachusetts Avenue, near the corner of Cameron in Cambridge, MA 02139, tel. 617-868-5454* **www.marino-ristorante.com**

PROVISIONS

Just steps from the Copley Square Hotel, local farmers sell fresh produce and baked goods at the **Farmers Co-op Market** in Copley Square. From May to October, shoppers can find such items as homemade cranberry chutney or fresh maple syrup.

Bread & Circus has several locations in the Boston area. Each of these supermarkets has a bakery, natural foods grocery, and deli. Fresh organic produce is attractively displayed, and the stores sponsor environmental and nutritional programs. The Cambridge store is accessible from the Central Square T station on the Red Line. Check their Web site for other store locations and online organic offerings.

- *115 Prospect Street, Cambridge, MA 02139*
  tel. 617-492-0070, **www.wholefoods.com**

Six thousand members support the **Harvest Co-op** supermarkets in the Boston area. These two stores carry a full line of natural and gourmet produce, cheese, meat, and seafood. Each location has a delicatessen.

- *449 Cambridge Street, Allston, MA 02134*
  tel. 617-787-1416
- *581 Massachusetts Avenue, Cambridge, MA 02139*
  tel 617-661-1580

RESOURCES

Since 1979**, Friends of the Boston Harbor Islands** has worked to balance public use of the islands with the need to protect a fragile ecosystem and historic resources. Members support the islands through volunteer programs, public education, and advocacy. In particular, FBHI sponsors popular boat trips and island tours.

- *tel. 781-740-4290*

MassBike, the Massachusetts Bicycle Coalition, is a statewide bicycling advocacy organization working for better and safer bicycle transportation. For membership information and a copy of Mass Cyclist, write:

- *214A Broadway, Cambridge, MA 02139 tel. 617-491-RIDE,* **www.massbike.org**

With headquarters just a quarter mile from Walden Pond, **The Thoreau Society** fosters interest in the life, writings and philosophy of Henry David Thoreau. Members receive the quarterly *Thoreau Society Bulletin* and the *Concord Saunterer*, an annual publication of essays.

The Walden Woods Project has worked to preserve open space around Walden Pond. These two organizations have established the **Thoreau Institute**, with research facilities in a historic structure set in Walden Woods.

- *The Thoreau Society, 44 Baker Farm, Lincoln, MA 01773-3004, tel. 781-259-4750,* **www.walden.org**

FOR MORE INFORMATION

Tedd Saunders and Loretta McGovern describe strategies for creating profitable and environmentally sound businesses in *The Bottom Line of Green Is Black.* Published by Harper San Francisco, this book describes successful environmental initiatives in various industrial and commercial settings.

- *Harper San Francisco, hardback: 269 pages. $23.00*

The Nature of Massachusetts is an elaborate and carefully compiled account of the commonwealth's biological communities. Authors Christopher Leahy, John Hanson Mitchell, and Thomas Conuel describe the physiography and organisms of each community. The text is complemented by watercolor illustrations by noted painter Lars Jonsson.

- *Available from the Massachusetts Audubon Society; call 781-259-9661, or order through the Society's Web site,* **www.massaudubon.org**

Boston Naturally, The Green Map of Greater Boston, is an eco-friendly guide to the area's natural nooks and niches. Funded in part by The Lenox and Copley Square Hotels, this map is packed with information about public transit, open space, walking trails, bike paths, whale watching, and earth-friendly shopping. Special map symbols identify great places for birding and picnics.

■ *Call Eco-Logical Solutions at 617-425-0900, ext. 160 for more information.*

8

RHODE ISLAND

To me, this place allows you to be a child again. When you're up in the tower watching sailboats and tugboats and barges go by, it's as though you've been given permission to move into your tree house. You get to explore and create and do the kinds of clever things you recall from books like Robinson Crusoe *or* The Swiss Family Robinson.

— Charlotte Johnson,
Rose Island
Lighthouse Foundation

RHODE
ISLAND

LIGHTHOUSE-KEEPING ON NARRAGANSETT BAY

Rose Island Lighthouse, Newport, Rhode Island

Across the bay from Newport's Gilded Age mansions, a lighthouse on a small island stands as a symbol of the local community's commitment to historic preservation and environmental education. Here, adventurous overnight guests can practice conservation and self sufficiency. A wind turbine converts bay breezes to electricity, and rainwater is collected from the roof. Guests can try out the life of a lighthouse keeper, pitching in with chores and helping to operate the station.

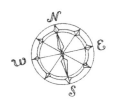

THE FACTS
Rose Island Lighthouse

address	Rose Island Lighthouse Foundation P.O. Box 1419, Newport, RI 02840
phone	401-847-4242 (fax 401-847-7262)
Web site	**www.RoseIslandLighthouse.org**
lodging	Two rooms for overnight guests, plus keeper's quarters for weekly stays.
rates	Upper moderate price (about $110 to $150 per night) helps to defray cost of lighthouse upkeep. Weekly prices vary from about $600 to $1,200, depending on the season. Ferry fare is an additional $10 per person round trip.
caveats	Early twentieth-century amenities with no running water. No pets. No wheelchair access. Arrivals and departures may be delayed by bad weather. Emergency phone only.
credentials	Rhode Island Historical Preservation Commission award. Listed on National Register of Historic Places.
special interest	Historic preservation, windpower, rainwater collection, birding, sustainable living.

RESTORATION

The island and its lighthouse have withstood centuries of history. Beginning in the 1700s, successive squads of British, French, and American soldiers built fortifications on the island. The ruins now serve as perches for herring gulls.

The Rose Island Lighthouse beacon first began illuminating the bay in 1870. Designed in the French Second Empire style, with a slate mansard roof, the lighthouse was from the start a classic example of American maritime architecture. The octagonal light tower and keeper's quarters were constructed for the grand sum of $7,500.

Over the next century, the lighthouse helped to keep vessels on course. In 1971 the lighthouse was deactivated by the Coast Guard. For the next thirteen years, the abandoned building was at the mercy of storms and vandals.

When the federal government offered to donate the property as a public site, enthusiastic local citizens formed the Rose Island Lighthouse Foundation. With a huge outpouring of financial support and volunteer labor, the foundation raised much of the money to restore the maritime landmark.

To raise restoration money, the foundation has organized clambakes, sold memberships, and secured grants. Area architects, engineers, carpenters, plumbers, contractors, students, and suppliers have contributed materials and thousands of work hours. Salvaged doors, cupboards, and drawers have been incorporated into the restored rooms.

By 1993, the lighthouse was once again ready for service. Fully automated, Rose Island Light has resumed its place on nautical charts as an official aid to navigation, and the lighthouse has become a popular destination for day visitors, overnight guests, and keepers.

The success of this endeavor is largely due to Charlotte Johnson's creativity and perseverance. Now executive director of the Rose Island Lighthouse Foundation, Charlotte also serves as the default off-season keeper. On nights when the lighthouse is unoccupied, she may cross the channel in the Foundation's old wooden lobster boat and stay on the island herself.

ACCOMMODATIONS

Staying on a small island is a challenge, and this is a place for adventurous, self-reliant people. Visitors can choose between an overnight stay, or a more ambitious week-long lighthouse-keeping stint. A cellular phone and marine radio are available for emergencies.

Open during the day as a museum, the first-floor rooms metamorphose into guest quarters for the night. Overnight visitors have the opportunity to experience a small dose of the life of an early twentieth-century light-house keeper.

The first floor includes two bedrooms, a library, living room, kitchen, and pantry/water closet. Described as "mostly bed," the bedrooms feature quilt-covered metal beds and nautical decor on the walls. Basins and pitchers are provided for washing up.

In keeping with the self-sufficient theme, guests are expected to make their beds and leave the quarters clean. Since the guest rooms serve as museum dioramas during the day, visitors need to keep their space tidy.

The Foundation also invites reliable people with basic mechanical skills and a conservation orientation to be lighthouse keepers for a week. While the beacon itself is fully automated, there are other responsibilities.

The keeper's duties include raising and lowering the flag, checking the water and electrical systems, and recording weather data. In addition, keepers agree to complete at least one hour of painting, compost turning, or other chores each day.

As keepers make entries in the lighthouse log, they become part of the island's history.

In contrast to the downstairs museum, the second-floor keepers' quarters have been modernized. The spacious bedroom has a queen-size bed. There's also a separate bunk room. The living area has a convertible sofa, a rocking chair, and a working wood stove. In the corner, varnished stairs climb the tower to the beacon.

"The Lighthouse is a symbol of all our good feelings towards islands and the sea."

Charlotte Johnson,
Rose Island
Lighthouse
Foundation

DINING

Bottled water is provided for overnight guests. However, "restaurant row" takes on a new meaning here, as the nearest dining establishment is a boat trip across the bay. Consequently, overnight visitors need to bring their own groceries.

Seafood is an exception. At low tide, visitors can gather mussels from the rocks along the shore. The lighthouse provides poles to surf-cast for Tautog (black fish), striped bass, bluefish, and flounder. Lobster pots by the dock also offer seafood potential.

The downstairs kitchen is dominated by a massive black stove, complete with an iron pot and a tea kettle. A working pitcher pump does duty at the sink, and a wash tub on the floor holds ice tongs and a washboard. Seashell-filled canning jars sit on the windowsills, and a wooden coffee grinder resides on the counter.

The kitchenette in the keeper's quarters is more modern, with a small refrigerator, coffeemaker, toaster, and microwave (adequate wind is needed, though, to generate enough electricity for their use). The kitchen is fully furnished with pans, dishes, and linens.

For downstairs guests, there's an abundance of pans and utensils. The massive stove is not in service, so cooking facilities are limited to a gas hot plate. In good weather, guests can fire up the gas barbecue grill outside the kitchen door.

The ambience makes all the preparation worthwhile. Twilight is the time for a seafood dinner, with antique china reflecting the candlelight while the lights of Newport form a necklace across the bay.

ACCESS

Rose Island is located one mile west of Newport, just south of the suspension bridge arching over the bay. The lighthouse is accessible by boat only.

A small passenger ferry operates from July to Labor Day, shuttling visitors to Rose Island from several points in Jamestown and Newport. At other times, Charlotte transports guests in "Light-A-Rose" from the Goat Island Marina, where a seasonal fee is charged for secured parking. This thirty-foot recycled lobster boat, now owned by the Foundation, often is greeted by gulls and oystercatchers at the Rose Island dock.

Once at the lighthouse dock, guests lug their gear and groceries up a path to their quarters, past beach roses and a lighthouse-shaped doghouse. Then the boat departs, and guests are on their own, although the director usually stops in daily to see if any assistance is needed.

It's good to plan a lighthouse visit with a broad margin, allowing for the whims of the elements. If the bay becomes too rough for safe passage, the Foundation will arrange alternate onshore accommodations, reschedule your visit, or provide a gift certificate for the full amount paid.

Once you're on the island, keep in mind that you may get weathered in at the lighthouse. The Foundation advises guests to plan for this possibility, particularly in the winter season. For visitors not on a tight timetable, this can have a fringe benefit, for the extra stay comes with no additional charge.

CONSERVATION

Overhead, a spinning wind turbine generates power for use in the building. Wind velocity suddenly has new meaning at the lighthouse, since the day's electrical use is dependent on output from the wind generator.

Likewise, the hydrologic cycle here is not a vague abstraction, but an immediate and vital concern. The water supply is collected from rain falling on the roof and directed by downspouts to the cistern in the basement.

Water is diverted into the cistern only after an initial downpour cleans the roof. A pitcher pump lifts water to the pantry sink.

To reduce use of electricity, the light fixtures have been outfitted with compact fluorescent bulbs. For atmosphere as well as practicality, guests can bring candles to place in wall sconces.

Outdoor solar showers are used in warmer months. During the winter, overnighters heat bathing water on the propane burner in the kitchen. Keepers have a propane water heater. In a concession to modern preferences, a radiant floor heating system provides comfortable temperatures, even during the winter.

Organic waste is composted or put into the lobster trap. Other trash accompanies guests on their trip back to the mainland, where paper, plastics, and metal are recycled.

ENVIRONMENTAL PROGRAMS

With its island location and self-sufficient tradition, the Rose Island Lighthouse is well-situated to serve as a resource-efficient environmental education center. Public tours and student programs demonstrate ecological awareness and the value of historic preservation.

The Foundation offers public tours from July to Labor Day. School tours are conducted in the spring and fall, teaching stewardship by direct example. Day visitors explore the station from the windmill to the cellar cistern, learning about the lives of lighthouse families. Old keeper logbooks and photographs provide glimpses of everyday life on Rose Island.

At one time, developers had plans to build a big marina and condominiums on the abandoned military base next to the lighthouse. However, local environmental groups rallied and encircled the island with a 3,500-ft. banner, staving off this threat. The foundation now owns the remaining land on the island, preserving the property as permanent open space for generations to come.

ACTIVITIES

The lighthouse property is perched on a small corner of the seventeen-acre island, and most of Rose Island is occupied by former military fortifications. The island's wild roses are busily reclaiming the brick ruins. They share the site with everlasting pea blossoms, Queen Anne's lace, honeysuckle, catnip, and other self-reliant species.

Because there are no mammalian predators on the island, this is a favored rookery for herring gulls, egrets, oyster-catchers, herons, and other avian species. From April to August, thousands of birds nest on the island and forage amid the sea grass along the shore.

The island's abundant bird life is a big attraction for birders. However, during the nesting season, unwary humans may be dive-bombed, Hitchcock-style, by feathered parents protecting their eggs and young. Hard hats are advised.

Beachcombers can stroll the island's shell-strewn shoreline. A post-industrial pastime here involves searching for beach glass — broken shards that have been rounded and polished by the surf. Visitors also can poke about the old barracks near the lighthouse (young children should be watched carefully here and elsewhere on the island).

Cold-water-tolerant guests can swim in the brisk surf. A two-person kayak is provided for paddling on the bay.

Winter brings the added attraction of harbor seals that like to loll about on concrete foundations jutting into the water. While storms can complicate access, the elements also provide drama for adventurous visitors who can watch storms sweeping across the bay.

During inclement weather, guests can relax inside, perusing the history of the lighthouse as recorded in old ledgers. Visitors can browse the bookshelves in the library or play old records on the wind-up Victrola. The living room houses a player piano and a stack of song rolls, with sing-along selections from "Bye, Bye Blackbird" to "Minnie the Moocher."

Telescopes and binoculars are strategically placed for visual exploration of the bay. Hammersmith Farm, of Kennedy-Bouvier fame, is within view. To the west is the shoreline of Jamestown, while Newport lies a mile east. There is an ongoing parade of vessels, with armadas of sailboats on summer days. On rare occasions, guests have sighted deer swimming across Narragansett Bay.

T o appreciate the ultimate
purpose of a lighthouse,
there's nothing like a soupy fog.
Sounds of mournful foghorns
and clanging buoys drift in the
mysterious thickness. Waves collide
with rocks as you stroll along the
shell beach. The apparitions of
military ruins fade, then re-appear.

Above you, the octagonal tower of
Rose Island Lighthouse stands firm.
The beacon reliably flashes
every six seconds, a confident
constant in a world
of change.

The National Center for Environmental Education
Whispering Pines Conference Center, West Greenwich, Rhode Island

In a classic climb up the corporate ladder, W. Alton Jones had gone from janitor to chief executive officer at Cities Service Corporation. For a retreat from his busy schedule, Jones built Whispering Pines Lodge in the forests of western Rhode Island. Here he entertained guests such as the King of Nepal, and spent weekends with his fishing buddy Dwight Eisenhower.

Today, this retreat is the W. Alton Jones campus of the University of Rhode Island. For travelers in southern New England, it's worth a little extra effort to seek out the Whispering Pines Conference Center for an overnight stay.

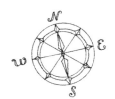

THE FACTS
Whispering Pines Conference Center

address	W. Alton Jones Campus 401 Victory Highway West Greenwich, RI 02817
phone	401-397-3361, ext. 6056, or 401-397-3304 [fax 401-397-6540]
Web site	**www.uri.edu/ajc**
lodging	A total of thirty-two rooms in four guest houses. A number of rooms are disabled-accessible.
rates	$185 single, $135 per person, per day, double occupancy includes all meals.
caveats	Individuals cannot book far in advance. The center is geared mainly to groups, although drop-in visitors are welcome when space is available.
credentials	Member, International Association of Conference Centers.
special interest	Environmental education, wooded lakeside setting.

THE CONFERENCE CENTER

Whispering Pines Conference Center is part of the National Center for Environmental Education, which covers 2,300 acres of white pine forests, sugar maple groves, pastures, streams and lakes. The Center's buildings on the shore of Lake Eisenhower have a friendly, noninstitutional feeling.

Many original furnishings are still in place, including a much-admired ornate chest in the lounge of Whispering Pines Lodge. Lodge memorabilia (such as photos of Ike in fishing gear) decorate the pine-paneled walls.

Guest rooms are in four separate buildings with rustic-chic decor. The main lodge has four rooms with private baths, while the remaining guest quarters are in three other buildings.

For groups, there are four well-equipped meeting rooms and a small auditorium. The Center sponsors specialized environmental programs such as the Women's Wilderness Weekend.

DINING

The Center serves meals buffet-style, and vegetarian options are available. Fresh-baked pastries are a highlight. Groups and individual guests typically are on Full American Plan (all meals included).

From the dining room, guests can watch the ducks on the 75-acre lake. As part of recycling at the Center, food scraps are fed to the domestic animals at Woodvale Farm.

NATURAL SETTING

Most of the site is woodland, and one thousand acres of the campus have been specifically protected as natural habitat. Here, scientists from the University of Rhode Island, Massachusetts Institute of Technology, and NASA conduct research projects.

A number of rare and uncommon plant species thrive in the 100-acre Nettie Jones Nature Reserve. This natural habitat serves as an outdoor laboratory for landscape architecture students at the University of Rhode Island. A local botanist conducts spring and fall wildflower walks for guests at the Conference Center.

WOODVALE FARM

The National Center for Environmental Education also offers youth camp programs at Woodvale Farm on the URI campus. This working farm dates back to the nineteenth century, when the Matteson family worked the land. The pastures, garden area, buildings, and cemetery from this earlier era have been preserved.

WOODVALE FARM
STUDENT WORKSHOP

Another nearby tract formerly was part of the state poor farm, where indigents once labored in the fields. Two certified organic gardens now have taken the place of the poor farm. Here, children attending summer programs help to tend the garden, pumpkin patch, and apple orchard. From the shelter of stone walls, sneaky woodchucks watch for an opportunity to purloin a carrot or rutabaga.

The Environmental Education Center puts the former barns to good use. Inner-city students learn firsthand about the farm as an ecosystem, as they assist in animal and crop raising, natural control of insects, composting, and recycling. Kids study the origins of pizza dough as they grow wheat and grind grain into flour. Seasonal activities include sheep shearing, cider pressing, horse-drawn hayrides, and caring for newborn animals.

Thousands of children visit the camp each year. At the Nocturnal Camp, kids study night ecology, then sleep during the day. Children in lower grades participate in the Farm Discoveries program, while the Living Farm and Farm Ecology programs are for older elementary students.

ACTIVITIES

Guests at the Center have free access to facilities and equipment for bocce, horseshoes, volleyball, basketball, croquet, and pickup softball. About twenty canoes are on hand for visitors to explore the lake's islands, beaver lodge, and coves. Tennis courts and a swimming beach are other recreation options.

For hikers, ten miles of trails wind through woodlands and wetlands. Many guests bring mountain bikes for rides around the property. In winter, visitors can snowshoe or ski cross-country along these trails.

For off-site excursions, guests at the URI campus can explore one of the largest uninterrupted forest tracts in southern New England. Trails extend across some forty thousand acres of woodland in the adjacent Arcadia and Pachaug State Forests.

ACCESS

The Whispering Pines Conference Center is located twenty-seven miles southwest of Providence, near Interstate 95. The Center is an hour and a half drive from Boston and about three hours from New York City. From Boston or Providence, take Interstate 95 south to Exit 5B, then follow Route 102 north 2.5 miles and look for the URI sign.

The T. F. Green Airport serving Providence and the rest of Rhode Island is less than half an hour away. No public transit is available to the Center, but the staff can recommend limo or taxi services.

I n late spring, showy ladyslippers emerge in the moist woodlands of the National Environmental Education Center, commencing their season of insect seduction. Using shady tactics, these pink blossoms trick gullible insects with a nectarlike scent wafting from the interior of the moccasin-shaped flower. But there's no nectar inside, and the disappointed insect works his way back out, picking up pollen on the way.

In the region ...
RHODE
ISLAND

While Newport usually brings mega-mansions to mind, the town also has walker-friendly cobblestone streets lined with antique shops and boutiques. Just east of Newport, the **Norman Bird Sanctuary** includes 450 acres of exceptional natural habitat providing shelter for nesting birds, rabbits, and foxes. Habitats include woodland, salt marshes, and craggy ridges. Children's programs include theme hikes and educational workshops. Trail fee for guided walks.

- *583 Third Beach Road, Newport, RI 02842*
  tel. 401-846-2577.
  www.normanbirdsanctuary.org

The **Narragansett Bay National Estuarine Research Reserve** includes Patience and Hope Islands, as well as big chunks of Prudence Island. Natural communities include forested uplands, rock cliffs grading into cobble beaches, salt marshes, and an extensive eelgrass meadow. Wildlife on Prudence Island includes eastern red fox, a seasonal colony of least terns, and a large herd of white-tailed deer. For humans, the reserve provides interpretive areas and walking trails, a deep water pier, and a swimming beach.

- *P. O. Box 151, Prudence Island, RI 02872*
  tel. 401-683-6780.

Long Pond-Ell Pond Trail is recommended for its diversity of natural habitat in a short walk. The path climbs through oak-hickory forest to rocky overlooks above two ponds. Ell Pond, a glacial kettlehole lake, is bordered on three sides by a red maple-Atlantic white cedar swamp. Unmarked trailheads are located at parking lots on North Road and Canonchet Road in Hopkinton.

- *For more information: Audubon Society of Rhode Island, 12 Sanderson Road, Smithfield, RI 02917 tel. 401-231-6444*

GREEN DINING

The shops, gardens, farmyard and international bazaar at the Fantastic Umbrella Factory have a vestigial Sixties ambience. Within this countercultural complex, the **Spice of Life Natural Foods Café** serves Mexican, Middle Eastern and vegetarian specialties. This family-friendly place on Route A1a emphasizes the use of natural and organic ingredients.

- *Box 254, Charlestown, RI 02813, tel. 401-364-2030*

Perched on the perimeters of Providence and Pawtucket, **Garden Grill Café and Juice Bar** combines healthy vegetarian and vegan food with a concern for the environment. The café makes a point of using organically grown products and recycled paper. The garden wraps made with spinach flour tortillas are a specialty; the Artichoke Heart Quesadilla ($5.95) is a standout. Dinner entrées such as the Tofu and Vegetable Pad Thai are in the $8 to $11 range. Smoothies and juices complete the healthy menu at the Garden Grill, located in the Blackstone Place Center at Lafayette Street. Open 10 am to 9:30 pm Monday through Saturday, noon to 8 pm on Sunday.

- *727 East Avenue, Pawtucket, RI, tel. 401-726-2826*

PROVISIONS AND SHOPPING

Located just off Bellevue Avenue near the International Tennis Hall of Fame, **Harvest Natural Foods and Catering** is a handy place to stock up for an expedition to Rose Island. Here you'll find organic produce and local goods, such as goat milk from Misty Willow Farm. Lunches are mainly takeout with fresh-made muffins and sandwiches. Hot soups are popular when a brisk breeze is blowing off the bay. Open seven days a week.

- *One Casino Terrace, Newport, RI 02840
  tel. 401-846-8137*

Boris Bally, Atelier, specializes in artwork made from old highway signs and other recycled objects. The owner has served as a professor at various universities around the country, and his work has been featured in publications from the *Wall Street Journal to Vogue.* Check the Atelier's splendid Web site at **www.BorisBally.com**.

- *The Ryan Post Building, 789 Atwells Ave., at Academy
  Avenue, Providence, RI 02909, tel. 401-277-8464*

The **Alternative Food Cooperative** serves the University of Rhode Island community in the Kingston area. Open seven days a week, the cooperative offers a variety of produce and personal care products, such as honey from local hives, milk from neighborhood goats, rice almond bread, organic blueberries, and vanilla body lotion. Stop for a peanut butter pretzel before venturing into the nearby Great Swamp.

- *357 Main Street, Wakefield, RI 02879*

Just a few miles from the Whispering Pines Conference Center, **Meadowbrook Herb Garden** sells hundreds of varieties of herb and flower seeds, along with wreaths, dried flowers, suncatchers, and topiaries. Visitors can browse in the greenhouse or attend numerous workshops. Open daily; about one mile east on Route 138 from Interstate 95's Exit 3A. Watch for the sign on the south side of the road.

- *Route 138, Wyoming, RI 02898, tel. 401-539-7603*

Located in a residential neighborhood near Brown University, **Bread & Circus Whole Foods Market** has an impressive selection of organic produce, natural foods, and eco-friendly products, including seafood and meats. This and other Bread & Circus stores support the Northeast Organic Farming Association's efforts to aid farmers in the transition from conventional to organic farming. The chain's Web site offers on-line shopping for natural foods and products.

- *261 Waterman Street, Providence, RI 02906*
  tel. 401-272-1690, **www.wholefoods.com**

RESOURCES

Quahoggers, teachers, fishermen, and others concerned about Narrangansett Bay have joined forces to form **Save the Bay**. The organization's Habitat Program is helping to protect and restore marsh grass and submerged eelgrass beds in the bay. Send "Eel-mail" to <u>savebay.savebay.org</u>.

- *434 Smith Street, Providence, RI 02908*
  tel. 401-272-3540, **www.savebay.org**

Supported by donations and memberships, the **Rose Island Lighthouse Foundation** maintains the light-house and its natural surroundings. The Foundation also offers educational programs for children and adults. Public tours and picnics are scheduled from July to Labor Day.

- *P.O. Box 1419, Newport, RI 02840, tel. 401-847-4242*
  www.RoseIslandLighthouse.org

FOR MORE INFORMATION

Ken Weber's *Walks and Rambles in Rhode Island* provides a choice of forty outings, including woodland, wetland, island, and beach walks. Each selection has a map, hiking time, distance, and directions to the trailhead.

- *Woodstock, VT: Backcountry Publications,*
  1993 (second edition).

9

CONNECTICUT

Our thoughts and sentiments
answer to the revolutions of the
seasons as two cog-wheels fit
into each other. A year is made up
of a certain series and number of
sensations and thoughts, which
have their language in nature.
Now I am ice, now I am sorrel.

— Henry David
Thoreau

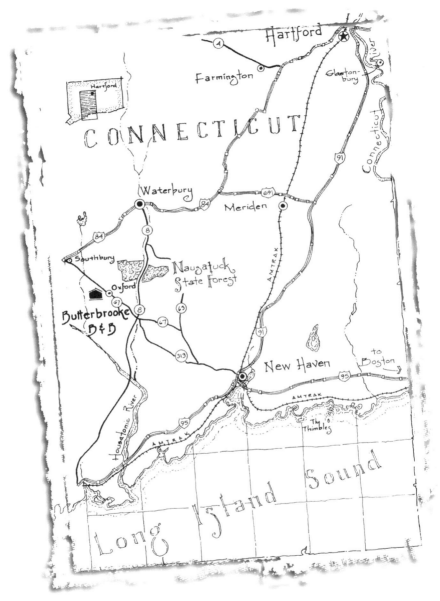

CONNECTICUT

Colonial Solar in Connecticut

Butterbrooke Bed & Breakfast
Oxford, Connecticut

CERTIFIED ORGANIC VEGETABLES.

This roadside sign is the only hint that you've reached the Butterbrooke Bed & Breakfast, a deliberately low-key inn in the wooded hills northwest of New Haven. Indeed, owner Tom Butterworth doesn't do any advertising at all, relying instead on word of mouth for guests to find this historic retreat.

The environmental focus here dates clear back to 1711, when the original builders had the foresight to orient the house for passive solar heating. Most of the windows face south, and the earth-sheltered home nestles into the hillside, turning its back on the north wind. Old sugar maples provide summer shade. In fact, the inn has been featured on solar tours, so that today's builders can learn from tradition.

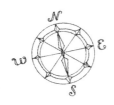

THE FACTS
Butterbrooke Bed & Breakfast

address	78 Barry Road, Oxford, CT 06478
phone	203-888-2000
lodging	One large guest suite with private entrance, bedroom, and sitting room
rates	$65 to $75 per night
caveats	House has a slight smoky aroma from the old fireplaces. No credit cards.
credentials	The inn's garden provides certified organic produce.
special interest	Organic gardening, historic architecture.

THE INN

Two ancient farmhouses were connected at one time to form the present inn. Three centuries of history are evidenced by the slightly slanted plank floors and a heavy tomahawk-resistant door with original hand-wrought hardware.

The spacious guest suite has the benefit of a separate entrance. Antique furnishings give the flavor of long-ago New England, comfortable without being precious. An extra bed can be placed in the room. Two fireplaces in the guest quarters are complete with an eighteenth-century bake oven and a cooking crane.

ACCESS

The inn is twenty-two miles northwest of New Haven, just west of Route 67 on Barry Road near the town of Oxford. From New York City, the Butterbrooke is just an hour and a half northeast via Interstate 84. The owner can arrange to pick up New York visitors who arrive at Exit 14 on I-84 via Bonanza Bus, or a travel shuttle will transport guests from the bus station to the inn.

KITCHEN AND GARDEN

The highlight of the menu here is Tom Butterworth's multigrain pancakes, which metamorphose by the season. Depending on what's ripening in the garden, Tom's berries, apples, cantaloupes, or other produce may be blended with batter and orange juice. Tom purchases grains from organic natural food sources, and he welcomes vegetarian guests.

The garden supplies a variety of other produce, including Tahitian squash (a long-necked type of butternut), daikon radishes, and Tom's highly touted super-sweet corn. Solar "grow chambers" with plastic water jugs have been in use for two decades to jump-start the spring garden. Wild blackberries and other untamed edibles grow in the woods on the property.

With his unassuming manner, guests may not realize that the owner is a professor of biology with a doctorate from Columbia University. Visitors find that Tom is a good source of information on the area's plants and wildlife.

However, the garden is Tom's forte. He has developed a "sheet composting" technique for soil improvement, using manure and a cover of leaves. Also, he makes long compost piles that require no tilling. Recyclables are taken to town, and the inn ends up with very little solid waste.

ACTIVITIES

Many of the guests are freeway refugees from nearby I-84, stopping for a break on their way to Maine. Others are exhausted New Yorkers seeking peace and quiet. "Some people come up here and sleep the whole time," Tom laughs. As a result, Tom serves breakfast as late as 12:30 in the afternoon.

The spring-fed pond is a good place to cool off on a hot summer day. The dock has a built-in bench where you can watch beavers at work or gaze at the reflections of autumn foliage. In winter, the pond provides a venue for ice skating. Elsewhere on the site, you can stroll by the brook, or search for birds' nests in the brambles.

OWNER TOM BUTTERWORTH HARVESTING ORGANIC PRODUCE

The sugar maples are turning
salmon orange, and the harvest
moon signals the close of the garden
season. The first cold snap has
frosted the Jerusalem artichokes,
a favorite of Tom's. He spades
the soil, collects the knobby tubers,
adds some Tahitian squash to
the wheelbarrow, and heads
for the house.

It's time to put things by.
Tom stores, cans, and freezes
produce to last through the long
winter. Until the next garden season,
guests at Butterbrooke can dine by
the fireside and appreciate
these reminders of long
summer days.

In the region ...
CONNECTICUT

Nearby **Naugatuck State Forest** has extensive hiking paths. To see some of the best scenery in the state, take the Spruce Brook Ravine Trail. This misnamed path winds through conifers (hemlocks, not spruces) enroute to a waterfall.

Giant reptiles once roamed south of Hartford, leaving fossilized footprints at **Dinosaur State Park**. A geodesic dome exhibit center is the largest enclosed dinosaur track site in North America, with prints dating back nearly 200 million years. Or make your own tracks along the nature trails winding through the park. The park is open daily, but the exhibit building is closed on Mondays.

■ *400 West Street, Rocky Hill, CT 06067*
  tel 860-529-8423, **www.dinosaurstatepark.org**

GREEN DINING

Across from the Yale campus in central New Haven, **Claire's Cornucopia** is located in a pedestrian-friendly area of art galleries and cafés. Open from breakfast to 9 or 10 p.m. daily, Claire's has a diverse menu with a Mexican emphasis. Their *pizzettes* are ten-inch flour tortillas topped with sun-dried tomatoes and other good stuff. Claire's has a friendly collegiate atmosphere with counter service.

■ *1000 Chapel Street at College, New Haven, CT 06510*
  tel 203-562-3888

PROVISIONS

Located down the road from Butterbrooke B&B, **Catnip Acres Herb Nursery** has been in operation for more than two decades. Summer visitors can tour a butterfly garden and other herb displays, while winter shoppers can pause for a cup of spiced tea by the fireside. Herb seminars, book signings, and herbal luncheons are offered throughout the year.

- *67 Christian Street, Oxford, CT 06478*
  tel. 203-888-5649

Edge of the Woods, a natural foods supermarket in New Haven, includes a kosher vegetarian restaurant and food to go. Macrobiotic foods are available. Open seven days a week.

- *379 Wailey Avenue, New Haven, CT 06511*
  tel 203-787-1055

RESOURCES

The Connecticut Forest and Park Association (CFPA) is a nonprofit organization dedicated to the conservation and enhancement of the state's natural resources. The Association plans, builds, and maintains

the statewide Blue-Blazed Hiking Trail System. The CFPA's *Connecticut Walk Book* is the ultimate guide to this trail network.

- *16 Meriden Road, Rockfall, CT 06481*
  tel. 860-346-2372, **www.ctwoodlands.org**

FOR MORE INFORMATION

Sixty Selected Short Nature Walks in Connecticut by Eugene Keyarts is a useful guide. The book includes maps for each hike, along with practical information and some details about local plants and wildlife.

- *Old Saybrook, CT: Globe Pequot Press. 180 pages. $9.95*

10

ADIRONDACKS

*... We had been out for two or three hours
but had seen nothing; once we heard a tree fall
with a dull, heavy crash, and two or three times
the harsh hooting of an owl had been answered
by the unholy laughter of a loon from the bosom
of the lake, but otherwise nothing had occurred
to break the death-like stillness of the night;
not even a breath of air stirred among
the tops of the tall pine trees.*

*Wearied by our unsuccess we at last
turned homeward when suddenly the quiet was
broken by the song of a hermit thrush; louder
and clearer it sang from the depths of the grim
and rugged woods, until the sweet, sad music
seemed to fill the very air and to conquer for the
moment the gloom of the night; then it died
away and ceased as suddenly as it had begun.*

— Theodore Roosevelt, notes on a visit
to the Adirondacks, 1877

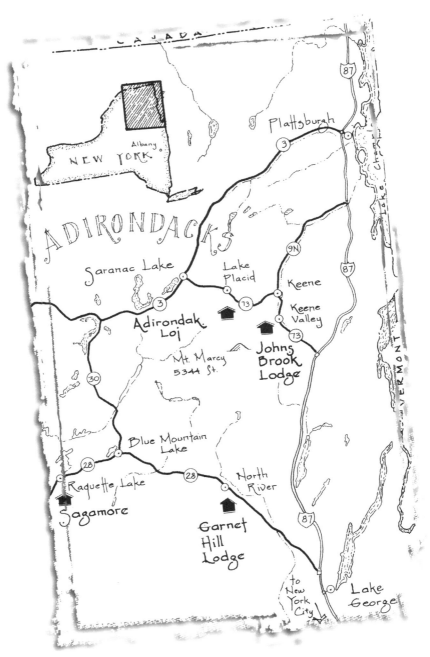

ADIRONDACKS

A North Woods Retreat
Adirondak Loj, Lake Placid, New York

Relaxing in Adirondack chairs, a family watches
from the shore as the last canoeists return to the shore
of Heart Lake. The water reflects fading midsummer
light as a full moon rises through the
pines behind the lodge.

Inside, folk musicians are tuning their guitar and bass.
Rustic light fixtures cast a mellow glow on knotty pine
ceilings. Day hikers, back for the night, are reading
or playing cards in the library. This is Adirondak Loj,
a congenial place to stay in the mountains
of northern New York.

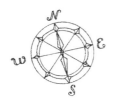

THE FACTS
Adirondak Loj

address	Box 867, Lake Placid, NY 12946
phone	518-523-3441
e-mail	adkinfo@adk.org (general information) loj@adk.org (membership information)
Web site	**www.adk.org** Select *Lodging and Camping,* then *Adirondak Loj.*
lodging	Open year around. Main lodge houses 46 guests in combo of four private rooms, four family-sized rooms or co-ed bunkroom. Two cabins accessible by foot trail, plus several lean-tos and a campground. One cabin is designed for disabled access.
rates	Bunkroom space in the Loj begins at about $30 per night, including breakfast. Cabins rent at a group rate of about $90 to $200 per night. Off-season specials and reduced rates for members are available.
caveats	No public transportation. Shared communal bathrooms.
special interest	Adirondack lakeside setting, environmental programs, hiking.

THE LOJ

Operated by Adirondack Mountain Club, the Loj is nestled among the pines on the shore of Heart Lake. While there are many rustic accommodations in the region, the Loj stands out as a focal point for environmental information and programs.

The cozy library has a wide selection of books on the region's natural setting and history. Box files along one wall hold issues of *Adirondack Life* and conservation magazines. A stone fireplace provides warmth on winter evenings.

A poster announces upcoming presentations such as "Butterflies of the Adirondacks" and "Life Cycle of the White Tailed Deer." The Loj hosts educational workshops throughout the year, from children's programs to Elderhostel events.

The main building houses up to forty-six guests. Options include four private rooms, four family-sized rooms and the large co-ed bunkroom. All rooms share communal bathrooms. Bedding and towels are provided for lodge guests. In addition, free earplugs are available for snore-sensitive dormitory dwellers.

> *Please recycle your cups — it will make a tree smile.*
>
> hand-lettered sign by the coffeepot at Adirondak Loj

THE CABINS

The two cabins are a short distance from the Loj. The *Campground Cabin* sleeps four people. The larger *Wiezel/Trails Cabin* holds up to sixteen guests and is disabled-accessible. (This cabin is not available in summer.) Canvas cabins, each with six bunk beds, are another option.

Cabin guests need to bring their own bedding and towels. The cabins are designed as functional sleeping quarters,

An Adirondack Mountain Club lean-to

with no fireplaces and minimal decor. The living room areas have couches, with extra tables in the Wiezel/Trails Cabin.

ACCESS

The Loj is about eight miles south of Lake Placid via Route 73 and Adirondak Loj Road. If you're arriving by car, pay heed to the deer crossing signs. Try to be off the road by twilight, when deer often are on the roads.

Adirondack Trailways (800-225-6815) provides bus service to Lake Placid, from whence ambitious visitors can hike to the Loj. Also, Amtrak offers connecting bus service to Lake Placid from the Westport train station.

DINING

Meals are served at the Loj throughout the year, including breakfast, a brown-bag trail lunch, and dinner. Family-style meals are served in the pine-paneled dining room.

Food is planned with hungry hikers in mind, including ample portions of homemade breads and soups. Breakfast may include staples such as blueberry pancakes, oatmeal, and scrambled eggs. Vegetarian options are available. For do-it-yourselfers, the Loj has a hostel-style kitchen, with a full complement of cookware, electric stove and a portly refrigerator.

ACTIVITIES

Low-impact summer recreation includes canoeing, fly fishing, swimming in the lake, white-water kayaking, and rock climbing. In winter, the Loj rents skis and snowshoes.

Adirondak? Loj? No, it's not a misspelling. Melvil Dewey, a former owner (and originator of the Dewey Decimal System for libraries) was a fanatic about phonetic spelling.

There is a small natural history museum at the Loj, staffed by a resident naturalist in summer. An aquarium displays the newts and small fish of Heart Lake, while geology exhibits explain the history of the Adirondacks.

The Loj is the staging area for organized hikes planned for various ages and interests. A popular trail destination is Mt. Marcy, the highest peak in New York, a fourteen-mile trip from the Loj. However, because this route is overused at times, park officials are encouraging visitors to try less-traveled trails.

For example, the Avalanche Pass Trail takes you to a narrow lake wedged between steep rock faces. In places, the trail actually is bolted into the sides of the cliff. And then there are the paths to Mount Jo, where a steep climb rewards hikers with a spectacular High Peaks panorama.

*B*y mid-September, the first
snow has dusted the
High Peaks, and frost has trimmed
the insect population. After a hike,
this is a prime time to relax on the
Heart Lake dock and take in the
conifer-framed view.

Off to the right is a stand of white
birches, with Mount Jo in the
background. To the left, backed
by the majestic MacIntire peaks,
crimson sugar maples are
highlighted by the late afternoon
sun. The sun sinks toward the
horizon, marking the approach
of the equinox and the conclusion
of another summer at
Adirondak Loj.

ALMANAC

CAR-FREE IN THE HIGH PEAKS
Johns Brook Lodge, Keene Valley, New York

For people who really want to get away from traffic, but still prefer a roof over their heads, Johns Brook Lodge beckons. The lodge and cabins are located in the Keene Valley, three and a half miles from the nearest road and 750 feet above the trailhead. Because the lodge is in a wilderness area, no vehicles are allowed. Guests typically pack lightly, since they haul in their gear on foot.

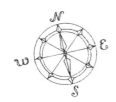

THE FACTS
Johns Brook Lodge

address	Box 867, Lake Placid, NY 12946
phone	518-523-3441
e-mail	adkinfo@adk.org
Web site	**www.adk.org** Select link to *Lodging and Camping*, then select *Johns Brook Lodge*.
lodging	With two family rooms and two co-ed bunkrooms, the Lodge can accommodate up to twenty-eight guests.
rates	Co-ed bunkroom space goes for about $30 in peak season, half that at other times, including breakfast. Depending on size and season, cabins rent for group rates of $60 to $120 per night.
caveats	All gear must be packed in via a 3.5-mile trail. No showers or other indoor running water. No phone.
special interest	Hiking, car-free setting, solar water heating, remote mountain location.

THE LODGE

In addition to being car-free, the lodge also is phoneless, (although there is radio communication for emergencies).

In place of these modern conveniences, the rushing water of Johns Brook provides background accompaniment for guests chatting on the porch. The accommodations include two family rooms and two co-ed bunkrooms. Combined, these facilities can accommodate up to twenty-eight guests.

The lodge is open with reduced service during the spring and autumn midweeks, and during the winter for groups. A warm sleeping bag is essential for most of the year.

Two recent-vintage cabins provide year-round spartan accommodations, with mattresses on bunk bed frames. Camp Peggy O'Brien has propane-powered lights and stove, while Grace Camp also has a wood stove. Running water is of the outdoor variety, meaning that guests desiring water need to scoop it from Johns Brook, haul it indoors, and treat it before use. As with the lodge, the cabins are accessible only by foot trails.

There is no electricity at Johns Brook. Solar panels provide hot, warm or cool water, depending on the cloud cover, while the lights and stove are propane-powered.

ACCESS

Since no cars are allowed, all gear must be packed in via a 3.5 mile trail. Adirondack Trailways (800-225-6815) provides bus service to Keene Valley. While the lodge parking area is not a scheduled stop, it is rumored that friendly bus drivers will stop to let off hikers.

DINING

No fancy tablecloths here, but full-course meals are served during the summer months and autumn weekends. Homemade ice cream is a Saturday evening tradition.

ACTIVITIES

Here at the epicenter of the Adirondacks, guests at the lodge can select from hundreds of miles of paths through the northern forest. The Brothers Trail is a favorite of locals for its ridgeline views. From Johns Brook Lodge, this sometimes-rocky path gradually ascends and descends the Brothers peaks, affording prime views along the way.

S pring is a quiet season here, and few guests are on hand to observe as spring slowly gathers strength along Johns Brook. By May, trilliums, trout lilies, and violets carpet the forest floor, and the stream is bubbling with pent-up energy. Trees tentatively send out buds, then burst into leaf as the days turn warmer. In the distance, a long ridge stands silently, a backdrop to the renewal of life in the High Peaks. For people craving solitude, this is a prime time to follow the path to Johns Brook Lodge.

ALMANAC

STAYING AT A GREAT CAMP
Sagamore, Raquette Lake, New York

At the turn of the twentieth century, Sagamore was a star in the Gilded Age's flamboyant fling of rustic architecture in the Adirondacks. The Vanderbilts entertained here, at the interface of elegance and wilderness.

A century later, the coachmen and butlers are long gone, but the tradition of the Great Camps continues at Sagamore in a more egalitarian vein. Now operated by the nonprofit Sagamore Institute, the lodge's nationally renowned programs provide awareness of the natural environment and the human heritage of the Adirondacks.

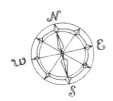

THE FACTS
Sagamore

address	Box 146, Raquette Lake, NY 13436
phone	315-354-5311 [fax 315-354-5851]
e-mail	Sagamore@telenet.net
Web site	**www.sagamore.org** Extensive information on programs, history, and facilities at Sagamore and the area.
lodging	Double-occupancy rooms in historic buildings and cottages, with shared baths.
rates	An overnight stay (about $100) includes all meals. Most guests stay at Sagamore as part of an organized multi-day program, where the cost (in the $200 to $600 range) typically includes instruction, lodging, and all meals. Volunteers can come for a work weekend and stay for just a nominal fee. (Parents note: On a Great Camp vacation, you don't have to keep shelling out money for games and rides.)
caveats	No television. No room phones. No pets. Closed mid-October to mid-May.
credentials	National Historic Landmark. Adirondack Park Heritage Award. New York State Millennium Arts and Business Partnership Award.
special interest	Historic architecture, Adirondacks setting, environmental programs.

THE LODGE

This secluded setting includes 1,526 acres on Sagamore Lake. The Sagamore complex includes 27 of the original buildings. Accommodations are mainly for guests in an organized program. However, overnight visitors are welcomed on a space-available basis, with a two-night minimum stay.

Guest rooms are in three lodges, each accommodating about twenty people. In addition, there are three seasonal cottages. Sagamore will not guarantee specific room requests, except for Gloria's Cottage, which can be reserved on a limited basis.

Rooms typically have twin beds. Quilts on guest beds are sewn by volunteers. Shared bathrooms are down the hall, complete with claw-foot tubs. Guests are directed to return their linens and towels to the laundry room at the conclusion of their stay. One cottage can be adapted for disabled access.

An inexpensive way to stay at Sagamore is to join the Friends of Sagamore and volunteer for the annual Memorial Day work weekend. For $25, you can join crews to clean up or make repairs, getting a first-hand view of the place in the process and a chance to meet other Great Camp aficionados.

ACCESS

Sagamore is in the central Adirondacks. Visitors typically arrive by private vehicle. From Albany and points south, take the Northway (I-87) to the Warrensburg exit (#23). Follow Route 28 west about sixty miles to Raquette Lake. At the crossroads, watch for signs to the lodge, which is located four miles south of Raquette Lake via graded road.

PROGRAMS AND SPECIAL EVENTS

Visitors contribute to the preservation of the property. Upkeep is mainly funded by visitor fees. The Sagamore

Web site provides details on current programs, which typically last two to five days.

Sagamore's staff suggests the Adirondack Outdoor Weekend for an introduction. For independent-minded guests, the Heritage Program is loosely structured; visitors can choose from several hands-on options. Expert craftspeople teach classes such as rustic furniture construction, blacksmithing and rug braiding.

Guided tours are available for day visitors in the morning and early afternoon during July, August, and weekends through Columbus Day. A small admission fee is charged.

Try Thoreau's technique for creative pond loafing:

1. *Row a boat out to the middle of Walden Pond (a small Adirondack lake may be substituted).*

2. *Lie in bottom of boat.*

3. *Drift until you bump against one of the shores.*

4. *Repeat.*

Special events round out Sagamore's calendar. June's eco-friendly No Octane Wooden Boat Regatta includes a barn dance and barbecue, and other summer events feature local cloggers and musicians.

Sagamore has a student intern program where students can gain experience in outdoor education and retail management. Volunteer work weekends are scheduled for Memorial Day weekend and again in the fall.

BOATHOUSES AND BARK SIDING

In 1897, William West Durant began work on Sagamore. In addition to the main lodge building, with its wraparound porches, the camp grew to include a blacksmith shop, boathouse, henhouse, wagon shed, and numerous other outbuildings. The Vanderbilts purchased the lodge in 1901, and entertained here in grand style for the next half century. After a stint as a Syracuse University conference center, the lodge now is owned by the nonprofit Sagamore Institute.

The structures share a common use of rough-hewn local wood and stone. Many exterior walls are surfaced with northern white cedar bark — a sort of exterior wallpaper. This technique, adapted from Native American practice, was elevated to a decorative craft. Some of the weather-resistant bark siding is nearly 100 years old, although snowbanks have caused deterioration in places.

Replacement of bark siding is a laborious process. Bark is harvested from standing trees, then applied in four-foot strips or two-foot shingles.

BEARS IN THE GARDEN

The Sagamore staff recycles kitchen waste for composting and use on the grounds. A conventional compost pile was ruled out, since this would likely raise expectations among bears and create a major feeding site. Instead, a covered cage system is used. Its durability is commemorated by claw marks where bears have unsuccessfully tried to gain entry. One staff member, nicknamed "the compost queen," is responsible for aerating the mix with a special compost paddle.

DINING

When the camp bell at Sagamore announces that it's time to eat, guests line up for meals served buffet style under the lofty ceiling of the paneled dining room. The long tables foster entertaining dinner conversation. Vegetarian options are available. Diners are expected to clear their own dishes. In addition to the main dining area, a coffee shop is open for day visitors from 9:30 a.m. to 4:30 p.m. in summer.

ACTIVITIES

Visitors have a choice of tennis, croquet, volleyball, canoeing, or swimming in the lake. Guests also can trade off pinsetter duty at the self-service open-air bowling alley, complete with a stone fireplace and overhead log trusses.

Hikers can explore twenty miles of trails that wind through the site and connect with the regional trail system. The harsh Adirondack winter weather reaps benefits here, for there are no reported Lyme disease problems, poison ivy, or poisonous snakes on the property.

Local guides lead nature walks, sometimes wielding a magnifying glass to zero in on details. En route, guides describe the traditional use of Adirondack plants, such as the rolling of mulleins in pitch or tallow to use as torches.

Ongoing crafts demonstrations may include construction of Adirondack guideboats. A weaver often is in residence, ripping used clothing into strips for rugs. Woodwork often is in progress in the Wigwam, one of several workshops.

Wildlife sightings are common. Black bears are in the area, but the most common sighting is described by the staff as "back end disappearing into brush." After a long absence, moose are returning to the area from Canada and Vermont; the nearby Moose River plains are prime habitat for these massive ungulates.

During Sagamore's peak season, the gift shop is open daily, carrying regional crafts, books and audiotapes. Former employees collect and donate recycled plastic bags to the gift shop for use at the checkout counter.

D ressed in period costumes, guests descend on Sagamore each August for the Grand Tour, a chance to return to the Gilded Age in the Adirondacks.

For this event, the buildings are decorated in rustic Adirondack style. The event may begin with croquet and cocktails, followed by performances by the Vintage Dance Society. The multi-course dinner follows, concluded by cutting a Main Lodge-shaped cake. Guests then retire to sip port on the porch. Profits from this revelry go to maintain and restore Sagamore.

In the region ...
ADIRONDACKS

The Adirondack Park is a vast sanctuary, larger than Yellowstone, Glacier, Olympic, and Yosemite National Parks combined. The state of New York established the park in the late nineteenth century after decades of logging threatened water supplies for downstate cities.

Today, the Adirondacks offer one of the best outdoor recreation settings in the eastern United States, with plenty of room for hiking, skiing, canoeing, and kayaking. The park has two visitor information centers at Paul Smiths and Newcomb.

■ *Box 3000, Paul Smiths, NY, tel. 518-327-3000*
   www.northnet.org/adirondackvic

At nearby Blue Mountain Lake you can rent canoes, sailboats, and rowboats at **Blue Mountain Lake Boat Livery**, an ancient sagging structure along the shore, complete with sleeping dogs on the porch.

Another way to get out on the water is to ride the **Raquette Lake Mailboat.** This aquatic mail route makes deliveries to cabins that are accessible only by boat.

■ *Bird's Adirondack Marine, Rt. 28*
   Raquette Lake, NY 13436, tel. 315-354-4441

Ensconced on 32 acres overlooking Blue Mountain Lake, the **Adirondack Museum** has well-designed indoor and exterior exhibits of regional camping, logging, and mining history. Guideboat enthusiasts will find no less than sixty-eight of these craft on display. The museum shop specializes in Adirondack books, prints, and crafts. Open seven days a week from Memorial Day weekend to mid-October.

■ *P.O. Box 99, Blue Mountain Lake, NY 12812*
   tel. 518-352-7311, **www.adkmuseum.org**

GREEN DINING/OTHER PLACES TO STAY

Located in a former garnet-mining area, **Garnet Hill Lodge** is named after the semi-precious stones that sparkle in the fireplace masonry; minuscule garnets even gleam in the driveway gravel. The lodge offers naturalist programs to guests and day visitors, including a two-day guided snowshoe walk. In winter, the highly rated Garnet Hill cross-country ski center provides access to more than 50 kilometers of groomed trails plus 100 kilometers of backcountry skiing. Winter rates are in the $100 to $160 range, Modified American Plan; skiing packages offer substantial savings. Rates are substantially lower in non-skiing months.

The lodge's Log House Restaurant features fresh-baked pastries and Mary Jane's Onion Pie, along with exotic fare such as Yucatan corn-and-bean stew. Vegetarian entrees are prominently featured on the menu. The wood-paneled dining room overlooks Thirteenth Lake.

- *Garnet Hill Lodge, Thirteenth Lake Road, North River, NY 12856, tel. 518-251-2444,* **www.garnet-hill.com**

Along the main access route from the south, the inexpensive **Four Seasons Natural Foods Café** is open for lunch and dinner six days a week, with lunch only on Sunday. The main action is at the buffet, where diners can find miso soup and quinoa dishes.

- *33 Phila Street, Saratoga Springs, NY 12866 tel. 518-584-4670*

PROVISIONS AND SHOPPING

The **Adirondack Mountain Club** operates trading posts at Heart Lake and Lake George, purveying publications and hiking gear. The AMC Lake George Information Center is near Interstate 87's Exit 21. Merchandise also can be purchased via a toll-free number and an on-line shopping center.

- *814 Goggins Road, Lake George, NY 12845 tel. 800- 395-8080,* **www.adk.org**

Next door to Plattsburgh's City Hall, the **North Country Co-op** is a provision point for natural foods. The store is near Exit 37 on I-87; follow signs to the historic district.

- *13 City Hall Place, Plattsburgh, NY 12901*
  tel. 518-561-5904

RESOURCES

The **Adirondack Mountain Club** is dedicated to the protection and responsible recreational use of the Adirondacks and other wild places in New York. Since 1922, members have supported conservation efforts, education, and natural history programs, while gaining access to recreation facilities. Twenty-six chapters provide local programs in New York and nearby states.

- *814 Goggins Road, Lake George, NY 12845*
  tel 518-668-4447, **www.adk.org**

FOR MORE INFORMATION

Author Howard Kirschenbaum recounts Great Camp history in *The Story of Sagamore*, a slim volume with old photos, a site plan, and an annotated list of the numerous buildings on the property.

- *$4.95; available from the Sagamore Institute,*
  Sagamore Road, Raquette Lake, NY 13436

The Adirondack Mountain Club publishes the **Forest Preserve Series** of guidebooks and maps, as well as specialized guides that focus on Alpine summits, native forests and trees, canoeing, rock or ice climbing, skiing, mountain biking, and winter backpacking. *The Adirondack Wildguide: A Natural History of the Adirondack Park* is a well-illustrated overview of the North Country. Published by the Adirondack Conservancy and Adirondack Council, this guide features the forests, lakes, and mountains of the region, with watercolors and pen-and-ink drawings by Anne Lacy.

- Order online or call the Adirondack Mountain Club at 800-395-8080. **www.adk.org**

11

FINGER LAKES

The woods lay in calm repose after the
grateful shower, and large rain-drops
were gathered in clusters on the
plants. The leaves of various kinds
receive the water very differently:
some are completely bathed, showing
a smooth surface of varnished green
from stem to point .... On others,
like the syringa, the fluid lies in
flattened transparent drops, taking
an emerald color from the leaf
on which they rest.

— Susan Fenimore Cooper,
Rural Hours

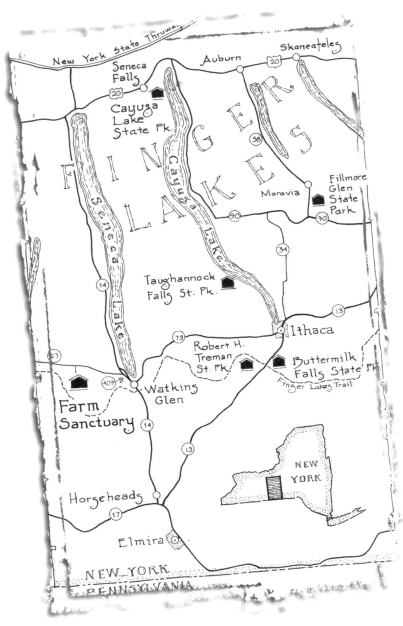

FINGER
LAKES

An Animal-Friendly Inn
Farm Sanctuary Bed & Breakfast
Watkins Glen, New York

Pigs root in a pasture. Turkeys peck at bugs, and cattle are silhouetted on a ridge. These are common sights in upstate New York. However, this is no ordinary rural scene, but rather the Farm Sanctuary, a nonprofit operation that rescues, rehabilitates, and provides life-long care for ill-treated farm animals.

The mission of Farm Sanctuary extends far beyond individual cases of mistreatment. This national organization works to end the exploitation of animals used for food production, calling attention to systematic abuses in the way that animals are treated on factory farms and feedlots. As part of the Sanctuary's education program, visitors can stay overnight at the farm.

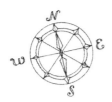

THE FACTS
Farm Sanctuary
Bed & Breakfast

address	P.O. Box 150 Watkins Glen, NY 14891
phone	607-583-2225, ext. 25 fax 607-583-2041
Web site	**www. farmsanctuary.org**
lodging	Three cabins, each with two double beds.
rates	$60 per night for first person, $10 for each additional person (four maximum per cabin). Breakfast is included. Sanctuary members receive a $10 discount.
caveats	Bed & breakfast cabins and day tours are available May 1 to October 31 only, although the Sanctuary is open for members year-round. Some visitors may be uncomfortable with the photo displays and advocacy positions of the Sanctuary.
credentials	Featured in *Vegetarian Times* and in national newspapers.
special interest	Animal rights, environmental advocacy.

THE SANCTUARY

Farm Sanctuary's 175 acres are home to more than five hundred pigs, goats, cattle, turkeys, and other farm animals housed in twelve shelter barns. Human visitors stay in three bed-and-breakfast cabins. The recently constructed sleeping quarters are clean and comfortable, with basic furnishings. Heaters are provided on cold evenings. Young cedars planted around the cabins will in time add a woodsy ambience.

Reservations are recommended, since the cabins often are booked up in advance during the summer months. Check with the Sanctuary first if you want to bring a companion animal with you. In addition to individual stays, the Sanctuary hosts camps and conferences for groups of twelve or more.

Overnight guests are given complimentary tours; day visitors can take the Sanctuary circuit for a nominal fee.

The People Barn is an education center with exhibits and a gift shop. On one wall is an extensive display of the many celebrities who have contributed talent and money to the cause. Also in the barn are photo exhibits that document the mistreatment of caged chickens, calves, and other animals.

Anyone who eats meat or any animal products should prepare to be challenged here. This is definitely a place with an opinion.

ACCESS

The Sanctuary is located at 3100 Aikens Road. From Watkins Glen, take Route 409 west to Route 23, then take this road eight miles. Turn left on Aikens Road, continue for 1.5 miles, then turn in at the Sanctuary sign. The access drive is a gravel farm road that may be dicey during mud season.

DINING

The Sanctuary serves plant-based vegan breakfasts in the People's Barn. No eggs or dairy products are used in food preparation. A typical breakfast includes vegan muffins, juice, and soy milk.

PROGRAMS

Farm Sanctuary operates the largest public shelters in the country for victims of "food animal" production. The organization provides emergency rescue, rehabilitation, daily care, and adoption services for abused and neglected farm animals.

The Adopt-a-Farm Animal monthly sponsorship program provides the funding for feed, bedding, veterinary costs, and caregiver staff. The shelter also places animals with people who will give them proper care.

The Sanctuary has provided information to millions of people about food animal production through a variety of educational programs and campaigns. Each year, several thousand people have toured the New York and California shelters.

Working with law enforcement officials and humane enforcement agents as part of the Watch Hog Project, the Sanctuary has monitored farm animal cruelty cases. Animal abandonment and neglect, which have been common agricultural practices, now are being prosecuted as animal cruelty cases in the courts.

ACTIVITIES

Most of the on-site recreation relates to the animals. The Sanctuary encourages visitors to give a hog a belly rub, feed a sheep, and generally get to know the farm animals.

Farm Sanctuary is located in the scenic Finger Lakes Region, next to the Sugar Hill State Forest and miles of hiking trails. Nearby is the Finger Lakes Trail, which stretches nearly 560 miles from the Pennsylvania border to the Catskills.

TONI AND DAWN, TWO RESIDENTS
AT THE FARM SANCTUARY

For an unconventional Fourth of July "Pignic," the Sanctuary hosts an Oinky Open House. This is a day of shelter tours, hayrides, food, and fun. Needless to say, vegetarian rather than conventional hot dogs are served.

Beneath the surface of these festivities is a radical critique of the food-animal industry. The Farm Sanctuary's setting is appropriate, for upstate New York has a tradition of activism dating back to the genesis of the women's suffrage movement and the abolition of slavery. Whether or not visitors subscribe to a vegan philosophy, Farm Sanctuary is a thought-provoking place to link animal rights and environmental concerns with the food on your table.

In the region ...
FINGER LAKES DISTRICT

During the Ice Age, continental glaciers invaded this region from the north, reaming out ancient river valleys and creating the Finger Lakes. As the earth warmed, glacial runoff gouged out gorges or glens in the adjacent hillsides, creating numerous waterfalls.

Watkins Glen State Park offers an interactive waterfall experience. A path in the glen winds past some of the park's nineteen waterfalls, then through the spray of the Cavern Cascade.

■ *Watkins Glen State Park, Watkins Glen, NY, tel. 607-535-4511.* **http://nysparks.state.ny.us/parks**

Taughannock Falls, eight miles north of Ithaca, is the highest vertical single-drop waterfall in the northeastern United States. Water flowing over a sandstone ledge cascades more than two hundred feet into a glen that opens to Cayuga Lake.

■ *Taughannock Falls State Park, Box 1055, Trumansburg, NY 14886, tel. 607-387-6739.* **http://nysparks.state.ny.us/parks**

OTHER PLACES TO STAY

The New York State Park system contains hundreds of cabins. In the Finger Lakes region, several parks have unheated cabins for rent from May to October, and Cayuga Lake State Park also has heated cabins. Typical prices are about $30 per night for a four-person unit ($122 per week) to about $60 nightly ($239 weekly) for a cabin that sleeps six.

Buttermilk Falls State Park (seven cabins). Trails lead to the falls, where there is swimming in a natural pool. A nature trail also encircles the Larch Meadows wetland.

- *Route 13 south of Ithaca, tel. 607-273-5761*

Cayuga Lake State Park (fourteen heated cabins near the swimming beach). A few miles away, Montezuma National Wildlife Refuge is a favored spot for birding.

- *Route 89, three miles east of Seneca Falls*
  tel. 315-568-5163

Fillmore Glen State Park (three cabins). A trail leads to five waterfalls and to the Cowsheds, a huge cavity in a shale cliff.

- *Route 38, one mile south of Moravia, tel. 315-497-0130*

Robert H. Treman State Park (fourteen cabins near the waterfalls in Enfield Glen). A handsome stone-stepped path leads to Lucifer Falls.

- *Five miles south of Ithaca on Route 13*
  tel. 607-273-3440

Taughannock Falls State Park (sixteen cabins near the western shore of Cayuga Lake). The park's waterfall is thirteen feet higher than Niagara Falls.

- *Route 89, eight miles north of Ithaca, tel. 607-273-3440*

Park accommodations vary in quality. If you're particular about your lodging, an advance inspection is advisable. A master list of cabins is available from the New York State Department of Environmental Conservation.

- *50 Wolf Road, Albany, NY 12233, tel. 518-457-2500*
  Cabin reservations: 1-800-456-CAMP
  www.ReserveAmerica.com

GREEN DINING

Cooperatively owned and managed, the **Moosewood Restaurant** is nationally known for its series of cookbooks featuring healthy food and vegetarian recipes. Occupying an ivy-covered brick building in downtown Ithaca, the Moosewood has a friendly atmosphere and seasonal outdoor dining. The café carries nitrate-free beers and ales, as well as a selection of Finger Lakes wine. Soups are a standout. Open daily; dinner only on Sunday.

- *Dewitt Building, Buffalo at Cayuga Streets*
  Ithaca, NY 14850, tel. 607-273-9610
  www.moosewoodrestaurant.com

Influenced by the animal-rights visitors headed for the Sanctuary, the small community of Watkins Glen has several restaurants offering vegetarian and vegan options. Located in a brick building on the town's main street, **Glen Mountain Market** sells a variety of vegan and vegetarian options including the Sanctuary Special sandwich (with seitan salami). The Market's products are preservative-free; breads and pastries are handmade from scratch daily. Also for sale are specialty items such as Sally's Sassy Sauce and the "Wall of Flame" line of hot sauces. Open seven days a week.

- *200 N. Franklin St., Watkins Glen, NY 14891*
  tel. 607-535-6900

PROVISIONS

Down the hall from the Moosewood Restaurant is The **Oasis Natural Grocery,** also located in the Dewitt Building. The Oasis carries books and magazines as well as a selection of natural foods.

- *215 North Cayuga, Ithaca, NY 14850, tel. 607-273-8213*

Located on the west side of downtown Ithaca, **Greenstar Co-op** is a member-owned whole foods grocery featuring fresh produce, with an emphasis on local and organically grown food. Also on hand are a multifarious selection of nori, curry paste, stuffed grape leaves, herbs, spices, vitamins, herbal remedies, housewares, and recycled paper products. The deli serves knishes, sushi, and such. A community bulletin board provides information about environmental and other regional issues. Open seven days a week, from mid-morning into the evening; closes earlier on Saturdays and Sundays.

- *701 W. Buffalo St., Ithaca, NY 14850, tel. 607-273-9392*

RESOURCES

The Finger Lakes Trail System extends across upstate New York. To promote the building, maintenance and corridor protection for these hiking routes, the **Finger Lakes Trail Conference** was organized in 1962. The Conference coordinates groups and individual volunteers who help to build and maintain the trails. The Conference Store sells trail maps, guidebooks, hats and other hiking paraphernalia.

- *FLTC Service Center, P.O. Box 18048, Rochester, NY 14618, tel. 716-288-7191*
   www.fingerlakes.net/trailsystem

FOR MORE INFORMATION

The **Animal Rights Resource Site** provides information about the Farm Sanctuary and more than one hundred other organizations worldwide that are working on animal adoption, shelters, rescue, protection, and welfare. Listings range from Santa Barbara-based All for Animals to the Swedish Defend the Elephant Society (a bilingual site).

- **http://arrs.envirolink.org**

Throughout the country, Moosewood cookbooks are found on the shelves of environmentally conscious cooks. While most recipes are vegetarian, some seafood meal ideas are included. The Moosewood Collective's *Moosewood Restaurant Cooks at Home* offers fast and easy recipes, with non-dairy and vegan sections and kid-pleaser options.

- *Fireside, NY: Simon & Schuster, 1994*
   Paperback, 416 pages, $15

12

NEW YORK'S
SHAWANGUNK
MOUNTAINS

*To an ecologist a dead tree, whether it be stand-
ing or lying under a blanket of moss, is just as
beautiful as a sprouting seedling or a living tree
in full autumn color. Each state of growth and
decay is a part of the tree's destiny, and has
a beauty which may only become evident when
one is conscious of it as a step in the cycle of life,
death and rebirth. Is it possible that, through a
gain in understanding and appreciation of the
natural processes, we searching humans might
grow in our relation to the seven ages of man?*

— Virginia Smiley, *Mohonk Bulletin*, 1965

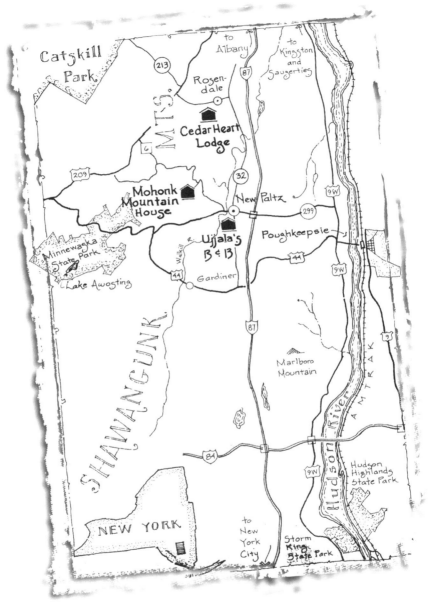

SHAWANGUNK
MOUNTAINS

A Sojourn in the Shawangunks

Mohonk Mountain House
New Paltz, New York

Photo: Ruth Smiley

View of hotel from Sky Top Path

The grandfather of today's earth-friendly inns rises from rock cliffs on the shores of Mohonk Lake. At a time when America was obsessed with subjugation of nature, this hotel was planned as a place to appreciate and respect natural values. Mohonk thus serves as the grandfather of today's earth-friendly inns.

Albert and Alfred Smiley, twin Quaker brothers, began work on Mohonk Mountain House in 1869. Four generations of the Smiley family have continued the original commitment of the hotel's founders, making additions to the buildings and expanding the surrounding natural preserve. Today, this fanciful assemblage of local stone and timber stands as a symbol of American efforts to reconcile the natural and built environments.

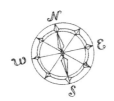

THE FACTS
Mohonk Mountain House

address	Lake Mohonk, New Paltz, NY 12561
phone	800-772-6646, 914-255-1000 (fax: 914-256-2100)
Web site	**www.mohonk.com**
lodging	261-room Victorian castle; also four kitchenette cottages open seasonally. Some rooms are disabled-accessible.
rates	Singles range from about $175 to $350. Double occupancy rates start at about $305, with the Tower Suites in the $550 range. Also add a 13% service charge plus sales tax. Special Value Rates and Packages available throughout year. Full American Plan: three meals included daily plus afternoon tea.
caveats	Traditional rules of decorum and attire. No pets.
credentials	Honored by the United Nations Environment Programme. Member: National Trust, Historic Hotels of America. National Historic Landmark.
special interest	Historic preservation, natural habitat conservation, low-impact recreation.

THE HOTEL

Crowned with a flourish of towers, gables and chimneys, Mohonk Mountain House zigzags more than an eighth of a mile along the shore of Mohonk Lake. Unlike most National Historic Landmarks, the hotel's designation also includes the surrounding land.

Mohonk historically has been a national focal point for key social issues. The hotel was the site for a series of meetings to address concerns about treatment of American Indians, and the Lake Mohonk Conference on International Arbitration reflected the owners' peace traditions. Notables of the day such as president William H. Taft, orator William Jennings Bryan, and author Edward Everett Hale attended these meetings.

Woodcut: Mohonk Mountain House

MOHONK MOUNTAIN HOUSE

Victorian, Edwardian, and Craftsman decor at the hotel reflect its evolution, and tradition permeates the public parlors. A great-grandfather clock marks the passage of time. Portraits of Rutherford B. Hayes, Andrew Carnegie, and miscellaneous ministers gaze down from the walls. Fireplaces and period furnishings complete the tableau of rustic refinement.

Mohonk is a place to appreciate fine woodwork, from yellow pine trim to the oak flooring and chestnut paneling. The central staircase is particularly notable, with ornately carved newel posts.

Most rooms are individually designed, with balconies and fireplaces. Televisions are conspicuously absent. The spacious cottages are open from about Memorial Day through Columbus Day.

ACCESS

The hotel is located west of the Hudson River Valley, about seventy miles north of Manhattan. An Amtrak and Metro-North station is in nearby Poughkeepsie, with frequent train service. The rail trip north from Manhattan's Grand Central Station is one of the most scenic passenger routes in the East; the tracks hug the Hudson for most of the way, with views of the Palisades across the water. These trains approach European rail travel in their frequency, scenery, convenience, and comfort.

Adirondack Trailways buses also serve New Paltz just a few miles from the resort. With advance notice, Mohonk drivers can meet guests at nearby bus or train stations, or at Stewart (Newburgh), Albany, and New York airports. For visitors living in the region, the hotel staff may even provide transportation from your home! Rates for these services are available on request.

By car, the lodge is six miles west of the New York State Thruway. At Exit 18, turn west on Route 299, follow this route through New Paltz and watch for Mohonk signs. After crossing the Wallkill River bridge, take the first right turn. In about 1/4 mile, bear left at the fork onto Mountain Rest Road. Continue up the mountain for about four miles to the Mohonk gatehouse.

DINING

Mohonk offers fine dining, as evidenced by the awards captured at international competitions by the culinary staff. The hotel purchases organic produce from a nearby farm. "Sound Choice" menu items appeal to health-conscious guests, and vegetarian entrees are available. A typical buffet may feature specialties such as salmon Wellington, and the array of desserts might include almond cloud cake with raspberry sauce.

The three dining rooms are a visual feast, with a soaring two-story ceiling supported by ornate wood columns. The panoramic mountain view from the dining room is framed by foreground birches.

ROCKING CHAIRS ON PORCH.
MOHONK MOUNTAIN HOUSE

Mohonk maintains its dining traditions, and guests dress accordingly. Men are required to wear jackets at dinner. There is no public bar at Mohonk, although beer, wine, and a full bar are available at meals and through room service.

At four in the afternoon, the staff brings out the china, along with tea and cookies. Other ancillary cuisine at the hotel includes an old-fashioned ice cream parlor and soda fountain, where a "fizzician" fashions floats and sodas.

Day visitors are welcome for dining; reservations are required. Breakfast and lunch prices are in the $21 to $33 range while dinner prices extend from $33 to $50.

CONSERVATION

The hotel puts environmental principles into practice on the extensive grounds. Each year, over 115 tons of food waste, 105 tons of horse manure from the stables, and 150 tons of wood chips are composted and then used in the gardens and on the golf course.

Our advice to all who care for scenery, at once grand and beautiful, is by all means go to Lake Mohonk. There you will find a view equal to any ... a lake which is a perfect gem of beauty; an atmosphere almost intoxicating in its strength and purity; geologic records that will excite your unbounded wonder ...

Prof. S.W. Buck, 1891,
in the *New York Independent*

Other conservation measures include a full recycling program. The laundry and maintenance workers use biodegradable products and non-aerosol cleaning materials.

ENVIRONMENTAL PROGRAMS

Mohonk's long tradition of environmental education has continued up to the present. The staff naturalist leads frequent nature walks, introducing visitors to the natural world around the hotel. As part of the "Garden Dreams" weekend, staff members demonstrate how they apply environmental stewardship in Mohonk's award-winning gardens.

Evening events include nature talks and slide shows, as well as classical music concerts, sing-alongs, dancing, movies, and dramatic readings. The hotel library has a large selection of natural history and the environment. For children, the Mohonk Kids' Club program features fossil and frog hunts, rock scrambles, and other nature-oriented adventures.

In recognition of Mohonk's earth-friendly efforts, the United Nations Environmental Programme has granted an award to the Smiley family and Mohonk Mountain House "for generations of dedicated leadership and commitment to the protection and enhancement of the environment and for their inestimable contribution to the cause of peace, justice, and sustainable human development."

ACTIVITIES

This is a place with plenty of recreational choices. Hikers and joggers can choose from ninety miles of trails, with more than one hundred gazebos strategically placed at key overlooks. A hike to the Sky Top Tower observation point provides a view that can extend across the Hudson Valley to the Taconics on a clear day. Near Sky Top Peak, a rock outcropping named "Washington's Profile" bears some resemblance to the first President.

Natural encounters don't require a strenuous hike, however. Just a short stroll from the hotel entry, paths wind through forests of hardwoods, hemlock, and pine. The massive rock formations are trimmed in lichen, and quartz crystals glint in the sun. Wood thrushes and wrens weave through the tree canopy, and it's common to see tracks of foxes, porcupines, and other woodland wildlife.

The diversity of habitats on the property is a plus for birders. Hawk migration watching is popular at the Trapps and elsewhere. Scarlet tanagers nest in the area. Birders also may spot pileated woodpeckers, wild turkeys, ruffed grouse, or rare finches from Canada.

Lake Mohonk is half a mile long and as much as sixty feet deep. Canoes, rowboats and paddleboats are at the dock for guests to use. Swimming and fishing also are options.

The Labyrinth by the lake is the setting for rock scrambles, where hikers can edge their way through cramped passages and crevices to reach Sky Top. For serious climbers, the Trapps are cliffs offering outstanding rock climbs.

In winter, over thirty miles of groomed paths are available for cross-country skiing, snowshoeing and snow tubing. Ski equipment is available free of charge to overnight guests; day visitors can rent equipment at White Cedars Lodge on the site.

For traditional transportation, guests can tour the grounds in a carriage drawn by Percherons, or in mule-drawn mountain wagons. Overnight visitors can bring their own horses by advance arrangement. Horse history is housed in the Barn Museum, crammed with fifty-plus antique carriages, old tools, a working blacksmith shop, and other Mohonk memorabilia.

Photo: Ruth Smiley

STONE GAZEBO.
MOHONK MOUNTAIN HOUSE

Rounding out the recreation alternatives are tennis, golf, croquet, lawn bowling, shuffleboard, and horseshoes. Hundreds of rocking chairs await visitors on the verandas. Horticultural enthusiasts can tour the ornamental gardens and greenhouses. For indoor exercise, guests can head for the fully equipped fitness center, complete with sauna. Massage services are available on site.

The hotel grants day visitor passes for general admission to the Mohonk resort grounds from early morning to one hour before dusk. Weekend and holiday passes are $12 (children $8), with reduced midweek rates.

A*s the holiday season approaches, the hotel is decorated with evergreen swags and wreaths. Inside, the hotel has organized craft activities. One family is constructing gingerbread houses, while another group is recycling old menus into Victorian picture frames.*

Outdoors, light snow drifts down from the sky, trimming the boulders and dusting the stone summerhouses. In the forest, each twig captures an allotment of flakes, occasionally shaking them loose and releasing a tiny snow shower. From Sky Top, a lone hiker looks down on a quintessential Victorian scene, as ladies seated in runner-equipped chair skates are guided by gentlemen across the frozen surface of Mohonk Lake.

In the region ...
SHAWANGUNKS

The Gunks, as they're locally known, include a cluster of parks and preserves protecting more than twenty thousand acres of forested ridges, rock outcrops, and glacial lakes. **Mohonk Preserve** is the largest private natural refuge in New York State, extending over 6,000 acres of the Shawangunk Ridge. The Visitor Center on Mountain Rest Road provides hiking information and serves as a trailhead for hikers headed for the northern part of the Preserve. Over 150 guided nature programs are offered each year, and a new interpretive center is located near the Trapps.

Towering more than one thousand feet above the Hudson, **Storm King Mountain** was the focal point of a prolonged environmental battle over a proposed power plant. The project at the mountain's base eventually was abandoned, and the mountain now is preserved as state parkland and a natural area owned by Harvard University. Stillwell Trail passes through Black Rock Forest en route to prime hawk-watching sites on the summit.

GREEN DINING

Operating in an old frame building on Rosendale's Main Street, the **Rosendale Cafe** combines good dining with a healthy mix of community entertainment. The mostly-vegetarian menu incorporates many vegan dishes such as black bean chili served over brown rice. Organic foods are used whenever possible. On Friday and Saturday evenings, the cheerful space is the setting for everything from jazz quartets and improvisational troupe comedy to films, puppet shows, and African dance, all at a reasonable price. Prices for sandwiches are in the $5 range, while entrees are about $10. All desserts are made daily at the cafe — with free whipped cream.

- *434 Main Street, Rosendale, NY 12472
  tel. 914-658-9048*

PROVISIONS

On the east side of the New Paltz historic district, **Earthgoods Natural Foods** is a compact but well-stocked store offering mainly vegetarian and vegan items. Cereals, canned goods, a small organic produce section and personal-care items are displayed on shelves between blue cast-iron columns. The deli case holds pre-made sandwiches such as "unchicken salad" pitas stuffed with soy protein and vegetables. In keeping with the town's German tradition, Earthgoods offers a selection of sauerkraut and veggie sausages.

- *71 Main St., New Paltz, NY 12561, tel. 914-255-5858*

The **New York State Guide to Farm Fresh Products** links farmers and consumers, listing nearly two thousand farm markets, stands, "U-Pick" farms, on-farm outlets, wineries, and community farmers' markets statewide. The well-organized listings indicate available products and seasons, with locations, phone numbers and notation of organic farming practices. The free guide is published in four regional editions, available by calling for a copy, stopping at a state tourist information center, or online.

- *New York State Department of Agriculture and Markets
  tel. 800-554-4501,* **www.agmkt.state.ny.us**

OTHER PLACES TO STAY

Just a few miles from Mohonk Mountain House, **Ujjala's Bed & Breakfast** is a cheerfully painted 1910-era cottage set in a grove of pear, quince, and apple trees. The inn has four guest rooms (three rooms share a bath), and a studio also is seasonally available. A longhouse sanctuary next to the house provides a place for writing, yoga, or Tai-Chi.

Owner Ujjala Schwartz formerly coordinated the Holistic Way Program at the Mohonk Mountain House. She treats guests to gourmet vegetarian breakfasts with homemade breads made from rice flour, along with fresh fruit, herbal teas, and other healthy cuisine.

Rock-climbers have a special interest in the inn, since the barn on the property holds a private climbing wall with more than one thousand hand-holds. A Finnish sauna is available for post-climb relaxation. Rates are about $78 to $98, double occupancy.

■ *2 Forest Glen Road, New Paltz, NY 12561*
   tel. 914-255-6360, **ujjalasbnb.com**

The solar-powered beam of the **Saugerties Lighthouse** sweeps across the Hudson River. The lighthouse, restored by the Saugerties Lighthouse Conservancy, includes two bedrooms for overnight stays. A bathroom with composting toilet is shared with the keeper's quarters. Guests need to consult a tide table before taking a hike along the adjacent nature trail, since the path floods at times. The room rate of $140 per night helps to support the ongoing work of the Conservancy.

■ *P.O. Box 654, Saugerties, NY 12477*
   tel. 914-247-0656 or 914-246-8893

On the northern crest of Shawangunk Ridge, **CedarHeart Lodge** is an environmentally oriented lodge and retreat center. A hunting lodge in a previous incarnation, this inn now is being renovated with native, locally milled fallen red cedar and recycled building materials. The lodge uses non-toxic cleaning materials, recycled paper products, and cooperatively grown organic coffee. The seventeen-acre wooded site offers privacy for bed-and-breakfast guests, workshops, celebrations, and retreats. All seven guest rooms are furnished with all-cotton bedding and bath linens. Vegetarian and traditional meals are served. Room rates start at $60 for singles, with doubles and family suites priced at $100 to $125.

- *22 Hillcrest Lane, Rosendale, NY 12472*
  tel. 914-658-8556; hotline 914-687-0757 for vacancies.

RESOURCES

The **Catskill Center for Conservation and Development** is a nonprofit conservation and advocacy organization serving the Catskill region. The Center promotes environmental quality, encourages economic and cultural development, assists in environmental planning, and helps to build a constituency for the protection of the region's resources.

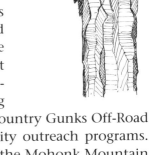

- *Arkville, NY 12406*
  tel. 914-586-2611 or
  800-721-2662
  www.catskillcenter.org

Mohonk Preserve, Inc. is a nonprofit organization that manages the 6,300-acre natural area and works to protect land in the Shawangunks. Volunteers support the Preserve's operations by helping with trail maintenance, leading nature hikes, serving on the backcountry Gunks Off-Road Patrols, and conducting community outreach programs. The Preserve's Visitor Center near the Mohonk Mountain Lodge carries gifts, bug boxes, and books about the region.

- *1000 Mountain Rest Road, Mohonk Lake*
  New Paltz, NY 12561, tel. 914-255-0919

In 1966, Clearwater was launched to focus attention on the need to clean up the Hudson River. Since then, this 106-foot sloop has traveled up and down the Hudson, focusing attention on environmental problems and opportunities. Members of **Clearwater Inc**. act as river watchdogs. Volunteers can serve as crew members, hoisting the sails and taking water quality samples.

- *112 Market Street, Poughkeepsie, NY 12601
  tel. 914-454-7673,* **www.clearwater.org**

FOR MORE INFORMATION

Mohonk, Its People and Spirit, by Larry E. Burgess, traces the history of the hotel from its founding through four generations of the Smiley family.

The book has many vintage photos of the inn and its natural setting.

- *Paperback: 122 pages, $15.00. Available from the hotel gift shop, local bookstores, or Purple Mountain Press, Fleischmanns, New York.*

The National Trust for Historic Preservation publishes *Historic Hotels of America*, a directory of more than one hundred quality American hotels and inns, such as the Mohonk Mountain House, that have faithfully maintained their historic architecture and ambience. The 150-page guide includes color photographs, rates, history, and amenity information.

- *Paperback: $3.00. Available from National Trust for Historic Preservation, 1785 Massachusetts Avenue, NW, Washington, DC 20036, tel. 202-588-6295.*

For a video preview of Mohonk Mountain House, *The Road to Wellville* is a rather odd movie filmed in part at the lodge. The Mohonk buildings serve as a stand-in for Dr. John Harvey Kellogg's eccentric Michigan clinic. The hotel also has been featured on Arts and Entertainment's American Castles series.

NEW YORK CITY

Northbound hawks tend to disperse over a wide migratory path in the spring. But on the journey back in the fall hawks concentrate most predictably over certain natural formations, such as mountain ridges. That is where they are likely to find rising columns of hot air known as thermals, which allow them to save energy by soaring rather than arduous flap-flap-flapping.

The hawks flying over Central Park have no natural mountains there to help them on their way. But they have thermals, nevertheless, created by the man-made ridges of tall city buildings. That is why fall hawkwatching has always been part of the park's birdwatching scene.

— Marie Winn, *Raptors in Love: A Wildlife Drama in Central Park*

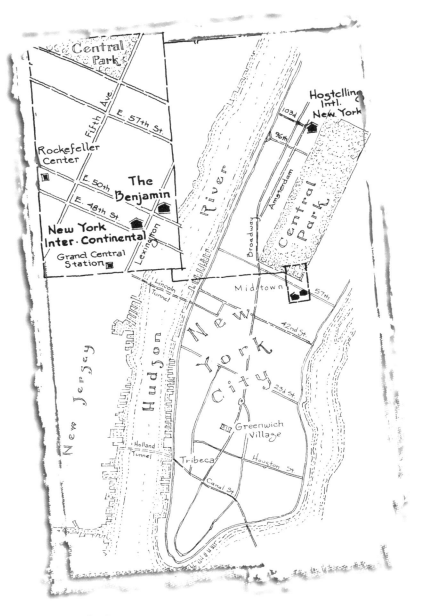

MANHATTAN ISLAND,
NEW YORK CITY

THE BIG APPLE'S
ECO-FRIENDLY HOTEL
The Benjamin, New York, New York

From her apartment near the corner of Fiftieth and Lexington, artist Georgia O'Keeffe looked out at the hotel across the street. Rising thirty stories was an eclectic assemblage of Romanesque arcades, crenelated parapets, Gothic-style rose windows, and terra cotta birds. She painted these eccentric details, capturing the hotel on canvas.

Illustration: Manhattan East Suites

Recently, the building has undergone a much-needed renovation, preserving its architectural character for future generations. Renamed The Benjamin, An Executive Suite Hotel, this elegant hotel also incorporates sophisticated systems for resource conservation and waste management, along with employee environmental training programs. As a result, The Benjamin has been certified as one of the few five-globe ECOTELs™ in the Northeast.

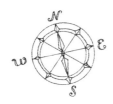

THE FACTS
The Benjamin

address	125 East 50th Street New York, NY 10022
phone	212-715-2500 reservations: 1-888-4-BENJAMIN
e-mail	access via Web site
Web site	**www.thebenjamin.com**
lodging	209 renovated guest rooms, including 97 one-bedroom suites and a deluxe two-bedroom suite.
rates	Guest rooms start at $320 per night.
caveats	Not much greenery nearby, although Central Park is within walking distance.
credentials	Five-globe ECOTEL™ certification
special interest	Resource conservation, waste management, midtown Manhattan location

Illustration: Manhattan East Suites

THE HOTEL

The lobby's background of marble and velvet sets an elegant tone for the hotel. The attention to detail is evident in the raised metal leaf reception desk, Venetian glass mirrors, and the grand staircase that leads to the guest lounge.

The Benjamin caters to business executives. All suites include ergonomic chairs, generously proportioned desks, and the latest in technology and business amenities. Internet access is provided in guest rooms and meeting rooms.

Decorated in warm tones, the rooms may include custom armoires, oversized club chairs, and sleep sofas. Galley kitchens feature state-of-the-art appliances, glass door cabinets, and granite countertops. The wedding-cake shape of the Benjamin enables many guest rooms to have abundant natural light, balconies, and full terraces. Guests can choose from no less than eleven pillow options.

ACCESS

In the heart of Manhattan, The Benjamin has access to one of the world's most elaborate public transportation systems. More than forty percent of the nation's mass transit operates in the New York City metropolitan area.

The city's trains, subways, buses, and taxis make a private vehicle unnecessary in Manhattan. Many of New York's favorite destinations are within walking distance of The Benjamin. For visitors arriving by train, connections at Grand Central and Penn stations are nearby.

RENOVATION

The hotel, originally named the Beverly, was designed by architect Emery Roth and completed in 1927. The recent restoration by Manhattan East Suite Hotels has restored the building's original elegance.

The architectural firm of Ronald Schmidt & Associates directed the renovation, with interior design by Di Leonardo International. This team has taken great care to preserve the integrity of the original design, unobtrusively integrating security devices and other necessary additions.

Photo: Manhattan East Suites

CONSERVATION

From the beginning, the design team and staff have worked to weave environmental considerations into the renovation. As a result, The Benjamin earns high marks for energy efficiency, solid waste management, and water conservation.

The hotel has one of the city's most complete recycling and waste management programs, based on a "zero-waste" goal. Each guest room contains an attractive wicker recycling bin. All staff members receive special training in ways to conserve resources and to minimize trash. Post-consumer recycled papers are used throughout the hotel for cards, stationery, and other products.

ACTIVITIES

The hotel's Woodstock Spa and Wellness Center offers progressive treatments, pampering products, and holistic philosophy. The twenty-four-hour fitness center has a full range of equipment for strength training and workouts.

Rockefeller Center, Fifth Avenue shops, and Broadway theaters are near the hotel, and Central Park is within walking distance.

I n late April, daylight lingers on the streets of Manhattan. Orioles return from their winter homes in Latin America to take up residence in Central Park. With careful site planning, the female oriole selects a slender branch inaccessible to the park's raccoons and squirrels. She then works with hemp, milkweed silk, and other plant materials to weave an intricate nest. As real estate brokers ply their trade in the surrounding city, the orioles raise a family in this prime New York location.

In the region ...
NEW YORK
CITY

One of the world's great urban open spaces, **Central Park** provides an abrupt contrast to the concrete and glass canyons of the surrounding city. Designed by Frederick Law Olmsted and Calvert Vaux, the park offers a sylvan setting for hiking, bicycling, and sports. Surprisingly, Central Park is known as one of the best birdwatching venues in the United States.

Part of the Gateway National Recreation Area, the **Jamaica Bay Wildlife Refuge** is one of the few major natural preserves accessible by subway and elevated train. The refuge includes about nine thousand acres of salt marsh, freshwater ponds, upland woodland, and mud-flats. Wigeons, glossy ibis, and more than three hundred other avian species have been recorded here, not counting the numerous aircraft from nearby JFK International Airport.

■ *Floyd Bennett Field, Building 69, Brooklyn, NY 11234*
tel. 718-318-4340, **www.nps.gov/gate**

The Cathedral Church of St. John the Divine is a testament to the overlapping territories of spirituality, ecology, and architecture. Construction work has been underway since 1892; the rough-cut rock ribs in the transept lend a cave-like quality to the unfinished interior. This is an inclusive sacred setting with a strong emphasis on environmental issues. Visitors can take an environmental tour past recycling bins and aquariums with Hudson River fish. The gift shop has an unusual mix of books on religion, science, and ecology, plus cast-plaster devils, gargoyles, and angels.

- *1047Amsterdam (at 112th Street), New York, NY 10025 tel. 212-316-7540, 932-7347 (tours)* **www.stjohndivine.org**

OTHER PLACES TO STAY

Just a few blocks from the Benjamin, **Hotel Inter-Continental New York** has undergone a twenty-million-dollar facelift, including major upgrading of systems to conserve water, save energy, and recycle waste. The hotel's Midtown location is convenient for access to Broadway plays, museums, and Rockefeller Center. Near Grand Central Station, the hotel is well served by public transit. Room rates start at about $270.

- *111 East 48th Street, New York, NY 10017 tel. 212-755-5900,* **www.new-york.interconti.com**

Near Columbia University on Manhattan's Upper West Side, **Hostelling International – New York** has been certified as a Sustainable Living Center, with recycling and conservation programs. The facility includes a cafeteria and kitchen. Subway stops are nearby, although a taxi ride to the door may be safer after dark. The garden is an urban oasis, with birches, fountain, brick paving, and a stone wall topped with barbed wire. Don't expect perfection at this mammoth urban hostel, but the price is right at $22 to $24 per night.

- *891 Amsterdam Avenue, New York, NY 10025 tel. 212-932-2300,* **www.Hostelling.com**

GREEN DINING

An American Place, one of the nation's highest-rated restaurants, now has taken up residence at The Benjamin. Chef and Proprietor Larry Forgione has been named by the Culinary Institute of America and the James Beard Foundation as the top chef in the country. Here, diners can expect creative reinterpretations of classic American cuisine, with frequent use of organic produce. A dinner here might begin with a field salad of organically-grown lettuce and greens ($9.00) and a crisp Hudson Valley goat cheese pancake appetizer ($9.50), followed by a seared mignon of venison with black pepper-lavender crust and wild huckleberry sauce ($32.00). The handsomely-crafted light fixtures are a notable feature of the interior. Open daily for breakfast, lunch, and dinner; check the restaurant's Web site for details.

- *565 Lexington Avenue, New York, NY 10022*
  tel. 212-888-5650, **www.anamericanplace.com**

With large windows facing the street, **Angelica Kitchen** has a bright, cheerful atmosphere. The intelligentsia who dine here select from macrobiotic meals such as the Dragon Bowl, with rice, beans, tofu, seaweed, and fresh vegetables. Dairy products and refined sugar are banned from the premises. The menu changes with each solstice and equinox. Watch for the tasty red lentil soup. Expect lunch or dinner to cost about $8 to $15.

- *300 East Twelfth Street, New York, New York 10003*
  tel. 212-473-0305

Retro coffee shop decor sets the stage for **Josie's** culinary juxtaposition of popular culture and environmental concern. Wearing "free-range staff" tee shirts, waitpersons at this high-energy café serve such fare as organic-beef hamburgers on focaccia buns, sweet potato ravioli, and dairy-and-wheat-free raspberry custard tarts. Meats are certified free-range or farm raised; grains, beans, and flour are certified organic, and water is triple-filtered. Josie's is just two blocks from the 72nd Street subway station on Broadway.

- *300 Amsterdam at 74th Street, New York, NY 10023*
  tel. 212-769-1212

For travelers on a tight schedule and a budget, **Vegetarian Paradise 2** offers healthy, inexpensive fast food. A light meal and juice can cost less than $5, with speedy service. All dishes are free of animal products, cholesterol, artificial color, refined sugar and preservatives. The

Magic Carpet combines Chinese cabbage, ginkgo nuts, sea moss, wood ear, and vegetables on a lotus leaf bed. Try the banana date tofu pudding for dessert. VP2 is on a quiet side street in Greenwich Village, near the southwest corner of Washington Square.

- *144 West Fourth Street (near Sixth Avenue), New York tel. 212-260-7049*

Rated "Best Organic Restaurant" by *New York Magazine*, **Herban Kitchen** offers omnivorous cuisine such as lentil loaf with sweet potato mash. Cooks use filtered water, cold-pressed oils, non-irradiated herbs, and unrefined sweeteners in food preparation. Vegan menu options are available. Candles, dried flowers, and seasonal outdoor seating add to the romantic SoHo atmosphere. Soup is served in miniature iron kettles, and bread comes with a mysterious, tasty lentil-mushroom spread. Open daily for lunch, dinner, and weekend brunch. A well-designed Web site provides current menus.

- *290 Hudson Street, New York, NY 10013 tel. 212-627-2257,* **www.herban.com**

PROVISIONS

Along with the abundance of natural food stores in New York City, twenty-six **Greenmarkets** are scattered throughout Manhattan. Along with typical farm produce, vendors at these open-air markets sell golden beets, honey, wine, smoked trout, syrup, baked goods, and much more. The Union Square Greenmarket (East Seventeenth at Broadway) is one of the largest authentic farmers' markets in America.

- *Information on Greenmarket locations and group tours can be arranged by calling 212-477-3220.*

RESOURCES

With more than half a million members, the **National Audubon Society** is an international leader in environmental advocacy and education. Audubon House, the Society headquarters building in Manhattan, is a century-old structure famed for its earth-friendly renovation. The Society's Web site describes this achievement of sustainable architecture in an urban setting.

- *700 Broadway, New York, NY 10003, tel. 212-979-3000*
www.audubon.org

FOR MORE INFORMATION

The *Green Apple Map* is a color guide to hundreds of eco-resources in New York City. The map lists locations for markets, restaurants, and other green businesses, along with information on public transportation, infrastructure, and other topics. This free map, produced by Modern World Design, is available from the New York City Environmental Fund, Hudson River Foundation, 212-924-8290. Online, the guide is part of the Green Map system.

- **www.greenmap.com**

New York, Naturally, A Resource Guide for Natural Living in New York is an alternative directory emphasizing New Age products and services. This guide includes an extensive list of restaurants and natural foods stores, along with coupons.

- *City Spirit Publications, 7282 Sir Francis Drake Boulevard, PO Box 267, Lagunitas CA 94938 tel. 212-966-8842 or 800-486-4794.*

The Big Apple's birds and birders are wryly depicted in *Redtails in Love: A Wildlife Drama in Central Park*. Author Marie Winn describes the resilient avians who somehow carry on courtship and nesting in this urban setting. Along the way, the author shares naturalist lore of Central Park, such as the annual arrival of the saw-whet owls in the Shakespeare Garden.

- *New York: Pantheon Books, 1998. Hardback, 295 pages, $24.00.*

PENNSYLVANIA'S POCONOS

... Perhaps when it's seed-time

the stars look arranged, dutifully sown,

but at peak of drought in the crop-blistering heat

who could do otherwise but despise

thoughts of pattern. Flung like stellar wild thyme

upon the slopes, ripped and burst into bloom

then abandoned as rubbish whole galaxies wide.

— Jim Schley, from "Urania"

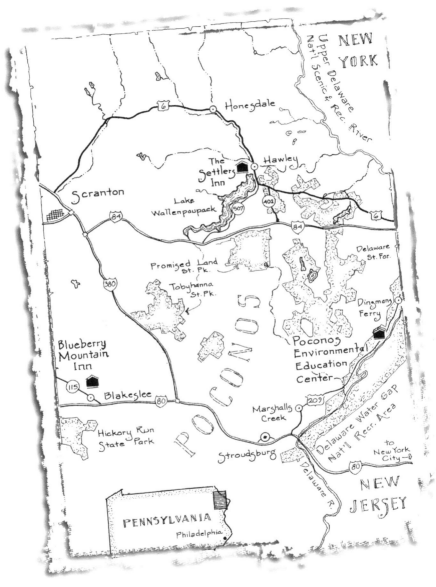

THE POCONOS

Protecting the Poconos
Blueberry Mountain Inn, Blakeslee, Pa.

Distinct from the rest of Pennsylvania, the Poconos are a lake-dotted glacial landscape. Because of the region's concentration of endangered and threatened species, the Nature Conservancy has designated the Pocono Highlands as one of the world's "Last Great Places."

The Blueberry Mountain Inn property near Blakeslee has a particularly diverse set of plant communities, including peat bogs, shrub swamp, spruce-tamarack-balsam swamp, and beech-maple forest. The site includes one of the largest native undisturbed spruce forests in Pennsylvania.

Grace Hydrusko, the environmentally minded owner of the inn, has granted a conservation easement on several hundred acres to The Nature Conservancy. This area is a key segment of the Thomas Darling Nature Preserve along Two Mile Run. Guests at the inn can appreciate the site's plants and wildlife, knowing that this unique landscape will be preserved.

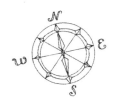

THE FACTS
Blueberry Mountain Inn

address	H.C. 1, Box 1102, Blakeslee, PA 18610
phone	570-646-7144 (fax 570-646-6269)
Web site	**www.blueberrymountaininn.com**
lodging	Five rooms and one suite, all with private baths. One room is disabled-accessible.
rates	Nightly rates for rooms are in the $90 range, while the suite goes for about $135. Rates include full breakfast. Special group rates and mid-week discounts are available.
caveats	Not accessible by public transit. Allergy-prone travelers should note that the inn has four resident cats.
credentials	Pocono Mountains Quality Assurance Award. AAA 3-Diamond rating. Charter Member of Green Hotels Association.
special interest	Land conservation, botany, skiing.

THE INN

Set among conifers, the inn occupies a small corner of the expansive site. Although the building is nearly new, the interior is largely furnished with family heirlooms handed down from Grace's Syrian ancestors. Urns are decorated with ornate tracery, and a pair of traditional wedding shoes inlaid with mother-of-pearl are a particular curiosity.

The spacious living room is dominated by a massive fireplace, built of stone from the property. The fireplace lintel was recycled from the owner's family home in New Jersey.

Upstairs, the library-TV room has a large skylight, plus windows framing the Poconos. Board games and environmental magazines are available for guests. In winter, strategically-placed solar cats are part of the decor, claiming sunny spots by south windows.

The inn's six rooms are furnished with antiques and fresh flowers. Each room has a queen bed, and most rooms have a full bath. Groups often stay at the inn, and visitors have included honeymooners and retired travelers. One guest has returned seventeen times.

ACCESS

Blakeslee is in the Poconos, just a few miles north of Interstate 80. The inn is about two hours west of the George Washington Bridge in New York City, and two hours north of Philadelphia's Ben Franklin Bridge.

From Interstate 80, take Exit 43, then follow Highway 115 north to Blakeslee. After the intersection with Route 940, continue north for 1.7 miles, turn right on Thomas Road and watch for the Blueberry Mountain sign. The inn is located at the end of a long, winding drive through conifer forest.

There is bus service to Blakeslee Corners. However, guests typically need their own vehicle, since the inn doesn't serve dinner and there are no restaurants nearby.

DINING

The aroma of baking bread often greets guests in the morning. Breakfasts may include crepes with hot strawberry sauce, oven roasted potatoes, semolina french toast, and apple strudel. On Sunday, there is a special buffet breakfast. Vegetarian guests are welcome, and special dietary needs can be accommodated with advance notice.

The dining table appointments include Limoges china, linen napkins, and antique teapots. On crisp days, cocoa is served from chocolate pots specially designed for this purpose.

A pantry is available to guests for other self-service meals. The cat drawings adorning the refrigerator have been sketched by children who have stayed at the inn.

CONSERVATION

The innkeepers use earth-friendly cleansers made from grapefruit skin. To save on water and energy, guests are given the option of skipping a daily linen change. Refillable soap dispensers are used instead of soap bars.

Water from the inn's deep well is run through a charcoal filter. Since four cats share the inn space, special filters clean the indoor air, reducing allergy problems.

ACTIVITIES

The cedar-paneled indoor pool room is a favored attraction. A special filtration system and ozonation reduce the need for chlorine.

A walking trail extends for a full mile into the remote reaches of the property, where hikers can pick wild blueberries in season. When winter comes to the Poconos, the inn hosts a festive event to groom this route for cross-country skiing. For additional skiing, three resorts are located within fifteen miles.

A pond on the site is stocked with fish. Two canoes and a rowboat are available for guest use. Wild turkeys often roam through the property, and guests also may see bear, deer, and red fox. At night, coyotes howl in the distance.

E ach season has its own special features in the woodlands and wetlands on the Blueberry Mountain Inn property. In late May and early June, the wetlands along Two Mile Run are accented with the striking blossoms of the rhodora. This wild azalea is more typically seen in the Canadian wilderness or upper New England.

By July, blueberries are beginning to ripen. As fall approaches, bottle gentian and cotton grass are on display. The deciduous tamarack needles turn gold in October, and the upland beech-maple forest comes alive with autumn color. Winter snows then coat the branches of the balsam firs, completing the cycle of the year along Two Mile Run.

Rhodora . Rhododendron canadense
to 1 m. Three-lobed azalea-like magenta
flowers bloom in May before
grayish-green leaves appear.

HOME-GROWN HOSPITALITY
The Settlers Inn, Hawley, Pennsylvania

SETTLERS INN

Tucked away in the northeast corner of Pennsylvania, the Settlers Inn has the comfortable air of an English manor. With strong community roots, this small hotel serves as a focal point for the village of Hawley.

For guests strolling the grounds, the Inn's priorities soon become apparent. A former swimming pool has been filled with earth and converted to a garden. Nasturtiums, calendulas, dianthus and daylilies are grown as edible flowers, and the chef is often seen snipping away at herbs for the kitchen.

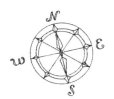

THE FACTS

The Settlers Inn at Bingham Park

address	Four Main Avenue, Hawley, PA 18428
phone	717-226-2993 reservations 800-833-8527
email	settler@ptd.net
Web site	**www.thesettlersinn.com**
lodging	Twenty rooms and suites, all with private baths.
rates	Rooms begin at about $85 per day for midweek and off-season times (November through June), and extend up to about $194 for peak season. Prices are based on double occupancy and include full breakfast.
caveats	No disabled access. No pets.
credentials	AAA 3 diamonds. Mobil 3-star-rated inn. Featured in the Innkeepers' Register of historic inns. Member, Green Hotels Association.
special interest	Historic architecture, regional cuisine.

THE INN

The Settlers Inn has shown resilience in the face of periodic reversals of fortune. In the optimistic Roaring Twenties, townspeople supported a community-based inn by purchasing shares in the Hawley Community Hotel. Just as the project was nearing completion, though, the Great Depression brought construction to a halt.

The forlorn building sat empty until the inn finally was completed after World War II. Then, in the 1960s, patrons deserted the inn in favor of new motels. More recently, as country inns are again "in," the refurbished Settlers Inn has enjoyed a renaissance under the current management.

The inn's country-manor theme is evident in the interior, where chestnut box beams and a native bluestone fireplace add to the ambience. East Coast Arts and Crafts detailing is displayed in the dining room light fixtures and the mural behind the lobby reception desk, with its fine oakleaf-pattern frieze.

Various design elements have been recycled from earlier incarnations. The ornate fireplace room partition was salvaged from an old bank. Many replacement windows have been rescued from building demolition, and the imposing Gothic dining room chairs were recycled from a cathedral.

In mild weather, the front porch and the fieldstone patio offer a congenial setting. The Tavern at the inn is a popular gathering place; the upstairs common room also has comfortable seating. Several conference rooms are available for groups; the local Audubon Society and the Delaware Highlands Conservancy meet regularly at the Inn.

The Inn's twenty rooms and suites typically are furnished with white wicker furniture. Quilted bed covers adorn antique brass beds. Some larger rooms have a sitting area. For business travelers, telephones with modems are available. The ample windows and beveled-glass oval mirror have made Room 9 a favorite with guests.

ACCESS

Hawley is located near the upper Delaware River in the northeast corner of Pennsylvania, about ninety miles west of New York City and forty miles east of Scranton. The inn is approximately ten miles north of Interstate 84, via routes 390, 507 and 6 (see the Inn's brochure for details). While most guests arrive by private vehicle, the inn can arrange to meet people arriving by bus or plane.

DINING

Room rates include a country breakfast featuring freshly baked breads and pastries. The Inn's elegant dining room is open to guests and the general public for lunch and dinner.

The restaurant offers regional cuisine, making seasonal use of local products. In particular, humble root vegetables are creatively featured in the inn's culinary creations.

The breads and desserts are all made in the Inn's own bakery. Organic herbs and vegetables are grown just outside the kitchen door, and other produce is procured from farmers in the area. A local hatchery keeps a special pool of Settlers Inn trout, custom-raised for the restaurant. Amish farm cheeses, local maple syrup, and Pennsylvania wines and beers also contribute to the cuisine.

A typical dinner might begin with baked onion soup and grilled portobello mushrooms, followed by vegetable pot pie topped with puff pastry. One of the Inn's signature desserts such as rhubarb cake with strawberry sauce and whipped cream would wrap up the repast.

ACTIVITIES

The inn's common rooms are comfortable places to relax with a book, to play chess or checkers, or to enjoy conversation with friends. Nearby Bingham Park provides a place for tennis, basketball, and play equipment for the kids. Guests can fish in the Lackawaxen River on the Inn's property or stroll through the carnival of summer color in the gardens. The inn's staff can provide information on local bicycling, cross-country skiing, and other recreation.

Hawley is located on Lake Wallenpaupack, the third largest reservoir in the state. Two wildlife sanctuaries are just a few minutes from the Inn. Recreation areas along the lake include extensive woodland and miles of trails for hiking, birdwatching, and photography. Local lakes and streams are summer settings for fishing, rafting, and sailing, replaced by ice skating and skiing in the winter.

As snow flurries fall on a December evening, guests arrive by horse-drawn carriage and gather around the massive fieldstone fireplace. After sampling hors d'oeuvres, the visitors take their places at the table and enjoy authentic Victorian cuisine. Holly sprigs, pine needles, and velvet complete this holiday scene at the Settlers Inn.

ALMANAC

In the region ...
POCONOS

The Poconos are survivors. Over the past two centuries, the region has withstood ill-advised forest clearing, mining and tacky tourism. Recent conservation efforts are contributing to the region's survival as a valued natural refuge and recreation area just a few hours from New York and Philadelphia.

As a unit of the Wild and Scenic River System, the **Upper Delaware Scenic and Recreational River** is a recreational highlight of the region. This part of the Delaware, considered one of the cleanest stretches of river in the Northeast, is an upstream continuation of the Delaware Water Gap National Recreation Area. Stretching for 73 miles along the border between New York and Pennsylvania, the Upper Delaware is particularly popular for canoeing and kayaking.

■ *RR 2, Box 2428, Beach Lake, PA 18405*
  tel. 570-685-4871, **www.nps.gov/upde/**

The boulder field in **Hickory Run State Park** is a geological curiosity. This thirty-acre area is strewn with stones, and the field is nearly devoid of vegetation. In addition to the boulder field, the state park includes more than 15,000 acres of forest.

■ *RR 1, Box 81, White Haven, PA 18661*
  tel. 717-443-0400

OTHER PLACES TO STAY

The **Pocono Environmental Education Center**, or PEEC, offers nature-oriented programs. Forty-seven cabins with wooden bunk beds hold two to fourteen people. Cabins have heat, electricity, showers, and modern bathrooms; meals are served in the dining hall. Family Nature Study Weekends cost about $94, and week-long stays are about $160 per person, including meals, lodging, and program activities. Guests need to bring or rent linens.

- *RD 2, Box 1010, Dingmans Ferry, PA 18328*
  tel. 717-828-2319, **www.peec.org**

PROVISIONS AND GREEN DINING

Set back from the highway, **Naturally Rite Restaurant and Cafe** is a refuge from traffic on a busy stretch of Route 209 near I-80. Inside, there's cheerful blue and white decor, with an outdoor terrace for summer dining. The restaurant serves low-salt, low-fat natural foods prepared without preservatives or additives. While much of the menu is vegetarian, seafood, buffalo, and poultry dishes also are featured. Involtini is a specialty; pasta spirals are layered with ricotta and mozzarella, then simmered in a cream and marinara sauce with fresh peas.

The adjacent **Naturally Rite Natural Foods Store** carries a wide selection of vitamins, organic produce and natural foods. On hand are lentil crisps, maple syrup, and organic chioccioli and other pastas. Store flyers are printed on recycled paper using soy-based ink.

- *Route 209, Marshalls Creek, PA, tel. 570-223-1133*
  www.naturallyrite.com

Nearby Honesdale, billed as the birthplace of American railroads, is noted for its Victorian architecture. Located on Main Street, **Nature's Grace Health Foods and Deli** supplies seasonal organic produce and free-range organic eggs. Raw milk (legal in Pennsylvania) is sold by the half gallon. The takeout deli offers inexpensive homemade soups, breads, salads, desserts and fresh-squeezed juices. Closed evenings and Sundays.

- *947 Main Street, Honesdale, PA 18431, tel. 570-253-3469*

Guests don't need to leave the Settlers Inn to stock up on eco-friendly wares. The inn sells its own home-baked bread made with organic flour. The Potting Shed gift shop offers an array of fun and functional items, from gardening supplies to whimsical jewelry and candles.

- *The Potting Shed at The Settlers Inn, Four Main Avenue, Hawley, PA 18428, tel. 717-226-2993*

RESOURCES

Working worldwide, **The Nature Conservancy** preserves plants, animals, and natural communities that represent Earth's diversity by protecting the land and water they need to survive. The Conservancy purchases some properties outright. In other cases, such as the Blueberry Mountain Inn, conservation easements protect fragile habitat. State and regional field offices are placed throughout the United States.

- *1815 North Lynn Street, Arlington, VA 22209 tel. 703-247-3720,* ***www.tnc.org***

Pocono Environmental Education Center (PEEC) is a residential environmental education center hosting twenty thousand visitors per year. The center serves mostly school groups, with three-day environmental camps, but residential programs also are available to adults and families. A gift store, natural history displays, and twelve miles of hiking trails are open to the public. Operated in cooperation with the National Park Service, PEEC is located off Route 209, midway between Stroudsburg and Milford.

- *RD 2, Box 1010, Dingmans Ferry PA 18328 tel. 717-828-2319,* **www.peec.org**

FOR MORE INFORMATION

The National Park Service publishes the *Official Map and Guide for the Upper Delaware Scenic and Recreational River.* The color brochure depicts facilities, public access points, camping facilities, local history and environmental information.

- *Superintendent, Upper Delaware Scenic and Recreational River, P.O. Box C, Narrowsburg, NY 12764*

15

BUCKS COUNTY, PENNSYLVANIA

*Not until June can the grass be
said to be waving in the fields.
When the frogs dream,
and the grass waves,
and the buttercups toss
their heads, and the heat
disposes to bathe in the
ponds and streams,
then is summer begun.*

— Henry David Thoreau

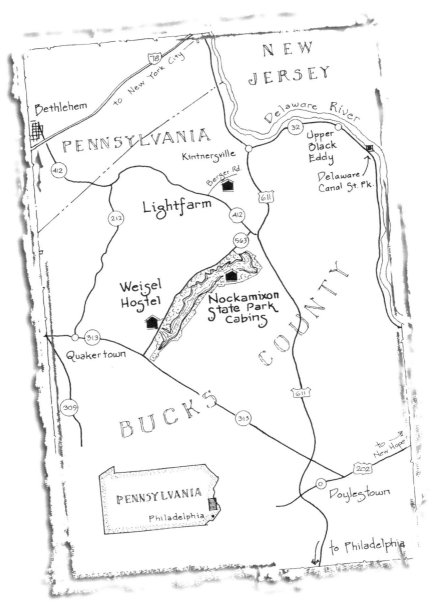

NORTHERN
BUCKS COUNTY

DIGGING BUCKS COUNTY

Lightfarm Bed & Breakfast
Kintnersville, Pennsylvania

Under the direction of an archaeologist, visitors at Lightfarm carefully remove soil from the excavation. Although nothing but dirt has materialized today, the workers hope to find another of the site's unusual sub-stemmed pipe bowls.

Lightfarm is a place for hands-on history of eastern Pennsylvania. Guests stay at a carefully restored working farm, and they have the option of participating in the continuing archaeological work on the site.

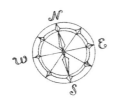

THE FACTS
Lightfarm B & B

address	2042 Berger Road Kintnersville, PA 18930
phone	610-847-3276 or 877-847-3276
email	litefarm@epix.net
Website	**www.lightfarm.com**
lodging	Four rooms with private baths.
rates	About $105 to $140 per night double occupancy, including breakfast. Special two-day and weekday rates.
caveats	Not accessible by public transit. No disabled access.
credentials	Member of American Bed and Breakfast Association; 1997 Award for Excellence. AAA 3-diamond rating. Featured in *Early American Life* and *Country Home*.
special interest	Archaeology, historic preservation, land conservation.

STENCILING PATTERN IN HALLWAY. LIGHTFARM

THE INN

Innkeepers Carol and Max Sempowski have an intense interest in the history of their property. The house dates back to about 1800, and their research indicates even earlier settlement.

Lightfarm even has its own small museum of pipe bowls, early redware, and other artifacts found on the property. The owners offer a tour of the museum and the historic structures on their property, including an ancient spring house that once was used to store dairy products. Other buildings on the site include a smokehouse and out kitchen.

OUT KITCHEN AT LIGHTFARM

The Sempowskis strive to restore structures using authentic methods. Wood timbers have been mortised and tenoned, for example, and beams have been hand-shaped with an adze.

The inn is carefully furnished with period decor. Some walls have Federal-era stenciling. A "hanging board" is original to the house.

All of the rooms have antique furnishings, with queen-size poster beds and private baths. Maria Sarah's Suite features a double pencil post bed, plus an adjacent sitting room with twin day bed.

ACCESS

The inn is located on a quiet country lane about fifteen miles southeast of Bethlehem. There is no public transportation to this rural location.

From the Philadelphia area, take Route 611 north from Doylestown to Route 412. Once on 412, watch for the

Lightfarm sign, and turn right on Berger Road. Lightfarm is the second farmplace along the road.

CONSERVATION

Lightfarm is registered in the local Heritage Conservancy's Significant Natural Areas Preservation Program. In cooperation with the Conservancy, the owners have agreed to protect Lightfarm from environmental intrusions.

A Pennsylvania Dutch foursquare garden occupies a south slope near the house. Characteristically, the vegetable garden is in the center, while the outer ring is planted to herbs and perennials, including some heirloom flowers such as ladyslipper. Elsewhere on the farm, grapevines and everbearing raspberries supply produce for the kitchen.

DINING

As part of the Lightfarm's historical emphasis, the innkeepers prepare traditional Pennsylvania Dutch breakfasts of sausage pie and other specialties. However, vegetarian and other special diets can be accommodated.

As cornbread bakes in a wood-fired bake oven, the innkeepers explain traditional methods of open-hearth cooking. Guests are served in the formal dining room or on an enclosed porch with countryside views.

ACTIVITIES

In addition to helping with historical and archaeological research at the inn, visitors can roam the 92-acre working farm, with its open meadows, creeks and wetlands. The seventeen-acre woodland is an inviting destination for birders and botanists.

Spring brings a display of violets, phlox, and other wildflowers, and autumn foliage provides a show later in the year. Guests can feed the farm animals, assist in sheep shearing, and make friends with the resident border collies and cats.

I *In late May, birdsong fills the hollow
at Lightfarm. Along Gallows Run Creek,
walnut and beech leaves sift sunlight,
shading the forest floor where the mayapple
is in bloom. Rising above each white flower
is a leaf-umbrella or two, as much as a
foot in diameter.*

*Over the next few months, a yellow-green
fruit will swell and ripen in the heat of late
summer. Some critics dismiss the fruit's
"sweetly mawkish" taste, or deride it as fit
only for pigs. Still, for one nineteenth-century
poet, the mayapple brought back vivid
memories of a rural boyhood.*

And will any poet sing

Of a lusher, richer thing

Than a ripe May-apple, rolled

Like a pulpy lump of gold

Under thumb and finger tips

And poured molten through the lips.

— James Whitcomb Riley
Rhymes of Childhood

In the region ...
BUCKS
COUNTY

This eastern Pennsylvania county combines a diverse set of natural communities with a richly textured historic landscape. However, its location just north of Philadelphia means that urban growth continues to pressure remaining open space.

Recognizing the need to protect the values that first drew people to Bucks County, local citizens and county officials have taken action to protect farmland and natural habitat. The county is nationally recognized for its pioneering work in rural planning and ecotourism development.

Long, skinny **Delaware Canal State Park** encompasses a sixty-mile stretch of the canal as it parallels the Delaware River. Towpath trails provide a level look at American history, and there's good birding along the reforested canal banks.

■ *Box 615A, RR 1, Upper Black Eddy, PA 18972*
tel. 610-982-5560

OTHER PLACES TO STAY

Twenty-eight Pennsylvania state parks include rental cabins and yurts. Just a few miles south of Lightfarm, **Nockamixon State Park** has ten family cabins for rent at about $47 to $118 nightly. Widely-spaced and surrounded by forest, the modern log cabins were constructed by the Pennsylvania Conservation Corps. Two cabins are handicapped-accessible.

Each cabin contains a furnished living area, kitchen-dining space, bathroom with shower, and two or three bedrooms. Cabins rent only by the week in summer, in the $400 to $500 range.

Visitors to the 5,000-acre park can rent bikes or head for Lake Nockamixon. Winter activities include cross-country skiing, sledding, fishing, and ice skating. The park offers environmental education and interpretive programs.

- *Nockamixon State Park, 1542 Mountain View Drive Quakertown, PA 18951, tel. 215-529-7300*
  www.dcnr.state.pa.us

Also within Nockamixon State Park is Hostelling International's **Weisel Hostel,** operated by the Bucks County Department of Parks and Recreation. A private room as well as dorms are available in this handsome restored stone building, formerly a country estate, for the low price of $10 per night ($13 for nonmembers). In peak season, the private room is the best bet here, as the dorms are a bit cramped. From time to time, naturalists give talks in the common room.

- *7347 Richlandtown Road, Quakertown, PA 18951 tel. 610-536-8749*

GREEN DINING

The well-known organic gardening and farming publications of Rodale Press are put into practice at the **Rodale Institute Research Center**. Guided tours of the Center's Experimental Farm are offered from May through September. The **International Cafe and Bookstore** at the Center offers visitors a chance to sample organic produce from the farm. After tasting the applesauce and pumpkin butter, you may want to take some home.

- *Rodale Institute Research Center, 611 Siegfriedale Road Kutztown, PA, tel. 610-683-1400*
  www.rodaleinstitute.org

PROVISIONS AND SHOPPING

The owners of **New Hope Natural Market** grow their own organic produce in season. The market carries a full selection of natural foods and supplements, plus some sandwiches and salads in the deli case. At the intersection of Routes 179 and 202, the store is open weekdays from mid-morning to 7 pm, with reduced hours on weekends. Look for the brightly-painted gazebo and perennial garden by the road.

- *415 Old York Road (Route 179), New Hope, PA 18938 tel. 215-862-3441*

A free directory, "Fresh from Bucks County Farms" lists dozens of local growers in the Lightfarm area, with special notation of organic sources such as **Solebury Orchards** near New Hope.

- *Available from the Bucks County Cooperative Extension tel. 215-345-3283*

RESOURCES

For nearly forty years, Bucks County's **Heritage Conservancy** has been acting to protect the area's land for agricultural use, wildlife habitat, and scenic value. The Conservancy works with landowners on various land conservation programs and educates the public about the values of open space preservation.

- *Heritage Conservancy, 85 Old Dublin Pike Doylestown, PA 18901, tel. 215-345-7020*

FOR MORE INFORMATION

Marsh, Meadow, Mountain: Natural Places of the Delaware Valley is a valuable guide to the region's key environmental sites. The book covers more than one hundred locations, including the Delaware Water Gap, New Jersey Pine Barrens, and open space oases in the Philadelphia area.

- *Temple University Press: 267 pages, $14.95*

16

PHILADELPHIA AND THE SCHUYLKILL RIVER VALLEY

How empty and silent the woods now,

before leaves have put forth

or thrushes and warblers have come!

Deserted halls, floored with dry leaves,

where scarcely an insect stirs as yet...

— Henry David Thoreau,
Journal, March 29, 1857

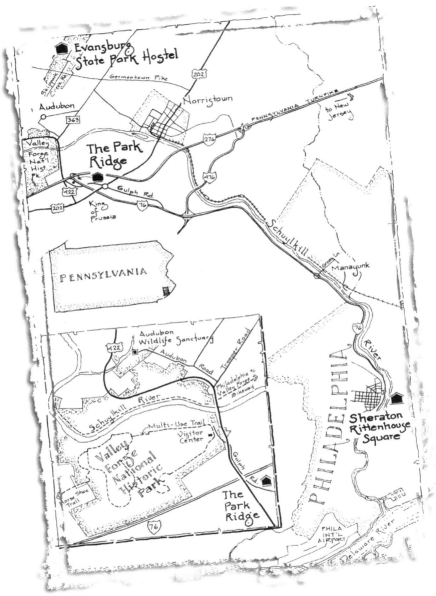

LOWER
SCHUYLKILL
RIVER VALLEY

A Suburban Ecotel
The Park Ridge at Valley Forge,
King of Prussia, Pennsylvania

Earth-friendly inns tend to be found either in rural areas or city centers. All too often, a suburban hotel is a bland building set in a sea of oil-stained asphalt — hardly a promising place to work on environmental improvement. Yet many travelers spend the night in hotels and motels in suburbia, and there's a real need for good examples of conservation in these locations.

The new owners of the Park Ridge near Philadelphia were interested in improving the hotel's environmental performance. After an intensive evaluation, the owners made major changes in the hotel's operation. As a result, the Park Ridge now is one of the few hotels in the United States that have received the ECOTEL certification, an industry standard developed with the help of the U. S. Environmental Protection Agency.

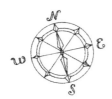

THE FACTS
The Park Ridge at Valley Forge

address	480 North Gulph Road, King of Prussia, PA 19406
phone	610-337-1800, 800-337-1801 fax 610-337-4506
e-mail	pridge@voicenet.com
Web site	**www.parkridgehotel.com**
lodging	Hotel with 265 guest rooms
rates	About $69 to $189 per night; reduced-rate packages available
caveats	Looks much like other suburban hotels; eco-friendly features are not readily apparent, but are embedded in the technical operation of the hotel.
credentials	One of the few U. S. hotels with an approved ECOTEL certification. Full-service hotel and conference center accredited by the International Association of Conference Centers.
special interest	Resource conservation, recycling

THE HOTEL

The Park Ridge caters primarily to business travelers, groups, and weekend leisure travelers. The hotel's conference center has nearly 15,000 square feet of meeting space, including a large ballroom and a number of smaller areas. A major renovation program includes complete remodeling of all guest rooms, new meeting and banquet facilities, and restyled restaurant and lounge.

Guest rooms are set back from nearby roads. Trees and earth berms help to buffer the hotel from the bordering highways. Inside, quilts soften walls in public spaces.

"Green Rooms" have been designed for travelers who want particularly healthy and eco-friendly overnight space. These rooms have special air and water purification systems. In addition, the hotel provides hypo-allergenic linen, towels, and toiletries.

ACCESS

The Park Ridge is located where the Pennsylvania Turnpike, Interstate 76, and other major routes converge. In light traffic, direct shuttle service to the hotel is just twenty minutes from Philadelphia's main Amtrak station, thirty minutes from the city center, or 35 minutes from Philadelphia International Airport.

Once on site, transportation options are limited. The busy highways bordering the site discourage walking or bicycling. Fortunately, the Park Ridge offers shuttle service or can arrange ground transportation to Valley Forge and other local destinations.

DINING

The Coppermill Harvest, a Zagat Award-winning restaurant, is open for breakfast, lunch, and dinner. After hours of headlight glare on the road, the low-key lighting is a welcome relief for travelers.

A breakfast specialty here is banana-pecan nut pancakes with warm maple syrup. Other offerings include granola and seasonal fruit. The hotel's Sunday breakfast lasts from 6:30 a.m. until noon, and includes made-to-order omelettes and Belgian waffles.

CONSERVATION

Recycling bins are conspicuously placed in guest rooms, but other environmental features at the hotel and restaurant are mostly behind the scenes. Employee training has been the first step; well-trained workers are knowledgeable about energy conservation, water savings, and recycling.

A well-planned recycling program has made a major difference in the hotel's operation. Each year, more than 100 tons of waste are diverted from the landfill, saving the hotel thousands of dollars. In fact, with these savings, the money spent in setting up the recycling program was paid back in just three months.

Consultants have evaluated the hotel's entire lighting system, and energy-efficient light fixtures have been installed or retrofitted. Occupancy sensors in empty rooms help to reduce lighting use.

Equipment throughout the hotel was replaced to conserve energy and water. Even small details in hotel operation now make a difference. For example, the staff frequently services refrigeration equipment, reducing the use of electricity.

To save on water and energy for laundering, guests at the hotel may choose to reuse their towels. Participating guests receive a packet of wildflower seeds.

ACTIVITIES

Conifers surround the hotel's outdoor swimming pool. Guests may play tennis on the hotel's courts or try out the exercise room. Indoors, Mad Anthony's Tavern in the hotel has billiards and darts. An eighteen-hole golf course lies across the road to the south.

The real recreation attractions are less than two miles away, at Valley Forge National Historic Park. In addition, bicyclists and hikers can travel to Philadelphia on the thirty-mile Valley Forge Bikeway.

A few miles from the Park Ridge, about seven hundred acres of grassland at Valley Forge National Historic Park are managed as tall-grass meadow, and are mowed just once a year. These meadows add to the historical authenticity of the park. Also, this tall-grass management reduces environmental and dollar costs, provides habitat and encourages the return of native species.

In early spring, little bluestem grasses carpet the fields at Valley Forge, providing shelter and sustenance for wildlife. Nearby stand massive oaks, still clad in faded autumn foliage. All winter, these leaves have hung tenaciously to their twigs. As warm weather arrives, new buds swell beneath the old leaves, achieving what blizzards and ice storms could not, as last year's leaves drop effortlessly with the arrival of spring.

In the region ...
PHILADELPHIA AREA

The meadows and woods of **Valley Forge National Historic Park** offer an open space respite from the region's urban sprawl. Valley Forge is best-known for its Revolutionary War history, but the 3,600-acre site also offers excellent nature-oriented recreation.

The park is a hub for biking and hiking trails that extend to Philadelphia and the Appalachians. The **Philadelphia to Valley Forge Bikeway** enters the park from the east, near the Betzwood Picnic Area. On the other side of the park, hikers on the **Horseshoe Trail** can head west to link up with the Appalachian Trail. Equestrians can bring their own horses and use designated bridle paths. The park's central multi-use loop trail is popular with joggers and cyclists. Bike racks are strategically placed at various stops on the trail.

Valley Forge's Environmental Center is open several days a week. A bird list is available here or at the Visitor Center.

- *Valley Forge National Historic Park, P.O. Box 954
  Valley Forge, PA 19482, tel. 610-783-1077*

Just north of Valley Forge is **Mill Grove**, the home where John James Audubon began his long career of bird illustration. Now a wildlife sanctuary, the site continues to be home for many species of birds, including descendants of the phoebes and swifts that Audubon studied.

- *Audubon Wildlife Sanctuary, P.O. Box 2
  Audubon, PA 19407, tel. 215-666-5593*

OTHER PLACES TO STAY

With its own interior bamboo forest, Philadelphia's **Sheraton Rittenhouse Square Hotel** uses plants to improve interior air quality. Guests tread on recycled granite flooring, and night tables are made from recycled pallets. Organically grown cotton bedding and bleach-free mattresses and covers add to the hotel's environmental appeal. The hotel has 193 rooms including some with disabled-access facilities. Room rates from $149 to $269.

■ *Eighteenth at Locust Street, Philadelphia, PA 19013*
   tel 215-546-9400, **www.sheraton.com**

The 12-bed **Evansburg State Park Hostel,** located just north of Valley Forge National Historic Park, is only thirty minutes from Philadelphia. Evansburg State Park offers canoeing on Skippack Creek and all sorts of other outdoor activities. In winter, the hostel is a good place to warm toes at the fireplace after a day of skiing. Evansburg is a member of Hostelling International's sustainable program, which emphasizes resource conservation and recycling. About $12 buys a bunk for the night. Don't dawdle too much on the way; the park gate may be locked after dusk.

■ *837 Mayhall Road, Collegeville, PA 19426*
   tel. 215-489-4326

GREEN DINING

A brief review can't do justice to Philadelphia's **White Dog Café**, one of the Northeast's best dining destinations. Located on a quiet street of brick rowhouses near the Penn campus, the café has received numerous awards and accolades. The chef seeks out suppliers of organic, fresh and seasonal ingredients for the kitchen, producing appetizers such as Amish farmhouse cheeses and local organic fruits with savory rosemary biscotti ($7.50), followed by oven-roasted organic free-range chicken with local wild mushrooms in rich thyme cream ($16.50).

These culinary achievements are combined with an outstanding record of environmental and social activism. Founder Judy Wicks organizes tours to focus on energy conservation, community gardening, and affordable housing. Each Monday, speakers on current issues hold forth on the enclosed porch.

The café is open seven days a week for breakfast, lunch, and dinner. Current menus and hours are available on the restaurant's Web site. The adjoining Black Cat gift store carries copies of the White Dog Café cookbook, as well as jewelry, crafts, and novelties made from recycled materials.

- *3420 Sansome Street, Philadelphia, PA 19104 tel. 215-386-9224,* **www.whitedog.com**

The **Manayunk Farmers Market** in northeast Philadelphia attracts a trendy, upscale clientele. Although some produce purveyors are present, this is mainly a place for casual dining. Around the central court, about two dozen booths sell everything from traditional Phillie hoagies to pine nut pizza, Venezuelan rice pudding and many vegetarian dishes. A deck overlooks the Schuylkill River — a splendid setting for a summer lunch.

- *4120 Main Street, Philadelphia, PA 19127, near the Manayunk station on SEPTA rapid transit line*

Several vegetarian restaurants are located in Philadelphia's Chinatown, a bustling area about six blocks northwest of Independence Hall. **Singapore Chinese Vegetarian Restaurant** has received widespread acclaim since its opening in the early 1990s. The owners have an Environmentally Clean Program in the restaurant, including filtered water. The strictly non-dairy vegetarian menu may include culinary exotica such as mock fish head molded from tofu and taro flour, with a cocktail cherry for the eye. Other unusual fare includes asparagus seaweed rolls, vegetable eel shreds, and ginkgo nuts (with the odorous outer pulp removed).

- *1029 Race Street (between 11th and 12th)*
  Philadelphia, PA, tel. 215-922-3288

PROVISIONS

Northwest Philadelphia's Manayunk District is bordered by a towpath on one side and a rapid transit line on the other. This historic milltown now is a center for eco-friendly dining and shopping. **Arnold's Way Natural Health Foods** offers snacks and natural sodas, take-out sandwiches and salads, along with bulk foods, cosmetics, and environmental products. The store also offers courses in yoga and nutritional counseling. A sign on the counter announces that free poetry and rubber bands are available on request.

- *4438 Main Street, Philadelphia PA 19127*
  tel. 215-483-2266, near Manayunk Station on SEPTA line

Nearby, a keystone arch welcomes visitors to **Down 2 Earth Naturals and Recyclables**, with its eclectic stock of fabrics, coconut foot cream, gardening supplies, concrete card holders, wheatgrass seed, banana fiber envelopes, recycled-object clocks, and sterilized hemp seed sold by the pound. Note the soybean-based counter top at the cash register.

- *4371 Main Street, Philadelphia, PA, tel. 215-482-4199*

Indigo is an international gift shop with natural glycerine soap, clothing and crafts. Don't miss the Guatemalan makeup mirrors with frames fashioned from recycled bottle caps.

- *151 North Third Street, Philadelphia, PA 19106*
  tel. 215-922-4041, **www.indigoarts.com**

In central Philadelphia, the **Ninth Street Market** is an exuberant melange of stalls selling about anything you need. In this remnant of old Philly, you can pick up regionally grown fruits and vegetables. Be prepared, though, for butcher shops complete with dressed goat and rabbits hanging in the windows.

RESOURCES

The **Keystone Trails Association** is an alliance of organizations and people interested in tramping through Pennsylvania. The KTA acts as a watchdog over government and private activities that might affect hiking. KTA trail crews help to keep the state's trails in good shape. Their Web site includes a hiking guide and map as well as statewide weather forecasts.

- *KTA, PO Box 251, Cogan Station, PA 17728*
  www.kta-hike.org

"Ride Hard, Be Heard" is a motto of the **Bicycle Coalition of the Delaware Valley.** The Coalition is working with planners to build a network of trails across the region and to provide safe bike parking. Kids at the Coalition's Youth Cycle and Recycle Program learn bicycle repair, maintenance, and safety.

- *252 South Eleventh Street, Philadelphia, PA 19107*
  www.bcdv.org

FOR MORE INFORMATION

Printed on recycled paper, the "Pennsylvania Trail of Geology" identifies rock formations along trails at Valley Forge. A map depicts the site's geology, including the karst valley where Washington's soldiers camped.

- *Free: 14 pages. Available from Valley Forge National Historic Park, P.O. Box 953, Valley Forge, PA 19481*

The Keystone Trails Association offers a number of guidebooks and maps useful for hiking throughout the state. *The Appalachian Trail in Pennsylvania,* now in its tenth edition, is the definitive guide to the state's 228-mile section of this famous hiking path.

- *Available from the KTA, PO Box 251*
  Cogan Station, PA 17728. 216 pages: $9.00

NEW JERSEY
HIGHLANDS

Home again; down temporarily in the Jersey woods.
Between 8 and 9 A.M. a full concert of birds, from
different quarters, in keeping with the fresh scent,
the peace, the naturalness all around me.
I am lately noticing the russet-back, size of the
robin or a trifle less, light breast and shoulders,
with irregular dark stripes — tail long — sits
hunched up by the hour these days, top of a tall
bush, or some tree, singing blithely ...

— Walt Whitman
"Birds – And a Caution",
May 14, 1888, from *Specimen Days and Collect*

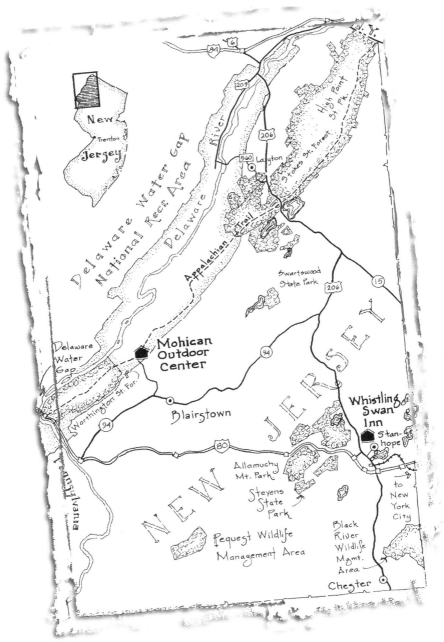

NEW JERSEY
HIGHLANDS

NATURALLY CLEAN
IN NEW JERSEY
Whistling Swan Inn, Stanhope, New Jersey

Photo: Whistling Swan Inn

This genteel inn is one of the region's noteworthy bed and breakfasts. Featured in the *New York Times* and other prestigious publications, The Whistling Swan is known for its superior service and high standards.

Owners Paula and Joe Williams-Mulay have taken many steps to conserve resources at the Inn. Concerned about the environmental effects of harsh cleaning products, they have returned to traditional maintenance methods. The innkeepers have found that simple, benign methods from their grandmothers' era provide the results they need to maintain their standards.

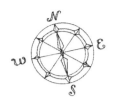

THE FACTS
Whistling Swan Inn

address	110 Main Street, Stanhope, NJ 07874
phone	973-347-6369 fax 973-347-3391
email	wswan@worldnet.att.net
Web site	**www.whistlingswaninn.com**
lodging	Ten guest rooms with private baths and queen-size beds.
rates	Standard rates vary from about $95 for the Cozy Rooms to about $150 for the two-room suite, including full breakfast. Weekly, monthly, and corporate rates also are available.
caveats	No pets. No children under 12.
credentials	Members of Professional Association of Innkeepers, Independent Innkeepers' Association, and Bed and Breakfast Innkeepers' Association of New Jersey.
special interest	Historic building renovation, eco-friendly inn maintenance.

THE INN

The Whistling Swan Inn is located in Stanhope's historic district, a comfortable neighborhood of turn-of-the-century homes and churches. In the nineteenth century, Stanhope boomed as a stop on a canal system which connected area lakes. Now Stanhope is a quiet town on the outer exurban fringe of the New York metropolitan area, and a handy base for exploring the Delaware Water Gap and the northwestern New Jersey lake district.

The Queen Anne-style home was completed in 1905 by one Mr. Best as a residence for his large family. The inn's office occupies the space where he once presided as a justice of the peace.

Situated on a full acre, the inn is framed by shade trees. The property provides plenty of room for Paula to indulge her interest in gardening. A red gazing globe recalls a common feature of Victorian landscapes. These bright spheres were placed in gardens as wintertime color accents, and they also allude to the Victorian fascination with crystal balls and mystery.

The inn's wraparound porch with stone pillars and double Ionic columns give the structure a substantial appearance. Inside, a three-story staircase provides visual drama. The period furnishings include many heirlooms from Paula's family. The front parlor alone holds an upright player piano, a working Victrola, and a Duncan Phyfe sofa.

Guest rooms are on the second and third floors of the inn. All rooms have private baths, telephone, and television. The queen-size beds have a variety of antique brass, iron, spindle, and high backboard frames. The inn caters to business travelers, with fax and other support services.

Rooms range from the smaller "Cozy Rooms" to a two-room suite. The Oriental Antiques Room is of special interest, with its collection of pieces brought by Paula's great uncle from Japan and Thailand. The room signs and tissue box covers were needle-pointed by Joe's father.

A two-room suite occupies the imposing octagonal turret at the corner of the house. With its appealing angular shape, the suite includes a sitting room with white wicker furniture, as well as a refrigerator.

ACCESS

Whistling Swan Inn is located just 45 miles west of New York City, and New Jersey Transit provides convenient train and bus service to Stanhope. It's just an hour and a half on the Boonton commuter rail line from Manhattan to the Netcong train station near the inn. Bus service is shorter, a little over one hour. Visitors can walk from the station through the tidy town of Stanhope, or the innkeepers will meet guests at the train or bus station with advance notice.

It's somewhat inconvenient to get around the area by transit, though, so most visitors arrive by car. The inn is just one mile north of Interstate 80.

DINING

The buffet breakfast includes fresh-baked breads and muffins, fruits and juices, yogurt, cereals, a hot main dish, and a variety of tea and coffee. Sample selections might include strawberry or peach soup, bread pudding, warm fruit compotes, baked French toast, or date banana bread.

The innkeepers will accommodate visitors with special diets or food allergies if notified in advance. Many guests are vegetarians, and the inn emphasizes vegetarian and healthy cooking. For example, jams and jellies have no added sugar, and low-fat cream cheese is served.

Guests can enjoy the elegant dining room setting, with its long oval table. In addition, they can choose to eat by a fireplace on winter mornings, or dine outdoors in mild weather.

REMUDDLING AND RENOVATION

Over the years, Paula says, a lot of "remuddling" had been done. As a result, the inn's renovation has been a free interpretation of the original Victorian styling. The current owners bought the house in 1985 and began improvements immediately, starting with the leaky slate roof.

The bathrooms at the Whistling Swan are a virtual plumbing museum. Some of the replacement toilets and pedestal sinks were salvaged from a seaside hotel on the Jersey shore. One tub sits in an iron ring.

The claw-foot tubs presented a special challenge. Paula and Joe prevailed on their friends for help. It took several men to de-claw, upend, and load the tubs into a van. Once the tubs were placed in their new home, the feet were reattached.

Although much of the original copper and brass hardware was intact, other items were missing. As a result, the owners have become adept at scouring salvage yards for everything from skeleton keys to caning supplies. A stained glass window was recycled from a doomed church.

ECO-FRIENDLY CLEANING TIPS FROM THE WHISTLING SWAN INN

Grandma's recipe for general cleaning: 1 cup baking soda and 1 cup vinegar to 1 gallon of water. Use rubber gloves.

Windows and mirrors: 1/4 cup vinegar to one quart water. Rub surface with old newspapers.

CONSERVATION

In addition to the owners' environmental sensibilities, the high cost of electricity was a prime motive for energy conservation. An energy audit provided a list of potential savings. As a result, the innkeepers use energy-efficient bulbs where possible. Motion sensors help to reduce unnecessary lighting. Outside, timers and night sensing devices provide light as needed. Guests are asked for suggestions for other ways to conserve. The result has been a substantial reduction in energy use.

Since high-tech cleansers are avoided, the inn is hospitable to people with chemical sensitivities. Common products such as baking soda and vinegar are effective in most situations.

The old porcelain tubs are sensitive to abrasives. The owners have found that baking soda is effective for most cleaning. Recycled plastic cleaning pads provide a backup when stronger measures occasionally are required.

As a result of their experience, Paula and Joe conduct training classes for prospective innkeepers, focusing on eco-friendly maintenance as well as other management techniques. Since innkeeping can be a tenuous economic enterprise, they point out that traditional cleaning methods often can save considerable cash.

ACTIVITIES

The inn provides bikes for guest use to explore the neighborhood or nearby state parks and forests. Swimming and fishing are popular pastimes at Lake Musconetcong, just a few blocks away, where boats are available for rental. Antique shops abound in Chester and other area towns. Or guests can simply relax in the hammock or porch swing.

In winter, there is cross-country skiing at Stevens State Park, and several golf courses within an eight-mile radius. There also are ample opportunities for downhill skiing in the area.

M ountain laurel, Kalmia latifolia, *is a common native shrub in the deciduous woodlands of the Delaware River valley. Its dark green foliage provides welcome winter color among the muted colors of deciduous forest. June is the best time to experience mountain laurel, however. In certain places around the Delaware Water Gap, it blooms so enthusiastically that the forest floor appears to be covered with a layer of new-fallen snow.*

ALMANAC

In the region ...
NEW JERSEY HIGHLANDS

Stretching for forty miles along the New Jersey and Pennsylvania banks of the middle Delaware River, the **Delaware Water Gap National Recreation Area** includes about 70,000 acres for hiking, boating, swimming and birding. On the New Jersey side of the river, the Lower Rattlesnake Swamp trail winds through hip-high ferns and native rhododendrons the size of small trees. Raccoon Ridge on the Appalachian Trail is a favored spot for hawk-watchers. Detailed information is available from the Park headquarters.

■ *Bushkill, PA, tel. 717-588-2451* **www.nps.gov/dewa/**

OTHER PLACES TO STAY

The **Mohican Outdoor Center**, operated by the Appalachian Mountain Club, is located on Catfish Pond in the Delaware Water Gap National Recreation Area. Co-ed bunkrooms hold four to ten people, with camp-style bathrooms and showers. The Center provides mattresses and pillows, but bring your own bedding, pillowcase, and towels.

The AMC recently has taken over operation of this facility after years of neglect, and renovation work is in progress. In the meantime, if you can put up with the somewhat-funky accommodations, costs are reasonable. For groups, weekend bunk space goes for $15 or $20 per night for members (a few dollars more for non-members). Individual weekend stays cost about $55 to $75. For the best deal, visitors can stay here for free, as part of a work-exchange arrangement.

■ *Mohican Outdoor Center, Blairstown, NJ*
   For directions, workshop and lodging information,

call 908-362-5670.
www.outdoors.org/Lodging/Delaware

GREEN DINING

For eco-friendly food, local residents and national news-papers recommend **Café Metro,** down the road in Denville. Ensconced in a refurbished nineteenth-century home, the restaurant emphasizes vegetarian and vegan selections. Open daily for dinner, as well as lunch on weekdays. Sample menu items: grilled chicken and egg-plant, veggie pizza made with organic unbleached flour. Lunch entrees run about $5–$11; dinner entrees around $7–$13. Less than a mile north of I-80's Exit 39, in pedes-trian-friendly Denville's downtown district. Watch for the big porch with blue trim.

■ *Café Metro, 60 Diamond Spring Road*
  Denville, NJ 07834, tel 973-625-1055

PROVISIONS AND SHOPPING

The **Peters Valley Craft Store and Sally D. Francisco Gallery** are located within the Delaware Water Gap National Recreation Area. The store and gallery include arts and crafts made from donated materials. The building is a renovated general store built in the mid-nineteenth cen-tury and listed on the National Register of Historic Places.

■ *19 Kuhn Road, Layton, NJ 07851, tel. 973-948-5202*

Along with a wide array of natural foods and organic produce, **Mrs. Erb's Good Food** includes a large take-out deli with hummus, salads, and sandwiches. Mrs. Erb's also offers "Student Care Packages," an assortment of healthy snacks, vitamins and nutrients to counteract the rigors of campus life. Weary shoppers can escape to the mezzanine for a therapeutic massage or facial. Located just a few steps from Café Metro in downtown Denville, Mrs. Erb's is open daily from mid-morning to early evening (10 am to 5 pm on Sunday).

■ *20 First Avenue, Denville, NJ 07834, tel. 973-627-5440*

RESOURCES/FOR MORE INFORMATION

The **New York-New Jersey Trail Conference** is an umbrella organization for hiking and environmental groups in the region. The Conference provides information about member organizations, distributes hiking-related books and produces a superior series of durable maps.

- *232 Madison Avenue #802, New York NY 10016, email NYNJTC@aol.com,* **www.nynjtc.org**

Nick Miskowski's *Hiking Guide to the Delaware Water Gap National Recreation Area* is the definitive guide to trails in the DWGNRA. This affordable book covers marked and unmarked trails and woods roads on both the Pennsylvania and New Jersey sides of the river.

- 112 pages, $7.95 plus postage and handling. *Available from the New York - New Jersey Trail Conference.*

THE CHALFONTE,
CAPE MAY

CAPE MAY

If birds are good judges of
excellent climate, Cape May has
to be the finest climate in the
United States, for it has the
greatest variety of birds.

— Alexander Wilson
ornithologist, c. 1811

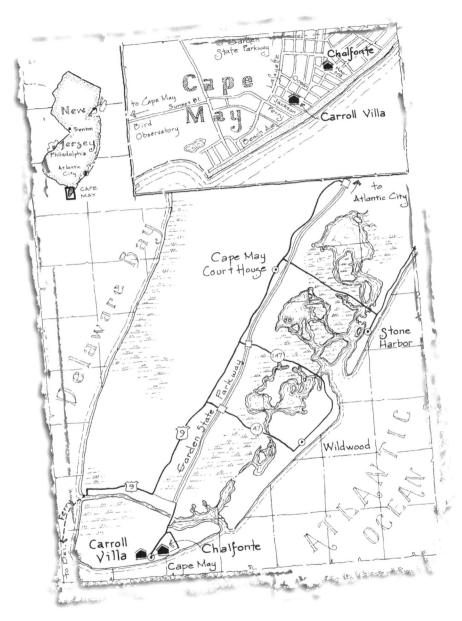

CAPE MAY

Eco-Victorian Hospitality
The Chalfonte, Cape May, New Jersey

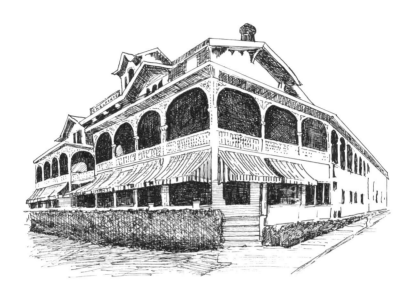

Cape May's beloved Chalfonte defies the conventional rules of hotel operation, and keeps guests coming back anyway. Built in the nineteenth century, this traditional summer hotel doesn't bother with new-fangled gadgetry such as heating, air conditioning, television, telephones, or hair dryers in the guest rooms. Instead, the hotel offers genteel Southern-style hospitality from a bygone era.

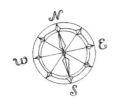

THE FACTS
The Chalfonte

address	301 Howard Street, P.O. Box 475 Cape May, NJ 08204-0475
phone	609-884-8409 fax 609-884-4588
e-mail	chalfontnj@aol.com
Web site	**www.chalfonte.com**
lodging	Seventy rooms in main building, plus two cottages. Ten rooms with private bath. Retrofitting for disabled access is planned.
rates	About $89 to $213 per night, including breakfast and dinner for two adults. Special rates for groups, events, mid-week visits, and long-term stays. Volunteers can exchange renovation work for an inexpensive pre-season or post-season stay at the hotel.
caveats	Ceiling fans rather than conventional air conditioning. No heating. Open Memorial Day through Columbus Day only, although the hotel office is staffed during the winter months.
credentials	Member, The Ecotourism Society.
special interest	Historic preservation, Victorian architecture, resource conservation, recycling, cultural programs.

THE HOTEL

Ornate gingerbread verandas and an Italianate cupola give the Chalfonte a distinctive profile. In addition to fifty rooms in the main building, accommodations are available in three historic cottages. The sixteen rooms in The Annex and the Howard Street Cottage are available at special rates to families with small children. The four-room Franklin Street Cottage is rented to families or groups of five or more.

Simplicity is the keyword in the guest rooms, which are furnished with marble-topped dressers and other period decor. Located on a corner, Room 40 is a favorite, with its sea breezes, balcony, and private bath with sitting tub. Ten rooms have private baths; other rooms share bathrooms on the hall.

Pesticide-free herb beds and a butterfly garden are on the property. The hotel's gardens are featured on a yearly tour of Cape May.

ACCESS

The Chalfonte is located in central Cape May. Most guests arrive by private vehicle, but the staff will pick up guests at the bus station on request; check with the hotel for details.

For travelers on the Garden State Parkway, go south to the end of the Parkway, then follow the signs to Cape May. After crossing the Canal Bridge and the Marina Bridge, make a left at the first light. Follow this street (Madison Avenue). Watch for the water tower (which proclaims that Cape May is a National Historic Site), then take the second right turn onto Sewall Avenue. The hotel is at the corner of Howard Street and Sewall Avenue.

DINING

The hotel capitalizes on Cape May's location near farm-land and the sea. Regional dishes incorporate local blueberries, sweet corn, tomatoes, peaches, apples, and fresh locally caught fish.

The cuisine at the Chalfonte has been described as "soul food with its Sunday clothes on." A Virginia-based family ran the hotel from about 1915 to 1970, and the current owners continue the tradition of Southern-oriented cuisine. The breakfast buffet ($8.50) includes such selections as spoonbread, grits, fresh fish, homemade biscuits, fresh-squeezed juices, and baked apples.

Dinner options ($21.00 fixed price) include a vegetarian entree, fresh fish of the day or a traditional Virginia-style entree of turkey, prime rib, or crab cakes, served with homemade rolls.

In keeping with the hotel's tradition, children under six years old dine in a separate supervised area. After meals, children can apply their artistic talents in coloring books designed and printed at the Chalfonte.

The Magnolia Room, the hotel's dining room, originally was a "shotgun" ballroom, so named because of its impressive length. Decor includes original plaster medallions on the ceiling, traditional ceiling fans, and lighting sconces.

In a traditional touch, pitchers of drinking water and recyclable or biodegradable drinking cups are set out for guests in the lobby. The King Edward Bar is available for other beverages.

CONSTRUCTION AND RENOVATION

The Chalfonte was constructed in 1876 by Colonel Henry Sawyer, a local Civil War hero. Originally planned as a boarding house, the Chalfonte has served for decades as Cape May's oldest continuously operating hotel and historic landmark.

An old building needs continual work, and the Chalfonte runs two innovative renovation programs. Students from the University of Maryland's School of Architecture come to Cape May each spring, assisting in the hotel's preservation and upkeep while gaining hands-on experience in architectural restoration.

In addition, loyal guests volunteer for work weekends. Each spring, this cadre helps to get the Chalfonte in shape for the upcoming season. The autumn work weekend puts the inn to bed for the winter. Depending on their skills, workers may paint, repair woodwork, or wield pruning shears in the garden.

CONSERVATION

The hotel extends the concept of a National Historic Site beyond conservation of the physical structure. The owners are committed to maintaining the traditional atmosphere of the hotel by limiting technological change. Visitors can enjoy a Victorian-era visit to the beach sans air conditioning, television, telephones, and other modern technology.

The hotel is not open in cold months when heating is needed. In summer, louvered doors and ceiling fans direct cooling sea breezes through the rooms. Most guests are well-acclimated to the lack of precise temperature control, and conserve energy by turning off unnecessary lights. As a result, the Chalfonte's electrical bill is considerably less than a typical hotel.

From the front desk and lobby to the kitchen and other areas, recycling is taken seriously at the Chalfonte. Office staff members collect blank-backed paper and cut it into notepads; they use cardboard and other paper scraps for packing materials. Surplus paper also is used for coloring pads and origami projects for young guests. The hotel emphasizes the use of recycled paper and soy-based ink for printed materials

To save on water for laundering, the hotel offers guests the option of re-using towels and washcloths. Signs in rooms remind guests to turn off lights and fans when not needed.

The Chalfonte is a member of The Ecotourism Society. The hotel actively supports the local Wetlands Institute, Cape May Bird Observatory, and other environmental organizations. A lobby display provides ecotourism information.

ACTIVITIES

The Henry Sawyer Room at the Chalfonte is the setting for frequent classical and jazz concerts and theater performances. The hotel also hosts art shows, massage workshops, and other events. The ocean is just three blocks down the street, but many guests prefer to relax on the veranda's rocking chairs.

A s the autumn equinox approaches, nature enthusiasts arrive at the shore for the Wings and Water Festival. Visitors can choose from dune walks, salt marsh safaris, boat cruises, bird walks, art and photography exhibits and workshops, quilt displays, fly casting demonstrations and folk music. Sponsored by the Wetlands Institute, the event has been honored as one of the top one hundred festivals in the United States and the best ecotourism event in New Jersey.

GREEN DINING ON THE
JERSEY SHORE
The Carroll Villa Hotel, Cape May, New Jersey

Mushroom *duxelle*.

Roasted eggplant.

Bell pepper. Spinach.

The chef combines these ingredients with fresh
mozzarella, then bakes the mixture in flaky puff
pastry, and adds a freshly made tomato sauce.
A waiter then serves the Vegetable Wellington to
diners on the terrace. This is a signature dish at the
Mad Batter Restaurant, associated with the Carroll Villa
Hotel, where environmental concerns are blended
with fine dining and innkeeping.

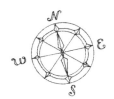

THE FACTS
Carroll Villa Hotel

address	19 Jackson Street, Cape May, NJ 08204
phone	609-884-9619 (hotel) 609-884-5970 (restaurant)
e-mail	mbatter@eticomm.net
Web site	**www.carrollvilla.com** (hotel) **www.madbatter.com** (Mad Batter Restaurant)
lodging	Twenty-two rooms.
rates	$105 to $175 range; lower rates for off peak and midweek stays. Rates include full breakfast at the Mad Batter.
caveats	Two-night minimum stay on weekends and during peak summer season in July and August.
credentials	Member, Green Hotels Association and Professional Association of Innkeepers. Highly rated by numerous travel guides and magazines. AAA-rated 2 stars
special interest	Eco-friendly dining and inn operation, Victorian architecture.

THE INN

Just half a block inland from the ocean, the Carroll Villa is flanked by other flamboyant Victorian hotels. A whimsical stuffed mannequin greets guests at the entry.

Guest rooms are on the second and third floors. Decor includes period antiques, Victorian-era wallpaper, and lace curtains. Rooms 21 and 28 have bay windows with the best ocean views. Three rooms each have their own private bath down the hall; all other rooms have a private, in-room bath. Room 20 has a private balcony.

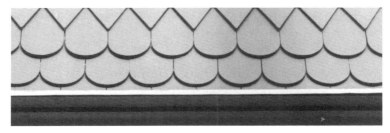

SHINGLE DETAIL, CARROLL VILLA HOTEL

ACCESS

The Carroll Villa is located in the historic heart of Cape May, on the southern tip of New Jersey. Although most guests arrive by private vehicle, bus service is available to Cape May, with Amtrak connections in Atlantic City.

For travelers on the Garden State Parkway, go south to the end of the Parkway, then follow the signs to Cape May. Stay on Lafayette until the road comes to a tee. Make a left on Jackson Street and look for the restaurant's yellow-and-white-striped awning.

DINING

Mad Batter, the hotel's acclaimed restaurant, offers a choice of seating in the skylit dining room or front porch. The glass-enclosed garden terrace also is seasonally opened for outdoor dining. A sun is painted on the terrace wall, and a fountain murmurs in the background. Visiting children and local artists have contributed artwork on the walls.

Vegetarian items are prominently featured on the menu. Local organic produce often is used in meal preparation.

The Mad Batter and Carroll Villa also emphasize recycling. The restaurant arranges for a farm to pick up food waste, and the staff buys recycled paper and other products for use in the hotel.

The breakfast menu may include orange and almond French toast, grilled and served with maple syrup. *Morgen Rostie* is a Swiss dish of panfried potatoes and fresh herbs enveloped in eggs and Gruyere cheese.

Sweet Rum Shrimp Cubano is a dinner specialty. Jumbo shrimp sauteed in garlic and fresh lime juice are served with a honey-rum sauce, saffron rice, and fried plantains.

Typical desserts at the Mad Batter include warm apple gallette, white chocolate mousse with raspberry sauce, and Italian-style warm bread pudding.

CONSERVATION

Built around 1882, the Italianate structure is capped with an ornate cupola. Over the years, though, the building had deteriorated until new proprietors came to the rescue in 1975. The owners scavenged through junk yards and basements for appropriate period fixtures and furnishings. Now, the restored hotel is a National Historic Landmark, and workers continue painting and patching in the off-season.

The hotel and restaurant take an active role in supporting The Nature Conservancy and other environmental groups through private fundraising functions at the hotel, as well as through donations and gift certificates. The Hotel is a business sponsor of the Cape May Bird Observatory.

ACTIVITIES

In this pedestrian-friendly setting, there are plenty of alternatives to driving. Visitors can take self-guided walking tours, and the inn staff can help to arrange tours of the historic district by carriage or trolley. Bicycles can be rented nearby, and whale-watch boats dock near the hotel.

Visitors can stroll along Cape May's picturesque streets or roam along the oceanfront. At nearby Sunset Beach, the surf curls onto the shore, then recedes, leaving the glint of "Cape May diamonds." These clear quartz pebbles were brought to southern New Jersey by runoff from Ice Age glaciers. An alert beachcomber might find ancient fossil fragments mixed with the quartz.

O*n an October weekday, most of the shops in Cape May are shuttered, and the tourist population is sparse. However, this is high season for raptors who are traveling south along the coast. An average of sixty thousand birds of prey are tallied at the official Hawk Watch each autumn, including red-shouldered hawks, ospreys, and peregrine falcons.*

Other migrating species include Swainson's thrushes, rose-breasted grosbeaks, black skimmers, and royal terns. Cape May's bird list includes more than four hundred species, and the area is known among birders as a "vagrant trap" where unexpected avians appear.

ALMANAC

In the region ...
CAPE MAY AREA

Cape May contrasts vividly with the typical tourist clutter of the Jersey shore. The narrow lanes lined with Victorian homes are vaguely reminiscent of Charleston, South Carolina, but with a distinct charm of their own. The large stretches of protected shore and marshland also commend the Cape May area to the discerning traveler.

The New Jersey Audubon Society's **Cape May Bird Observatory** conducts research on avian life, promotes conservation programs, and provides a wide variety of environmental education activities. Set among twenty-six acres of marsh and upland, The **Center for Research and Education** has displays, a lecture room, outdoor observation deck, natural demonstration landscaping, and a wildlife gallery. The **Northwood Center** is located at the north end of Lily Lake, a prime birding area. Bookstores at both locations specialize in natural history guides, high-quality optical equipment and other birding supplies. Each location is open 10 am to 5 pm daily.

- *Northwood Center, 701 East Lake Drive Cape May Point, NJ, tel. 609-884-2736*

- *Center for Research and Education, 600 Route 47 North, Cape May Court House, NJ, tel. 609-861-0466* **www.nj.com/audubon/abtnjas/cmbo.html**

PROVISIONS AND SHOPPING

Dozens of farm markets and stands in Cape May County are local sources of vegetables, berries, honey, herbs, and fresh-cut flowers. **Rifkin Farm**, 1.5 miles south of Woodbine on the Woodbine-Dennisville Road, carries pesticide-free asparagus, blueberries, and other produce.

RESOURCES

The nonprofit **Wetlands Institute** is located on 6,000 acres of coastal wetlands near Cape May. The Institute is dedicated to the conservation of intertidal salt marshes and other coastal ecosystems. The Diller Aquarium has hands-on exhibits featuring salt-water aquaria and life in the marsh. The Saltmarsh Trail provides an up-close look at the plants and animals that live in and around the marsh, and the spiral stairs of the Observation Tower lead to a panoramic view of the surrounding wetlands. The Tidepool Museum Shop sells books, gifts, and classroom items.

- *1075 Stone Harbor Boulevard, Stone Harbor, NJ 08247*
  tel. 609-368-1211, **www.wetlandsinstitute.org**

Since 1897, the **New Jersey Audubon Society** has been dedicated to fostering a conservation ethic, protecting the state's plants and wildlife, and promoting preservation of valuable natural habitats. The Society operates the Cape May Bird Observatory and the Nature Center of Cape May, as well as other centers and sanctuaries throughout the state.

- *790 Ewing Avenue, PO Box 125*
  Franklin Lakes, NJ 07417, tel. 201-891-1211
  www.njaudubon.org

FOR MORE INFORMATION

The New Jersey Audubon Society offers an impressive array of books on birding and the state's natural environment. Several titles are by noted author Peter Dunne of the Cape May Bird Observatory, including *The Feather Quest* ($25), his account of a year-long odyssey to discover the great birding locations of North America. Dunne also writes a weekly online essay, "Season's Passage." This is included along with a list of available publications on the Society's Web site.

- **www.njaudubon.org**

David Sibley's *The Birds of Cape May ($14.95)* is a focused and detailed guide to the Cape's bird populations. *Plant Communities of New Jersey* ($45 hardcover, $17 paperback), by Beryl Robichaud Collins and Karl H. Anderson, covers the state's varied natural habitat.

■ *Available from New Jersey Audubon Society bookstores, including the Cape May Bird Observatory.*
Call 609-861-0466 for ordering information.

BALTIMORE AREA

We recycle,

reuse and reduce ...

saving the planet

is an INN-side job.

— brochure, Celie's Waterfront
Bed & Breakfast

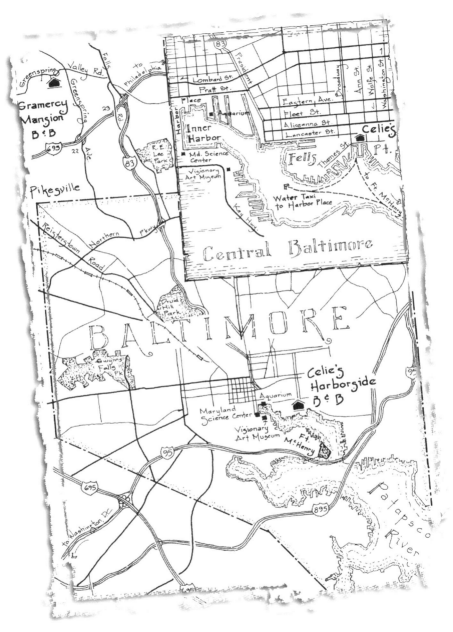

BALTIMORE

MARYLAND'S AROMATIC INN

Gramercy Mansion Bed & Breakfast, Stevenson, Maryland

An elegant mansion is a backdrop for
Gramercy's extensive organic gardens,
a place to explore tastes, sounds, and scents.
Orange squash blossoms vie for attention with
iridescent neon eggplant. Mixed greens are a
specialty here, a colorful blend of lettuces, arugula,
and edible flowers such as pansies, calendulas,
red bean flowers, and marigolds.

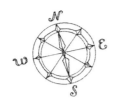

THE FACTS
Gramercy Bed & Breakfast

address	1440 Greenspring Valley Road Stevenson, MD 21153
phone	410-486-2405, 800-553-3404
e-mail	gramercy@erols.com
Web site	**www.gramercymansion.com**
lodging	Ten rooms, from economical singles to a luxury suite.
rates	About $65 to $275.
caveats	No disabled access for overnight guests. No public transportation.
credentials	Featured in regional and national publications. Certified organic farm.
special interest	Organic gardening, herb gardens, historic preservation.

THE INN

Gramercy Mansion's spacious grounds are an oasis on the edge of the Baltimore metropolitan area. The inn is set amid forty-five acres of woodland, fields, and gardens that are part of the Greenspring Valley Historical District.

The spacious Tudor-style house was commissioned by a railroad tycoon as a wedding present for his daughter. Since its origins, the property has gone through various incarnations, including stints as the home of a senator and a retreat for religious leaders.

An antique rocking horse greets visitors in the front entry. In the parlor, a huge gong from Hong Kong gets considerable use during parties. Complete with a grand piano, the living room provides an elegant setting for dances and classical music.

In addition to high-end suites and large rooms, the inn also offers five smaller but nicely furnished "back rooms," available for $65 single occupancy ($90 double occupancy), with shared bath. Elsewhere on the site, the Carriage House can be rented by groups.

THE FARM

Along with the inn operation, the owners grow herbs and specialty crops on the property. This continues a tradition of organic farming dating back several decades. The owners are members of the Maryland Organic Farmers Association. A nearby equestrian school supplies straw and manure for composting.

The commercial garden is a supplier to a number of supermarkets and restaurants in the region. Gramercy is the largest grower of organic basil in Maryland.

ACCESS

Gramercy Mansion is located on the northwest fringe of the Baltimore metropolitan area, about ten miles north of the Inner Harbor. No public transit is available; guests arrive by private vehicle or taxi. Check with the inn for exact directions.

The last part of the journey is the best. Chaperoned by stone walls, the access drive winds through woodland until the inn comes into view. In early summer, rhododendrons along the road provide a dramatic display.

DINING

The garden's products are put to good use in Gramercy's kitchen. Egg dishes are flavored with fresh organic herbs. Guests can custom-order their breakfasts from favorites such as fresh-baked muffins or raspberry pancakes, with a choice of omnivorous or vegetarian breakfasts. Unlike many inns, Gramercy accommodates late sleepers, with breakfast anytime from 7:30 until 10:30 a.m.

ACTIVITIES

In warm months, guests can swim in the large swimming pool or serve on the tennis court. Hiking trails wind through the wooded site. Children like to explore the small stream and investigate the Elf House, a large stump carved into a fanciful habitation.

The weekend at Gramercy has come to a close, and family members reluctantly pack their bags. Before leaving, they pay a final visit to the gardens. As crickets chirp in the background, they snip some sprigs of basil to take home as a reminder of their stay.

CONSERVING BY THE HARBOR

Celie's Waterfront Bed & Breakfast, Baltimore, Maryland

THAMES STREET, FELL'S POINT

With its brick row houses and cobblestone streets, Fell's Point is one of America's less-known but most notable historic districts. Celie's Waterfront Bed & Breakfast demonstrates earth-friendly innkeeping in this picturesque harborside setting.

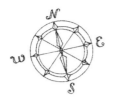

THE FACTS
Celie's Waterfront Bed & Breakfast

address	1714 Thames St., Baltimore, MD 21231
phone	410-522-2323, 800-432-0184 fax 410-522-2324
e-mail	celies@aol.com
Web site	**www.bbonline.com/md/celies** This B&B association Web site includes a brief summary of the inn.
lodging	Seven guest rooms. The Courtyard Room is disabled-accessible.
rates	$120 to $220 per night. Special rates for midweek business travelers.
caveats	No pets or small children. Limited night hours for check-in desk.
credentials	Selected by *Travel and Leisure* magazine as one of the top fifty affordable inns in the U.S.A. Member, Professional Innkeepers International. AAA 3-Diamond rating.
special interest	Harbor setting, historic district, pedestrian-friendly neighborhood.

THE INN

This three-story inn efficiently includes seven guest rooms, a dining room, sitting room, and two courtyards within its townhouse boundaries. Guests register in the sitting room, where a portrait of innkeeper Celie Ives' great-great grandmother presides above the fireplace.

Fresh-cut flowers accent the antique-filled guest rooms. Appointments include down comforters, flannel sheets, and thick terry robes. For business travelers, rooms have private telephones with modem capability, as well as ample desk space. Fax machines also are available at the inn.

Located on the street frontage, *Harbor Front Rooms 1 and 2* have picturesque harbor views. Each room has a wood-burning fireplace for use in season. To mask occasional street noise on weekends, clock radios are equipped with sounds of ocean waves.

Furnished with queen beds, *Atrium Rooms 3 and 4* overlook the center courtyard. These are quiet spaces on the second and third floors, with window boxes filled with flowers in summer.

Garden Rooms 5 and 6 each have an atrium door opening onto a private balcony overlooking the garden. The sunny bathrooms feature whirlpool tubs, and Room 6 has a skylight as well.

The cozy, ground-floor *Courtyard Room* is disabled- accessible. Furnishings include two twin beds. Although smaller than the others, this room has its own private courtyard, complete with table and chairs.

ACCESS

Located on Amtrak's Northeast Corridor, Baltimore has excellent train service. For visitors arriving at Baltimore's BWI Airport and headed for downtown, the Metro Rail link costs about one-tenth as much as a taxi — and no tip is needed.

Fell's Point is located just east of the Inner Harbor and central Baltimore. Water taxis stop at the landing across the street, offering a short and enjoyable ride across the harbor to the convention center and other destinations. The shops of Harborplace and other downtown attractions are within walking distance.

With these transit options, visitors don't need a car while staying at Celie's. Metro Rail and other public transit service information is available from the MTA, 410-539-5000.

DINING

Breakfast at the inn features delicacies such as poached pears, homemade granola, and fresh-baked cinnamon raisin bread, served with gourmet coffees and teas. For calorie-conscious guests, Celie's serves juice-sweetened preserves and lowfat options. In winter, a crackling fire adds to the cozy dining room ambience.

CONSERVATION

The inn actively participates in the local utility's conservation program, including the use of energy-efficient light bulbs. Where possible, natural daylighting reduces daytime need for artificial lighting, especially in the front rooms.

The owner actively promotes recycling, and the inn emphasizes environmentally friendly products and maintenance methods. Natural fabrics are used, signs encouraging conservation are placed in guest rooms, and pump containers dispense soap.

ACTIVITIES

Reminiscent of Mary Poppins, the view from Celie's roofdeck is more English than American, with timeworn brick buildings topped with chimney pots. This is Baltimore's oldest maritime neighborhood, the site of Colonial-era shipyards that produced the city's renowned clipper ships. Dating back to 1730, this harbor district once was home to Frederick Douglass and other notables.

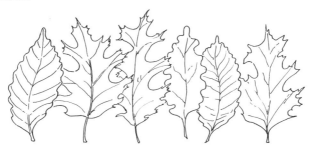

Visitors have ample opportunities to explore the cobblestone streets of Fell's Point. Eighteenth and nineteenth century houses built in the Federal and Greek Revival styles are intermingled with early Victorians. Walking tours are available. Shops, bars, and restaurants line the streets.

A brisk December breeze ruffles the holiday decorations along the streets of Fell's Point. Brilliant red-orange leaves drift down from the trees along Thames Street.

Inside Celie's, a cheerful fire greets guests gathering for breakfast in Celie's dining room. Concurrently, purple finches assemble for their morning meal at the feeder outside the dining room window. "Sparrows dipped in raspberry juice," Celie calls them.

ALMANAC

In the region ...
BALTIMORE AREA

Baltimore's highly-successful **Harborplace** has been a trendsetter in mixed-use center city developments, bringing new vitality to the downtown district and opening up recreational access to the harbor. Harborplace now is home to a cluster of science and maritime history museums and exhibits.

The **National Aquarium** is best-known for its huge central tank where sharks can be viewed at close quarters. The Aquarium also has an impressive array of exhibits from an Icelandic coast to a coral reef. In spite of its name, the Aquarium includes terrestrial habitats such as the rainforest where languid sloths ease their way through tropical foliage. Plan to obtain tickets early on busy weekends.

- *Pier 3, 501 East Pratt Street, Baltimore, MD 21202*
  tel. 410-576-3800, **www.aqua.org**

Across the harbor, the kid-friendly **Maryland Science Center** houses the Davis Planetarium, plus an IMAX theater and three floors of live science demonstrations. The Science Store carries an array of handcrafted items, books on nature and the environment, electronic jewelry, and science kits.

- *601 Light Street at Key Highway, Baltimore, MD*
  tel. 410-685-2370, **www.mdsci.org**

GREEN DINING

Ensconced within Baltimore's eccentric Museum of Visionary Art, **Joy America Café** features splendid harbor views and innovative interior design.

The museum and café are in a recycled warehouse. A burnished brass wall adds visual drama to the interior, and an outdoor deck overlooks the Baltimore harbor. While waiting at the bar, patrons can create their own chalk art on the slate counter.

- *800 Key Highway, Baltimore, MD 21230*
  tel. 410-244-6500, **www.avam.org**

Seafood and seaweed are featured at **Margaret's Restaurant** in Fell's Point. Crab cakes and local fresh fish are popular menu items. Vegetarian dishes include such fare as dulse or arame seaweed marinated in ginger-soy sauce with cabbage and carrots. Entrees generally are in the $9 to $18 range. Open Tuesday for dinner only; Wednesday through Sunday from mid-morning to late evening. Lots of art and artists hang out here; the associated Halcyon Gallery is upstairs.

- *909 Fell Street, Baltimore, MD 21231, tel. 410-276-5605*

One World Café successfully blends a friendly neighborhood feeling with global environmental concerns. Just south of the Inner Harbor, and part of the urban mix of rowhouses and antique shops on Federal Hill, the café has been voted Baltimore's best coffee house. This is a setting to slow down and sip organic coffee as your meal is prepared from scratch, a place for friends to play pool or admire the art on the walls of this renovated brick building. The mostly-vegetarian menu includes salads, sandwiches, smoked salmon, organic juices, vegan options, and the ever-popular black bean burrito ($5.25). For breakfast, the multi-grain pancakes served with blueberries or maple syrup are a standout. The One World Café Web site includes a current menu and hours, as well as an online opportunity to order organic coffee and tea blends.

- *904 South Charles Street, Baltimore, MD 21230*
  tel. 410-234-0235, **www.oneworldcafe.com**

The Sacred Submarine begins with half a baguette toasted with provelone and red onions, then is stuffed with baked tofu, organic baby field greens, tomato, mushrooms, basil, pickles, cherry hots and seasoning — all for $6.50 at **Liquid Earth.** This vegetarian restaurant, coffee and juice bar in Fell's Point assembles massive sandwiches, organic salads, fruit bowls and other healthy cuisine. Rock music reverberates in the brick-walled, art-filled interior. Open 7 am weekdays (9 am weekends) until late evening (except for 3 pm closing on Wednesdays and Sundays).

- *1626 Aliceanna Street, Fell's Point, MD 21231*
  tel. 410-276-6606

A few blocks from Celie's, the **Broadway Market** features a wide assortment of local produce and take-out food such as fresh-baked dimpfmeier rye bread and vegetarian black beans. The market shuts down at 6pm.

- *631-637 South Broadway, Baltimore, MD 21231*

Fresh breads and desserts are featured at **Puffins Cafe**, located in the northwest suburbs of Baltimore. This natural foods restaurant has a vegetarian bent, with dishes such as Japanese noodles with vegetables and tamari. Seafood entrees also are included on the menu; try the grouper in rolled oats and sesame seeds. A papier-maché zebra accents the black-and-white decor.

- *1000 Reistertown Road, Pikesville, MD 21208*
  tel. 410-486-8811

PROVISIONS

With a suburban location northwest of Baltimore, **Sunsplash** is a full-service natural foods store about two miles south of I-695. For travelers on I-695, take the #20 exit and follow Highway 140 two miles south to the Colonial Village Shopping Center.

- *7006 Reistertown Road, Pikesville, MD 21215*
  tel. 410-486-0979

RESOURCES

Maryland-based **Save Our Streams** is a nonprofit group that educates the state's citizens about the importance of cleaning and protecting the region's waterways. SOS focuses on education and common-sense projects as an effective way to involve people. *Revitalizing Baltimore*, a joint venture with government agencies, mobilizes people by planting trees, transforming vacant lots into community gardens, and conducting environmental education and job training programs.

- *8074 New Cut Road, Severn, MD 21144*
  tel. 410-969-0084 **www.saveourstreams.org**

FOR MORE INFORMATION

Chesapeake Almanac: Following the Bay Throughout the Seasons is an evocative guide to the changing natural rhythms of the bay. Author John Page Williams, Jr. describes the annual movements of ospreys, swans, and sea turtles. The book provides useful information for fishing, hiking, canoeing, and wildlife viewing. Sketch maps show where to find an elusive marsh flower or a favored spot for monarch butterflies.

- *Centreville, MD: Tidewater Publishers, tel. 800-638-7641*

20

UPPER
CHESAPEAKE BAY

SPRING GARDEN

The sun's languid pulsing,
Through the mist,
Turns drops of moisture
Warm and clear.
Where gently playing showers
Lave garden paths,
And growing vistas;
All belted round with blooming dogwoods;
And the pale new leaves
of the ghostly whiteoak
Hang their halo in a haze;
As earth and wet are surely merged,
In sensuous beginning innocence.

—William R. Stubbs,
from *Sounds of the Land*

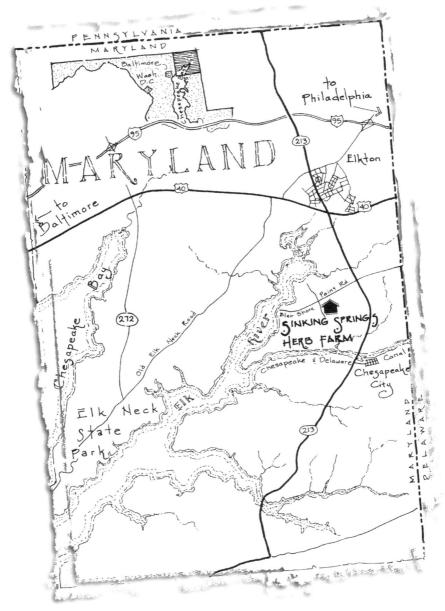

NORTHEAST
MARYLAND

HERBS BY THE BAY
Sinking Springs Herb Farm, Elkton, Maryland

THE GARDEN COTTAGE AT
SINKING SPRINGS HERB FARM

Long before ships landed at Jamestown and Plymouth Rock, when Elizabeth I was ruler of England, a sycamore seed sprouted near the shores of the Chesapeake Bay. Now, more than four centuries later, the Bristoll Sycamore shades the home of Ann and Bill Stubbs, owners of the Sinking Springs Herb Farm.

An official Maryland Champion Tree, the Bristoll Sycamore stands tall above the expansive gardens of lady's mantle, hyssop, feverfew and sweet woodruff.

Ensconced among these herbs is the cozy Garden Cottage, where guests can spend the night surrounded by soft fragrances.

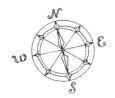

THE FACTS
Sinking Springs Herb Farm

address	234 Blair Shore Road Elkton, MD 21921 (entrance at 843 Elk Forest Road)
phone	410-398-5566 fax 410-392-2389
Web site	**www.cecilcounty.com** (Select Bed & Breakfast link)
lodging	One cottage with double bed and private bath
rates	About $93 per night (third person $25 extra)
caveats	Gardens closed on Sundays.
special interest	Herb gardening, historic buildings.

---

*Chesapeake Bay is a blend of
water from inland rivers and
Atlantic salt water.
As ocean currents sweep into the
bay, the earth's rotation curves the
salt water away from the west
shore. As a result, the east side of
Chesapeake Bay is saltier than the
western part of the bay.*

THE GARDEN COTTAGE

From the parking area by the barn, a path winds through the redolent landscape, past the Saffron Garden, the fish pond, the Ground Cherry Garden and an ancient apple tree to the cottage entry.

Although not an original structure at the farm, the cottage has the feeling of an historic building. The walls are recycled white pine boards rescued from an old house just before it was demolished.

The Garden Cottage includes a sitting room with fireplace, as well as the bedroom with double bed and private bath. Bordered with herbal aromas from the surrounding gardens, the Garden Cottage is a popular honeymoon hideaway.

HERBALICIOUS DINING

The Garden Cottage stay comes with a wholesome continental or country breakfast made with fresh local ingredients. But the real culinary highlights here are the periodic luncheons hosted by Ann and Bill. Described by the owners as "an herbalicious gourmet delight," these meals are prepared with fresh unprocessed produce and served in the the Stubbs' eighteenth-century home.

A sample luncheon menu includes poultry, seafood, and vegetarian menu options, along with additional herb-flavored dishes. Garden salads are made with the farm's freshly harvested vegetables and herbs, while dessert might be a homemade lemon-verbena cake accented with raspberry sauce. After the meal, Bill and Ann recount the farm's history as they lead a tour of the gardens.

Visitors in search of peppermint can choose among three varieties at Sinking Springs Herb Farm. Some of the owners' favorite herbs are winter savory, French tarragon, basil, oregano, pineapple sage, and white mint. No herbicides are used in the gardens, and composting returns nutrients to the soil.

VIOLET OR NASTURTIUM SALAD

(from Ann Stubbs' kitchen)

4-6 cups crumbled lettuce and other mixed greens

¼ cup garlic chives, minced

¼ cup fresh fennel greens, minced

3 tablespoons salad oil (sunflower, olive, or canola)

2 tablespoons tarragon vinegar

1 can (6½ oz.) tuna*
(Rinse several times to remove excess salt)

1 or 2 hard boiled eggs

½ cup violet or nasturtium flowers and/or borage

1 tablespoon mayonnaise (tofu mayo)

Hint of feta cheese, crumbled

Line salad bowl with violet or nasturtium leaves. Layer rest of ingredients in given order. Toss immediately before serving. Cover bowl with flowers!

*Could leave out tuna and have tomatoes and green pepper if you wish.

THE FARM

Bill Stubbs has deep family roots in this part of Maryland, with descendants dating back to the early 1700s. The Stubbs' home was built around 1712 as a two-room log cabin. Originally the rooms were separated by an open-air dog trot, but later were joined.

"Mux'n" is an Old English term meaning "to make a mess of." In the farm's rustic dairy barn, Ann Stubbs has a Mux'n Room where she arranges dried flowers. The barn also houses the numerous herbal incarnations and interpretations of the Sinking Springs gift shop: potted herbs, dried herbs, books on salt-free herb cookery, herbal soup mixes.

Herb oils are a special feature. Ann suggests anointing *cold* [not hot] light bulbs with a few drops of an essential or fragrant oil such as lavender, myrrh or wintergreen. When the light is switched on, the heat from the bulb diffuses the scent throughout the room.

ACTIVITIES

Sinking Springs is the setting for wreath and swag workshops throughout the year. Other offerings include autumn walks, a "Natural Santa" program as the winter holidays approach, and the Eighteenth Century Country Christmas in December.

The farm's mosaic of forest and field along the Chesapeake Bay offers abundant opportunities to explore locust groves, ponds, woodland paths, and an old graveyard. From late April to the end of October, flowers at the farm provide a continuous display. Late May is a favored time to visit the pond, where thousands of yellow lilies carpet the water for several weeks.

ACCESS

Located in the extreme northeast corner of Maryland, Sinking Springs is about ten miles south of Interstate 95. Take Route 213 about four miles south of Elkton, then turn west on Elk Forest Road and proceed past McKeown Road to the farm's main entrance.

Except for occasional charter bus groups, visitors arrive by auto in this rural setting, remote from public transit lines.

By mid-March, the gardens at the farm already are suggesting the herbs and flowers of high summer. Sinking Springs owner Bill Stubbs captures this time of year in his poem, "St. Patrick's Day."

As evenings grow longer,

The spreading midday warmth

Thaws peepers

From their frozen sleep;

And pussy willows glow;

Their soft chains of silver

Now pale jewels

Of yellow, green and pink

Mirroring lanes of gray houses

Bursting into banishing bloom;

As if this St. Patrick's Day

They would ban the snakes of time.

But the passing waters know

The saint never came that way.

— William R. Stubbs
from Sounds of
the Land

In the region ...
UPPER
CHESAPEAKE BAY

The Garden Cottage at Sinking Springs is a good base for exploring the upper reaches of the Chesapeake Bay and the Eastern Shore. Just a few miles to the south, several wildlife preserves are located along the Chesapeake and Delaware Canal.

Chesapeake City is a historic settlement along the canal connecting Delaware and Chesapeake Bays. Nearly wiped out at one time by ill-advised channel widening, the town core has survived as a unique example of a nineteenth-century canal town, with tiny storybook houses and shops.

GREEN DINING

Located near the University of Delaware campus in downtown Newark, **Sinclair's** has been selected as "Best Vegetarian Restaurant in Delaware" by a regional magazine. This place focuses on vegetarian dishes reasonably priced in the $3 to $5 range. The menu includes eggs, pancakes, sandwiches, veggie burgers, and salads, with occasional Thai, Indian, and Vietnamese specials. Sinclair's also produces and sells a line of "Moonlady Kitchen" pancake mixes, jellies, syrups, and salad dressings. Open for breakfast and lunch only. Inexpensive.

- *177 E. Main St, Newark, DE 19711, tel. 302-368-7755*

PROVISIONS AND SHOPPING

Near the University of Delaware campus, the **Newark Natural Foods** cooperative specializes in organic produce, locally baked fresh breads and hormone-free dairy products, as well as wheat-free, low-sodium, fat-free and macrobiotic items. The deli offers vegan and vegetarian soups, sandwiches and salads, mainly for takeout, but there are a few tables for on-site dining. Open Monday through Saturday, 9 a.m. to 8 p.m.

- *280 E. Main St, Newark, DE 19711, tel. 302-368-5894*

Chesapeake City Gift and Gourmet is crammed with handcrafted pottery, books, music, gourmet foods, and herbal soaps.

- *208 George Street, Chesapeake City, MD, tel. 410-885-2025*

OTHER PLACES TO STAY

Along the Chesapeake Bay, **Elk Neck State Park** is a diverse blend of beaches, marshland, and wooded bluffs. Extensive trails wind through forests of poplar, beech, and oak. During the summer months, a staff naturalist leads walks and programs.

The park's nine rental cabins are showing signs of deferred maintenance, but the scenic shoreline setting is a plus.

Each unit is equipped with a stove, refrigerator, table and benches, and four single cots with mattresses. The central washroom is a short walk away. Cabins are available for rental from early May to late October. In a separate location, the waterfront **Bowers Conference Center** accommodates up to thirty people for group events.

- *Elk Neck State Park, 4395 Turkey Point Road*
  North East, MD 21901, tel. 410-287-3172

FOR MORE INFORMATION

Sinking Springs innkeeper William Stubbs has written "Sounds of the Land," a collection of his original poetry and stories about the Eastern Shore. Many of the poems such as "Beech Leaves" and "River Morning" evoke the region's natural environment, while other poetry and essays highlight the area's history.

- *Available for $8 postpaid from Sinking Springs Herb Farm,*
  234 Blair Shore Road, Elkton MD 21921

21

SOUTHERN
DELAWARE

THE POINT

Beyond beige dunes;

Clutched by yellow-green grass,

There is a blue-slate horizon-haze

When August days are stormy.

Where the way is marked,

When the sea light blooms,

With bright pulsing pauses

Between sea and distant town.

— William Stubbs, *Sounds of the Land*

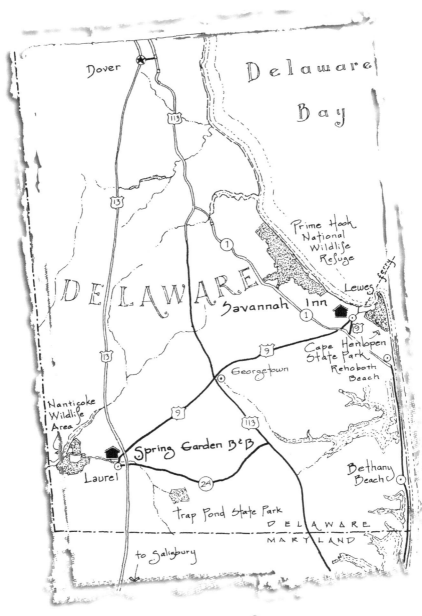

Dover

Delaware

Bay

113

13

1

Prime Hook
National
Wildlife
Refuge

DELAWARE

Savannah Inn

Lewes ferry

1

9

9

Cape Henlopen
State Park

13

Georgetown

Rehoboth
Beach

Nanticoke
Wildlife
Area

9

113

Spring Garden B&B

Laurel

24

Bethany
Beach

Trap Pond State Park

DELAWARE

MARYLAND

to Salisbury

SOUTHERN
DELAWARE

PROTECTING DELAWARE BAY
Savannah Inn, Lewes, Delaware

A distant relative of the spider, the horseshoe crab
(*Limulus polyphemus*) is a scientific oddity.
These marine invertebrates move about on five pairs of
walking legs, using modified pincerlike appendages
called chelicera to seize their prey. Literally
blue-blooded, these curious creatures have foraged
through the planet's mud for several hundred million
years, seeking worms and clams.

Along the window ledge of the Savannah Inn's
glassed-in porch is a Darwinian display of horseshoe
crab exoskeletons, arranged in ascending size.
These helmet-shaped shells are symbols of the
innkeepers' commitment to help protect the nearby
marshes and mudflats of the Delaware estuary.

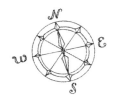

THE FACTS
Savannah Inn

address	330 Savannah Road, Lewes, (pronounced Louis) DE 19958
phone	302-645-5592
e-mail	mavs@panix.com
Web site	**www.panix.com/~mavs/** The inn's site has links to environmental, transit, and general tourist information for Delaware.
lodging	Seven rooms with shared baths.
rates	Rooms in the $70 to $80 range.
caveats	Shared bathrooms, natural ventilation and fans rather than air-conditioning, no phones in room, no pets, no breakfast provided during off-season.
special interest	Vegetarian dining, naturalist programs.

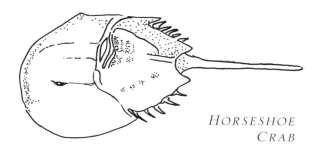

HORSESHOE CRAB

THE INN

Owners Richard and Susan Stafursky compare their inn to an ordinary European *zimmer*, comfortable but not pretentious. Built in 1910, the Edwardian building originally was a single-family home. Richard and Susan purchased the house, located in the historic district of Lewes, and created the town's first bed-and-breakfast inn.

Period furnishings and potted plants are in keeping with the original decor. An etched-glass window provides natural lighting for the registration desk.

Fans rotate overhead in the guest rooms. Bathrooms are down the hall, supplemented by in-room sinks. This child-friendly inn welcomes families. The larger rooms can sleep three or four persons. The angular-ceilinged north bedroom on the third floor features a neoclassic triple window.

The inn is framed by a huge American holly and a big beech with elephant-hide bark. Richard has designed a nail-free treehouse for the magnolia in the back yard. Perched in the tree, the house is built with clamps so he can remove it without arboreal damage.

ACCESS

The best way to reach the inn is by ferry, crossing Delaware Bay as gulls wheel overhead. Inn-bound guests coming from the north can save money on car ferry fees by leaving their vehicle in Cape May, New Jersey. The innkeepers will pick up guests at the Lewes ferry terminal.

Other guests arrive on their own boats. Mooring is available on the Lewes-Rehoboth Canal a few blocks from the inn. After docking, boaters pay a fee at City Hall.

Other options for inn visitors include arrival by bus (the innkeepers will meet guests at the Trailways terminal). Bus connections are available to the Amtrak station in

Wilmington, Delaware. Also, airborne visitors can take air-commuter service to nearby Georgetown.

For motorists, Lewes is just east of Delaware Route 1, about 5 miles north of Rehoboth. From Route 1, take Route 9 to Lewes. Once in town, Route 9 becomes Savannah Road. The inn is at the intersection with Orr Street, near the center of town.

Once at the inn, guests don't need a car if they are willing to do a little walking. The picturesque canal and downtown shopping district are just a few blocks away, the bay is less than a mile's walk, and ocean beaches are within three miles.

DINING

The inn serves generous continental vegetarian breakfasts, often featuring Susan's fresh-baked zucchini bread or bran muffins with raisins. A big bowl is filled with seasonal fruit. Granola, juices, and coffee or tea also are on hand. Food allergies usually can be accommodated with advance notice. Food scraps are sent to the compost pile.

ENVIRONMENTAL INFORMATION

As a biologist and president of the World Species List, Richard has undertaken the daunting task of compiling a comprehensive index of the earth's species data bases. Science-minded surfers from amateur lepidopterists to professional bacteriologists can access his Web site, **www.envirolink.org/species/**.

ACTIVITIES

Lewes was settled in 1631, about the time the Dutch were buying Manhattan. The Lewes Historical Society sponsors walking tours, or travelers can explore the historic downtown district on their own.

Guests at the inn can play board games or the vintage Chickering piano in the first-floor sitting room. A separate sitting room on the third floor provides a quiet spot for reading. The barn behind the inn includes a rustic observatory loft for art, music, or skywatching.

From time to time, Richard will take guests on Chesapeake Bay boating excursions. He serves as navigator and naturalist on these safaris to uninhabited Janes Island or Tangier Island, describing a trip to these isles as a "poor man's Caribbean vacation."

For individual exploration, Richard can refer guests to nearby uncrowded beaches for swimming, birding, and exploring. The inn's bulletin board is festooned with flyers about other local activities, such as whale-dolphin watches and sunset cruises.

Each spring, about the time of May's first full moon, hordes of horseshoe crabs begin to deposit as many as 80,000 eggs each in the sands and mudflats along Delaware Bay. This is fortunate timing indeed for a million or more exhausted migratory birds in search of sustenance. Arriving from points as distant as Tierra del Fuego, species such as willets, ruddy turnstones, semi-palmated sandpipers, and sanderlings descend on the bay to feast on horseshoe crab eggs and other estuarine delicacies.

By June, most of the migrants have resumed their journey, in some cases doubling their body weight before continuing north to the Canadian Arctic. The Lewes area provides prime vantage points where birders can witness this natural spectacle, one of the largest convergences of migrating birds in North America.

ALMANAC

Biking Inn to Inn
Spring Garden B&B, Laurel, Delaware

Level terrain, light traffic, and a pastoral landscape combine to make the back roads of Southern Delaware a prime place for bicycle touring. Adding to these incentives, innkeeper Gwen North has organized the award-winning Biking Inn to Inn program for earth-friendly travelers.

Cylists start at Gwen's Spring Garden Bed and Breakfast, traveling past a patchwork of fields and woodland on a loop to the coast and back to Laurel. Bikers can expect to cover 25 to 35 miles per day at their own pace, allowing time to check out the birds along the way. All tours include reservations at bed and breakfast inns, luggage transport, tour maps, cue sheets, and secure bicycle storage, plus breakfast and dinner daily.

THE FACTS
Spring Garden B&B

address   RD 5, Box 283A, Delaware Avenue Extended, Laurel DE 19956

phone   302-875-7015, 800-646-4402 or 800-797-4909 (Biking Inn to Inn)

lodging   Five rooms, including one suite.

rates $75 to $95 per night.

caveats   Not accessible by public transit. No disabled access. Children must be over ten years of age. Credit cards accepted for Biking Inn to Inn tours only. Smoking permitted in designated areas.

credentials   Delaware State Tourism Award for Excellence in Hospitality.

special interest Bicycling, historic preservation, canoeing, hiking, gardening, antiquing.

BARN AT SPRING GARDEN B&B

THE INN

This eighteenth-century home, now listed on the National Register of Historic Places, once was the home of a sea captain with a large family. By the 1950s, though, the once-elegant house had fallen into disrepair.

Gwen North, the current owner, can remember when her parents purchased the abandoned structure. Trees were growing through gaping holes in the living room floor when her family began the herculean task of refinishing, patching, and painting.

Today, guests can appreciate the restoration. The original section of the brick home was built circa 1780, with additions made in the Victorian era. The interior is filled with period detailing such as dentil mouldings, fluted mantels, and wide plank flooring.

The *Lewis Room*, named for the ancestral family of Spring Garden, has original details including beaded heart pine paneling, fireplace, canopy bed, and private bath with whirlpool tub. The *Song Bird Suite* has garden views, a private bath, and sitting room. The three other guest rooms also have antique appointments such as high-backed carved beds, pier mirrors and fainting couches.

ACCESS

The preferred means of access here is via bicycle. However, the innkeeper also will pick up guests at Salisbury Airport. There's no public transit to this rural inn.

By private vehicle, guests can travel to Laurel via Delaware Route 13. Follow the Laurel Historic District signs. Southbound, turn right at the second traffic light and go four-tenths of a mile. Northbound, go past the the traffic light at Junction 24, then turn left at the next light on Delaware Avenue Extended (County Road 466). Follow this lane about two-tenths of a mile to the inn on the right.

DINING

The inn's garden supplies organic herbs for the kitchen. A typical breakfast will include fresh fruit, whole-grain cereal, and a gourmet specialty such as Eggs Tarragon or Belgian waffles topped with fresh strawberries. A specialty is "Gwen's Concoction," an elaborate assemblage of bagels, fresh basil, Canadian bacon, tomatoes, and five different cheeses, devised one morning when the innkeeper ran out of eggs. Guests have the option of having a vegetarian breakfast (the innkeeper is vegetarian).

The dining room has a wealth of historic detail. Guests are served breakfast at a country hepplewhite table, flanked by original built-in cabinets, a pie safe, and a jelly cupboard. A woodburning stove provides warmth in the winter. In summer, guests have the option of breakfasting in the gardens.

ACTIVITIES

On a formal tour or not, bicyclists are welcomed at the inn. Spring Garden supplies secure storage, as well as color-coded maps identifying safe and scenic roads in the area.

Visitors can browse through the on-site antique shop, housed in the Civil War-era barn near the house. The shop's diverse inventory includes country primitives, folk art, and architectural elements such as old windows (good for mirror frames), iron fencing, corbels, and fireplace mantels.

Guests also can explore maple-shaded paths on the three-acre site in search of the Secret Garden. It's just a short walk into town to see Laurel's historic district, the largest in Delaware. Hundreds of homes display Colonial Revival and Victorian details such as jig-sawn balustrades, bargeboards, and fleur-de-lis bracket trim.

Birders are frequent guests, using the inn as a base for trips to nearby Nanticoke Wildlife Area or further south to the clusters of national wildlife refuges on Chesapeake Bay and the Atlantic Ocean. The inn has birding guides, tree books, and natural history information about the region.

Guests can put in canoes near the inn, paddling the quiet waters of Broad Creek to the quaint village of Bethel. Once bustling with shipbuilders at work, Bethel now has mellowed into a quiet haven of architectural treasures.

The waning sun illuminates the expanse of gourds, pumpkins, and Indian corn at Mr. Pepper's Pumpkin Patch, down the road from the inn. The owner has carved a maze through a sorghum field, where several visitors test their orientation skills as they twist and turn through the auburn-hued stalks.

The sun sinks to the horizon, and the group begins the return hike to the inn. The forest along James Branch dissolves into the October haze, providing a backdrop for deer grazing quietly in a meadow. Then, in the gathering dusk, the inn's familiar silhouette appears, and a lamp by the entry welcomes guests back to Spring Garden Bed & Breakfast.

In the region ...
SOUTHERN DELAWARE

Resilient Delaware Bay has survived industrial pollution, oil spills, and encroaching urban development. While additional progress is needed, water quality has improved, and considerable marshland along the bay's fringe now is protected within wildlife refuges.

Cape Henlopen State Park near Lewes includes more than three thousand acres of salt marsh, pine woodland, and other habitat. Along the shore, the dunes rise eighty feet above the Atlantic; further inland, the park's "walking dunes" continue to shift southward into stands of pine. The park's **Seaside Nature Center** offers environmental education programs.

■ *42 Cape Henlopen Drive, Lewes, DE 19958*
tel. 302-645-8983
www.dnrec.state.de.us/parks/

A few miles north of Lewes, the 8,000-acre **Prime Hook National Wildlife Refuge** is home to the rare Delmarva fox squirrel. Canoeists on Prime Hook Creek pass thickets of sweetbay magnolia, blueberry, and bayberry, as well as the rare seaside alder with its miniature pine-cone-like seeds. Hunting is occasionally permitted; check on details to avoid dodging stray bullets.

■ *Box 195, Milton, DE 19968, tel. 302-684-8419*

Home to the northernmost stand of bald cypress trees in North America, **Trap Pond State Park** offers a variety of naturalist programs. A canoe trail traverses the tea-colored water of James Branch, past trees that were old in Shakespeare's time.

■ *Box 331, Laurel, DE 19956, tel. 302-875-5153*

GREEN DINING

Serving the beach crowd, **Planet X** features organic cuisine in a self-described "artistically punky setting." The menu focuses on vegetarian and seafood dishes. Full bar and wine list; open seasonally Th-Su until 9 pm.

- *35 William F Street, Rehoboth Beach, DE 19971 tel. 302-226-1928*

PROVISIONS AND SHOPPING

Fruit stands and farmers' markets are common in this area of truck farms. In downtown Lewes, **Gertie's Green Grocer** carries organic fruits and vegetables, nuts, and bulk spices. In addition, the store has a good selection of vitamins and books on health and nutrition.

- *119 Second Street, Lewes, DE 19958, tel. 302-645-8052*

Located one mile inland from Bethany Beach, **Wild About Birds** carries items related to owls, butterflies, hummingbirds, ladybugs, bats, and assorted other flying critters. The shop also sponsors nature tours.

- *19 Atlantic Avenue (Route 26), Ocean View, DE tel. 302-537-7180*

RESOURCES

The Partnership for the Delaware Estuary, Inc. is a private nonprofit organization that coordinates environmental efforts and promotes the estuary as a regional resource. The Partnership publishes "Estuary News" to provide information about environmental issues.

- *P.O. Box 9569, Wilmington, DE 19809, tel. 800-445-4935 or 302-793-1701, e-mail:* partners@udel.edu

FOR MORE INFORMATION

Delaware Eco-Discoveries is a guide to low-impact recreation and natural attractions in the state, including parks and refuges, camping information, eco-events, tour guide operators, and nature-oriented organizations in the state.

- *Free: 16 pages. Order from Southern Delaware Convention and Tourism Commission, 800-357-1818, or e-mail* southdel@dmv.com.

As I ebbed with the ocean of life,
As I wended the shores I know,
As I walked where the sea-ripples wash you, Paumanok,
Where they rustle up, hoarse and sibilant,
Where the fierce old mother endlessly cries for her castaways,
I, musing, late in the autumn day, gazing off southward,
Alone, held by the eternal self of me that threatens
          to get the better of me, and stifle me,
Was seized by the spirit that trails in the lines underfoot,
In the rim, the sediment, that stands for all the water
          and all the land of the globe.

Fascinated, my eyes, reverting from the south, dropped,
          to follow those slender windrows,
Chaff, straw, splinters of wood, weeds, and the sea-gluten,
Scum, scales from shining rocks, leaves of salt-lettuce,
          left by the tide,
Miles walking, the sound of breaking waves
          the other side of me ...

— Walt Whitman, from *Elemental Drifts*

GENERAL INDEX

Acadia National Park, 23, 30
Adaptive re-use, explanation of, 11
Adirondacks,177-198
    map of, 178
Adirondack Museum, 196
Adirondack Wildguide: A Natural History of the Adirondack Park, 198
Adirondak Loj, Lake Placid, NY, 179-184
    environmental programs and workshops, 181
    illustration, 179
    museum and aquarium, 183
    organized hikes from, 183
Adirondack Mountain Club, 181, 182, 197
    Forest Preserve Series by, 198
Adopt-a-Farm Animal Program, 204
Agriculture, sustainable. *See also* Rodale Institute
    in Maine, 37-38.
    in Massachusetts, 120-121, 140
    in Vermont, 71, 74, 75. 93, 102
Agri-tourism, description of, 4
AMC,
    see Appalachian Mountain Club
AMC Mohican Outdoor Center, 4, 286
AMC Outdoors, 67, 68
Amtrak, 70, 73, 132, 216, 231, 269, 299, 314, 335
Anderson, Karl H., author, 304
Animals. *See also* Horses
    at Lightfarm, PA, 260
    Farm Sanctuary, in New York, 3, 201-206

    at Woodvale Farm, Rhode Island, 160-161
Animal rights, 201-206, 210
Antiques
    at Blueberry Mountain Inn, PA, 243, 244
    at Butterbrooke B & B, CT, 171
    at Carroll Villa Hotel, NJ, 299
    at Celie's Waterfront B & B, Baltimore, 313
    at The Keeper's House, ME, 20
    at Lightfarm, PA, 259
    at Blue Heron Farm, MA, 119
    at Mohonk Mountain House, NY, 215
    at Old Tavern, VT, 85-86
    at Savannah Inn, DE, 335
    at Whistling Swan Inn, NJ, 281-282
Antique shops
    in New Jersey Highlands, 284
    in Vermont, 96
    at Spring Garden B & B, Laurel, DE, 340, 341, 342
Appalachia Journal, 68
Appalachian Mountain Club (AMC), 10, 67
    Carter Notch Hut (illustration), 63
    cooperative stewardship, 61
    huts in New Hampshire, 62-64
    Mohican Outdoor Center, NJ, 4, 286
    Ponkapoag Camp, MA, 141
    publications by, 68
    trail network, 64, 65
Appalachian Trail
    in Massachusetts, 105, 107-109
    in New Hampshire, 61
    in New Jersey, 286

Blueberry Mountain Inn,
  Blakeslee, PA, 241-245
  antiques, 243, 244
  canoeing, 245
  photo, 241
  plant communities, 241, 245
  rhodora at, 245, 246
    (illustration)
  wildlife viewing, 245
Blue Heron Farm, Charlemont,
  MA, 117-121
  birdwatching, 121
  horses and goats, 120, 121
  maple syrup production,
    117, 121
  natural pest control, 120-121
  sugarhouse, 117 (illustration),
    119
Boats and boating. *See also*
  Canoeing; Kayaking
  access to Rose Island
    Lighthouse, RI, 152
  Chesapeake Bay, 337
  Delaware, 335
  mail boats, 19, 20, 196
  in New Jersey Highlands,
    284, 286
Bocce, 47, 161
Borie, Louis, 69
Boston and Boston Harbor area,
  MA, 127
  Blue Hills Reservation, 140
  Blue Hills Trailside Museum,
    140
  Boston Marathon, 134
  Copley Square, Boston, 138
  Drumlin Farms Education
    Center, 240
  Friends of the Boston Harbor
    Islands, 142
  Harbor Islands, 134
  map of, 128
  Museum of Fine Arts, 133
  National Recreation Area, 139

New England Aquarium,
  133, 139
Public Garden and Boston
  Commons, 138
subway system, 132, 137
Trinity Church, 138
The Bottom Line of Green Is Black,
  127, 143
Boughton, Jestena, landscape
  architect, owner of
  Colony Hotel, ME, 41, 46
Bowling, 194, 220
Buck, W. W., author, 218
Bucks County, PA, 255-264
  map of northern, 256
Burgess, Larry E., author, 226
Burke, Jeffrey, co-owner,
    The Keeper's House, ME,
    15, 17, 19, 32
Burke, Judi, co-owner, The Keeper's
    House, ME, 19, 22
Burns, Deborah E., author, 125
Business travelers
  at The Benjamin, NYC, 231
  at Celie's Waterfront B & B,
    Baltimore, 312-313
  at Park Ridge at Valley Forge,
    King of Prussia, PA,
    267-271
  at Whistling Swan Inn,
    Stanhope, NJ, 279-285
**Butterbrooke Bed and
  Breakfast**, CT, 169-173
  antique furnishings, 171
  as earth-sheltered dwelling,
    169
  illustration, 169
  organic gardening, 170,
    171-172
  passive solar heating, 169
Buttermilk Falls State Park, NY, 208
Butterworth, Tom, owner,
    Butterbrooke B & B, CT,
    169, 172 (photo), 173

Cabins, state park
Elk Neck State Park, MD, 330
Finger Lakes region, NY, 207-208
Nockamixon State Park, PA, 262-263
Camping, 3-4, 64, 141
Canoeing
in Adirondacks, 179, 183, 193, 196
in Evansburg State Park, PA, 273
in Poconos, 252
on Prime Hook Creek, DE, 344
in Rhode Island, 157, 161
in Shawangunk region, New York, 219
in Vermont, 75, 96
in White Mountains, NH, 59
Cape May, NJ, 289-304, 335
Bird Observatory, 296, 300, 302, 303
"diamonds," 301
fossils, 301
map of, 290
Nature Center, 303
Sunset Beach, 301
Victorian homes, 302
Wetlands Institute, 296, 303
Wings and Water Festival, 296
Carlson, Mary Ann and Wes, co-owners, West Mountain Inn, VT, 93
Carroll Villa Hotel, Cape May, NJ, 297-301
antique decor, 299
bicycling, 301
as historic structure, 300
horse-drawn carriages, 301
Mad Batter restaurant, 297, 299-300
photo, 301
recycled building materials, 300
Carson, Rachel, 33

Catskills Center for Conservation and Development, 225
CedarHeart Lodge, Rosendale, NY, 224-225
Celie's Waterfront B & B, Baltimore, 305, 311-316
energy conservation, 314-315
harbor setting of, 311, 312
recycling, 315
Central Park, NYC, 227, 233, 234, 238
Chalfonte, Cape May, NJ, 291-296
butterfly garden, 293
coloring books designed and printed at, 294
energy conservation, 295
herb garden, 293
preservation/renovation, 293, 294
work exchange program, 295
Cheese and cheese-making, 74, 75, 99
Chesapeake Almanac: Following the Bay Throughout the Seasons, 320
Chesapeake Bay, 321, 323, 324, 327, 337
Bowers Conference Center, 330
Elk Neck State Park, 330
Janes and Tangier Islands, 337
wildlife preserves, 329
Church, Frederic, landscape painter, 30
Cistern, at Rose Island Lighthouse, 153
Civilian Conservation Corps (CCC), as builders of Bascom Lodge, 107
Cleaning products, eco-friendly, 59, 124, 133, 244, 279, 283-284, 315
Clearwater Inc., Poughkeepsie, NY, 225-226

Coli, Bill and Norma, co-owners of Blue Heron Farm, 119-121

Collins, Beryl Robichaud, author, 304

Colony Hotel, Kennebunkport, ME, 41-48
coastal ecology, 47
Environmental Responsibility Program, 43-44, 47
herb gardens, 43
historic preservation, 39
landscape management, 46
recycling, 45, 46-47

Composting, 59, 120, 153, 161, 172, 218, 309, 325, 336
in AMC facilities, 59, 64
bear-resistant, 193

Composting toilet, at Saugerties Lighthouse, NY, 224

Concord, MA, 139
Great Meadows, 139
Museum, 139-140
Walden Pond, 138

Conference centers, 3-4
Bowers, MD, 330
Park Ridge at Valley Forge, 267-271
Rowe, MA, 123
Whispering Pines, RI, 157-162

Connecticut
Dinosaur State Park, 174
map of, 168
Naugatuck State Forest, 174
New Haven, 174, 175
Oxford, 174-175
Rocky Hill, 174

Connecticut Forest and Park Association, 175

Connecticut Walk Book, 175

"Consecration by Crow," 90

Conservation, 10, 51,198, 292.
See also Composting; Energy conservation; Land conservation; The Nature Conservancy; Recycling;

Solar; Water conservation
at Park Ridge at Valley Forge, 268, 270
in Pennsylvania and Poconos, 258, 254, 264, 268
at Shelburne Farms, VT, 73, 74, 75
at Stump Sprouts Lodge, MA, 114
in Vermont, 101, 102
West Mountain Inn program, VT, 92

Conservation Inns of Southwestern Vermont, 91

Conuel, Thomas, author, 143

Cookbooks
Folk and Fare, 95, 102
Kitchen with a View, 22, 23
Moosewood, 210
White Dog Café, 274

Cooper, Susan Fenimore, author, 119, 199

Copley Square Hotel, Boston, 129, 135-138
access by subway, 137
environmental programs, 129, 133
President's Gold Medal for Environmental Achievement, 136
recycled upholstery, 137
recycling, 137, 138

Cornucopia of Dorset, VT, 100-101

Crab, horseshoe, 33, 334, 337

Crafts
in Berkshires, MA, 122
at Colony Hotel gift shop, 45
in Delaware Water Gap National Recreation Area stores, 287
at Mohonk Mountain House, New York, 221
at Black Cat gift store, 274

Craignair Inn, ME, 31
organic garden, 31

Crawford, Suzanne (photo),
co-owner, Stump Sprouts
Lodge, MA, 111
Crawford, Lloyd, co-owner,
Stump Sprouts Lodge, MA,
111, 114, 115, 116
Crawford Hostel, NH, 61
(illustration), 63, 64
Croquet, 47, 75, 161, 193, 195, 220
Cross-country skiing
in Adirondacks, 197
in Bucks County, PA, 263
in Maine, 30, 39
in Massachusetts, 109, 111,
112, 113, 115
in New Hampshire, 60
in New Jersey, at Stevens
State Park, 284
in Poconos, 242, 245, 251
in Rhode Island, 161
in Shawangunk Mountains,
NY, 220
in Vermont, 88, 96

Delaware
bicycling, 340-342
Cape Henlopen State Park
Seaside Nature Center, 344
historic communities/districts
Bethel, 343
Laurel, 342
Lewes, 335, 336, 338
Lewes-Rehoboth Canal,
335, 336
map of southern, 332
Nanticoke Wildlife Area, 342
Partnership for the Delaware
Estuary, Inc., 345
Trap Pond State Park, 344
Delaware Bay, 335, 337, 344
Delaware Eco-Discoveries, 345-346
Delaware Canal State Park, 262
Delaware Water Gap National
Recreation Area, 281, 285,
286, 287, 288

DiLeonardo International, interior
designers, 232
Dining, 9. *See also* separate index,
Green Dining
Dryer lint, recycled, 45
Dunne, Peter, author, 304
Durant, William West, 192

Earth-friendly inns
definition of, 2
Mohonk Mountain House as
grandfather of, 213
suburban, 267
types of, 3-5
Earth-sheltered inn (illustration),
169
Eco-friendly hotels, 3
Eco-lodges, description, 4, 5
ECOTEL, definition, 5
Benjamin, NYC, 229, 230
Park Ridge at Valley Forge,
267, 268
Ecotourism
in Bucks County, PA, 262
events at Chalfonte, Cape May,
NJ, 296
standards, 5
The Ecotourism Society (TES),
5, 42, 44, 92, 292, 296
Education. *See also* Environmental
education
about farm animal rights, 203
science, at Shelburne Farms,
VT, 23
Elemental Drifts (Walt Whitman),
346
Elk Neck State Park, MD, 330
E-mail addresses for inns, 7
Endangered species, in Poconos,
241
Energy conservation, 44, 135, 131,
137, 232, 274, 283-284,
295, 314. *See also* Solar,
Windpower

Folk and visionary art, 141, 317, 342
Folk music, 78, 179
Foods, natural. *See* separate indexes for Green Dining and Provisions
Forgione, Larry, chef, 235
Friends of Acadia, 32
Friends of the Boston Harbor Islands, 142
Friends of Sagamore, 191
Full Moon Cafe, VT, 98

Galehead Hut, NH, 64
Gardening. *See also* Herb and herb gardening; Organic gardens
    community, for White Dog Café, Philadelphia, 274
    Pennsylvania Dutch foursquare, at Lightfarm B & B, 260
Garnet Hill Lodge, NY, 197
Geology
    of Berkshires, 104
    of Cape May area, 301
    of Champlain Basin, VT, 75
    drumlin field, Boston Harbor, 139
    exhibits of Adirondacks, 183
    Ell Pond, RI, as glacial kettlehole lake, 163
    of Finger Lakes, NY, 207
    garnets in Adirondacks, 197
    monadnocks, MA, 140
    of Penobscot Bay, ME, 25
    of Poconos, NY, 241
    of Shelburne Falls, MA, 122
    of Valley Forge, PA, 276
Goldberry's B & B, Williamstown, MA, 122
Golf, 47, 220, 271, 284
Goose Cove Lodge, Sunset, ME, 25-29
    astronomy, 29

Barred Island, 25, 26
    blueberries and organic produce, 27, 28
    birding, 28
    illustration, 27
    lobster bake, 27
    nature walks, 29
Grafton Conference Project, 87-88
Gramercy Mansion B & B, Stevenson, MD, 307-310
    antique furnishings, 309
    herb gardening, 309-310
    organic farm, 309
Great Works Regional Land Trust, ME, 39, 51
Green dining. *See* separate index: Green Dining
Green construction
    at Audubon Society hdqtrs., 238
    at Colony Hotel, 46-47, 49
    at Stump Sprouts Lodge, MA, 112
    at White Mountain Hostel, NH, 55, 57-58
Green Hotels Association, 6, 43, 44, 242, 248, 298
Greenleaf Hut, NH, 63-64
Green Mountain Club, 80
Green Mountain National Forest, 95-96, 98

Habitat, natural.
    See also Native plants
    in Bucks County, PA, 262
    in Maine, 24, 28, 46, 47
    at Mohonk Mountain House, NY, 214
    in Poconos, 241, 244, 245
    in Rhode Island, 159-160, 163
Hawks and hawk-watching
    in Cape May, NJ, area, 301
    in Central Park, NYC, 227
    in New Jersey Highlands, 286
Hawthorne, Nathaniel, author, 105

Herbicides. *See* Pest control
Herbs and herb gardening, organic
    in Connecticut, 174
    in Delaware, 342
    in Maine, 43, 46
    in Maryland, 308, 309, 319,
       323-327
    in New Jersey, 293
    in Pennsylvania, 247, 250
    in Rhode Island, 165
    in Vermont, 94
High Huts of the White Mountains,
    68
Hiking. *See also* Trails
    in Adirondacks, 179, 180,
       186, 196
    in Berkshires, 106, 108,
       109, 116
    in Connecticut, 174, 175
    in Finger Lakes region, 205
    at Gramercy Mansion, MD,
       310
    Greylock Ramble, 110
    guide by Keystone Trails
       Association, PA, 276
    in Maine, 23, 29, 30, 49
    in Poconos, 251, 254
    in Rhode Island, 161, 163-164
    in Shawangunk Mountains,
       NY, 211, 219, 222
    in Valley Forge National
       Historic Park, PA, 271, 272
    in Vermont, 75, 80, 93, 95-96
    in White Mountains, NH,
       60, 61, 64, 66, 68
Hiking Guide to the Delaware Water
    Gap National Recreation
    Area, 288
Hill Farm Inn, Arlington, VT, 101
Historic districts
    Fell's Point, MD, 311-316
    Laurel, DE, 342
    Lewes, DE, 335
Historic architecture
    at Butterbrooke B & B, CT, 170

    at Copley Square, MA, 138
    at Sagamore, NY, 190
    at Settlers Inn, PA, 248-249
    of Spring Garden B & B, DE,
       341
    of Vermont, 73, 84, 85-86,
       88, 100
    at Weisel Hostel, PA, 263
Historic Hotels of America, 84,
    214, 226
Historic preservation/renovation.
    See also Architcture
    at Chalfonte, NJ, 292, 294
    at Colony Hotel, ME, 42, 47
    at The Copley Square Hotel,
       Boston,135
    Fell's Point, Baltimore, 315
    at Gramercy B & B, MD, 309
    at The Lenox Hotel, Boston,
       131
    at Lightfarm B & B, PA,
       258, 259
    at Mohonk Mountain House,
       New Paltz, NY, 214
    at Rose Island Lighthouse, RI,
       147
    at Spring Garden B & B, DE,
       340
    at Shelburne Farms, VT, 73
    at Whistling Swan Inn, NJ, 280
Horses. *See also* Equestrian activity
    Fjords, at Blue Heron Farm,
       MA, 120
    Mohonk Mountain House, NY,
       220
    at Tatnic B & B, ME, 39
    Valley Forge National Historic
       Park, PA, 272
Horseshoe crab, 333, 334
    (illustration), 337
Horseshoes, 47, 162, 220
Hostel(s), 4, 6
    Crawford, NH, 61 (illustration),
       63

access to, by mailboat, 19-20
biking, 23
candlelight dinners, 23
hiking, 23, 24
island setting, 18, 19
organic garden, 23
photo, 17
Kellogg, Dr. John Harvey, 226
Keyarts, Eugene, author, 175
Kirschenbaum, Howard,
    author, 198
Kitchen with a View (cookbook), 23

Lakeside setting
    Adirondak Loj, 183
    Mohonk Mountain House, NY,
        213, 215
    Sagamore, NY, 191
    Shelburne Farms, VT, 75
    Whispering Pines Conference
        Center, RI, 158, 159
Land conservation/preservation
    in Bucks County, PA, 258,
        260, 264
    in Maine, 38-39, 51
    in Poconos, 241
    in southern Vermont, 81, 91
    by Vermont Land Trust,
        101-102
Landscape architects
    Boughton, Jestena, 41, 46
    Olmsted, Frederick Law,
        73, 140, 234
Laudholm Trust, ME, 51
League of New Hampshire
    Craftsmen, 67
Leahy, Christopher, author, 143
The Lenox Hotel, Boston,
    129-134
    cleaning products, 133
    employee training, 131
    historic restoration and
        furnishings, 132
    illustration, 129
    Presidential Gold Medal for

Conservation, 130
    recycling, 138
    water and energy conservation,
        131, 133
Lightfarm B & B, Kintnersville,
    PA, 257-261
    antique furnishings, 259
    archaeological work at,
        257, 259
    foursquare garden, 260
    illustrations, 257, 258, 259
    mayapples, 261
    Pennsylvania Dutch breakfasts,
        260
    redware, 259
    Significant Natural Areas
        Preservation Program, 260
Lighthouses
    Keeper's House, ME, 17-24
    Rose Island, RI, 147-156
    Saugerties, NY, 224
Llamas, 92, 93
Lodges, 5
    Adirondak Loj, NY, 179-184
    Bascom Lodge, MA, 106-110
    CedarHeart Lodge, NY, 224-225
    Garnet Hill, NY, 197
    Goose Cove Lodge, ME, 25-29
    Joe Dodge Lodge at Pinkham
        Notch, NH, 63
    Johns Brook, NY, 185-188
    Stump Sprouts Guest Lodge,
        MA, 111-116
    White Mountain Region, NH,
        61
Logging, sustainable, 37, 107,
    113, 114
Lonesome Lake Hut, NH, 64

Mailboat
    to Keeper's Inn, ME, 19, 20
    Raquette Lake, NY, 196
Maine
    Acadia National Park, 23, 30
    Blue Hill, 19

Mount Greylock, MA, 105, 107,
109, 110, 125
Mount Washington, NH, 66, 67
Mulay, Joe, co-owner, Whistling
Swan Inn, Stanhope, NJ,
279, 283, 284
Music, 75, 78, 100, 109, 179,
222, 296

Narragansett Bay National
Estuarine Research
Reserve, 163
National Audubon Society,
see Audubon Society
National Center for Environmental
Education, RI, 159, 160
National Historic Landmarks, 11,
190, 215, 294, 300. *See also*
National Register of
Historic Places
National Park Service, 80
guide to Poconos, 254
National Register of Historic Places,
73, 148, 287, 341
National Trust for Historic
Preservation, 11, 214, 226
National Wildlife Federation, 46
Native plants, 28, 46, 85, 241, 145,
271, 344. *See also* Habitat,
natural
Natural foods. *See* separate index:
Provisions
Natural ventilation, 38, 114,
137, 295
Nature reserves, RI, 160, 163
The Nature Conservancy,
241, 254, 300
The Nature of Massachusetts, 143
Nature programs, 106, 108, 197,
222, 263, 334, 344
Nature walks/tours, 11. *See also*
Hiking.
Delaware, 345
at Goose Cove Lodge, ME,
26, 28, 29

at Mohonk Mountain House,
NY, 218
at Sagamore, NY, 194
showshoe, 197

New Hampshire
Concord, 68
Conway, 56, 57
Franconia Notch State Park, 64
map of, 54
North Conway, 66, 67
Pinkham Notch, 62-65
Plymouth, 67
White Mountains, 59-60, 65
New Hampshire Guidebook, 67
New Jersey
Cape May (map), 290
Lake Musconetcong, 284
Stanhope, 281, 282
Stevens State Park, 284
New Jersey Highlands and
Delaware Water Gap
National Recreation Area,
281, 285, 286
map of, 278
Mohican Outdoor Center,
Blairstown, 286
mountain laurel in, 285
rhododendrons in, 186
New York. *See also* Adirondacks;
Shawangunk Mts.,
New York City
Adirondack Park, 196
Blue Mountain Lake, 196
Cayuga Lake State Park,
207, 208
Fillmore Glen State Park, 208
Hudson River Valley, 211, 216,
219, 225
Keene Valley, 185
Mohonk Lake, 213, 215, 221
Robert H. Treman State Park,
Ithaca, 208
State park system, 207

Earth-Friendly Inns: Northeast

Taughannock Falls State Park, 207, 208
Watkins Glen, 203
Watkins Glen State Park, 207
New York City
Cathedral Church of St. John the Divine, 234-235
Central Park, 140, 227, 233, 234
Green Apple Map, 238
Jamaica Bay Wildlife Refuge, 234
map of Manhattan Island, 228
restaurants, 235-237
New York, Naturally, A Resource Guide for Natural Living in New York, 238
New York-New Jersey Trail Conference, 288
New York State Guide to Farm Fresh Products, 223
Nockamixon State Park, family cabins at, 262-263
Nonprofit organizations/inns, 3, 5. *See also* names of individual organizations
Norman Bird Sanctuary, RI, 163
North, Gwen, innkeeper of Spring Garden B & B, Laurel, DE, 339, 341
Northeast Organic Farming Association, 165-166

Official Map and Guide for the Upper Delaware Scenic and Recreation River, 254
O'Keeffe, Georgia, artist, 229
Old Tavern, Grafton, VT, 83-89
dining room, 87
cross-country skiing, 88
equestrian activities, 88
historic setting, 83, 85-86, 87
garden, 86 (photo)
greenhouse, 87
Phelps Barn lounge, 87

wildlife, 85
works by Audubon, 85
Olmsted, Frederick Law, 73, 234
National Historic Site, 140
Open space preservation
Bucks County, PA, 264
Shelburne Farms, VT, 71
Valley Forge National Historic Park, 272
Vermont Land Trust, 101-102
Organic agriculture. *See* Agriculture, sustainable.
Organic wine, 12, 50
Organic gardening and farming. *See also* Herb gardens and gardening
in Berkshires, 114, 118
at Butterbrooke B & B, CT, 171
in Delaware, 342
at Gramercy Mansion B & B, MD, 307
in Maine, 23, 28, 31, 36, 37, 38, 43
in Massachusetts, 93, 124, 140
in New York state (guidebook), 223, and New York City, 235
at Rodale Institute Research Center, PA, 263
in Shawangunks, NY, 223
in Vermont, 87, 93, 98
at Woodvale Farm, RI, 160
Organic pest control, 44, 46, 120-121
Orton, Lyman, 81

Parisi, Dom and Joanne, owners, Goose Cove Lodge, 27
Park Ridge at Valley Forge, PA, 267-271
air and water purification systems, 269
conference center, 269
ECOTEL certification, 267
"green rooms", 269

Smiley family, 213, 219, 226
Smiley, Virginia, 211
Smith, Jane, co-owner,
    Tatnic B&B, ME, 35, 37
Smith, Tin, co-owner,
    Tatnic B&B, ME, 37, 38, 39
Snowshoeing
    in Adirondacks, 183, 197
    in Berkshires, MA, 109, 115
    at Mohonk Mountain House,
        NY, 220
    in Rhode Island, 161
    in Vermont, 88, 96
    in White Mountains, NH, 60
Snow tubing
    at Mohonk Mountain House,
        NY, 220
    in White Mountains, NH, 60
Society for Protection of
    New Hampshire Forests, 68
Solar, 10
    cats, 243
    domestic hot water, 38, 49,
        114, 153, 186, 187
    greenhouse, 49
    hot tub, 57
    passive, 35, 36, 37, 68, 169
    photovoltaic electricity,
        22, 153
Sounds of the Land, 321, 328,
    330, 331
Sow's Ear Winery, ME, 32
Spas, 4
Specimen Days and Collect
    (Walt Whitman), 277
Spring Garden B&B, Laurel, DE,
    339-343
    antiques, 341, 342
    bicycling, 339, 340, 341, 342
    canoeing, 343
    restoration, 341
Stafursky, Susan and Richard,
    co-owners, Savannah Inn,
    DE, 335, 336, 337
Stevens, Lauren, author, 125

Storm King Mountain, NY, 222
The Story of Sagamore, 198
Stubbs, Ann, co-owner, Sinking
    Springs Herb Farm, MD,
    323, 325, 326
Stubbs, William R., co-owner,
    Sinking Springs Herb Farm,
    MD, 321, 323, 325, 326,
    328, 330, 331
Stump Sprouts Guest Lodge,
    Hawley, MA, 111-116
    barn and silo (photo), 114
    cross-country skiing, 111, 113,
        115
    hiking, 116
    ice croquet, 115
    organic garden, 111 (photo),
        114
    passive solar, 114
    solar domestic hot water, 114
    sustainable logging, 113, 114
    wood-fired sauna, 115
Surfing, in southern Maine, 39
Sustainable agriculture, 71, 140, 238
Sustainable architecture, 238
Sustainable construction, 56
Sustainable logging, 37, 107,
    113, 114
Sustainable rural development,
    in southern Vermont, 83
Sustainable living, at Rose Island
    Lighthouse, RI, 148
Sustainable Living Centers,
    6, 235, 273
Swimming beaches, 47, 75,
    108, 337, 161, 183, 208,
    284, 286

Tatnic B&B, Wells, ME, 10, 35-40
    horses (illustration), 39
    land conservation, 38-39
    organic farming, 37-38, 39
    quilting lessons, 35 (photo),
        36, 37
    solar heating, 37, 38

Tanglewood Music Festival, 109
Taughannock Falls State Park,
    Ithaca, NY, 207, 208
Tennis, 75, 89, 161, 193, 220,
    267, 310
Thoreau, Henry David, 53, 67, 103,
    139-140, 255, 265. *See also*
    Walden Pond
Thoreau Institute, 143
Thoreau Society, 143
Tidepools, at Colony, ME, 47
Tombolos, 25
Trail(s)
    in Adirondacks, 183, 188, 194
    Appalachian, 61, 77, 96,
        107, 109
    in Berkshires, 115
    at Blue Hills Reservation, MA,
        140
    in Chesapeake Bay area, 330
    Finger Lakes, NY, 205
    at Gramercy Mansion, MD, 310
    Horseshoe, in Philadelphia
        area, 272
    around Narragansett Bay, RI,
        163
    in Pennsylvania, 276
    in Poconos, 244, 254
    in Shawangunks, 222
    in Vermont, 75, 77
    White Mountains, NH, 64, 68
Trail maintenance education, 109
Trailmaster mapping software for
    hikers, 80

Ujjala's B&B, New Paltz, NY,
    223-224
    longhouse sanctuary, 223-224
    rock climbing, 224
    vegetarian breakfasts, 224
United Nations Environment
    Programme, 214-215
"Urania," 239
U.S. Backyard Wildlife Habitat, 46

U.S. Environmental Protection
    Agency, 5, 267
U.S. Forest Service, 61, 80

Valley Forge National Historic
    Park, PA, 271, 273
    biking, 272
    bridle paths, 171
    Environmental Center, 272
    geologic guide and map, 276
Vaux, Calvert, 234
Vegan food. *See also* Vegetarian
    cookbooks featuring, 210
    in Denville, NJ, 287
    at Farm Sanctuary, NY, 204, 206
    in Maine, 50
    in Newark, DE, 329-330
    in New York City, 236, 237
    in Rhode Island, 164
    in Shawangunks, NY, 222
    in Watkins Glen, NY, 209
Vegetarian food
    in Adirondacks, 183, 193, 197
    in Baltimore area, 317-319
    at Butterbrooke B&B, CT, 171
    at Chalfonte, Cape May, NJ,
        294, 300
    in Chesapeake Bay area, 329
    cookbooks featuring, 210
    at Gramercy Mansion, MD, 310
    in Maine, 23, 28, 31, 43, 50
    in Massachusetts, 108, 123,
        124, 141
    in New Jersey Highlands,
        282, 287
    in New York City, 236, 237
    in Pennsylvania, 244, 260, 274
    in Rhode Island, 159, 164
    at Savannah Inn, 334, 336
    in Shawangunks, NY, 213, 222
    at Sinking Springs Herb Farm,
        MD, 325
    at Spring Garden B&B, DE, 342
    in Vermont, 73-74, 94
Vegetarian Times, 202

Vermont, northern, 69-80
    Burlington, 73, 77, 78-79
    Green Mountains, 77
    Killington, 78
    Lake Champlain, 72, 75, 77
    Long Trail, 80
    map of, 70
    Montpelier, 79
    Waterbury, 78
Vermont, southern, 81-102
    Arlington, 93, 101
    Battenkill River, 93, 95, 101
    Brattleboro, 98, 99
    Dorset, 100-101
    Grafton, 83-88, 99, 102
    Green Mountain National
        Forest, 98
    Manchester, 96
    map of, 82
    South Strafford, 98
    Vermont Country Store, 81
    Woodstock, 102
Vermont, University of, 85
Vermont Fresh Network, 94
Vermont Institute of Natural
        Science, 102
Vermont Land Trust, 101-102
Vermont Mozart Festival
        Orchestra, 75
Vermont Raptor Center, 102
Vermont Renaissance, 102
Volleyball, 59, 161, 193

Walden Pond, MA, 138, 140.
    See also Thoreau
Walden Woods Project, 143
Waldon, Dr. Ralph, 27
Walking. *See* Hiking
Walks and Rambles in Rhode Island,
        166
*Walks and Rambles in the Upper
        Connecticut Valley*, 68
Waste management, 10
    at Benjamin, NYC, 229, 232
    at Colony Hotel, Maine, 45

    at The Copley Square Hotel,
        Boston, 135
    at The Lenox Hotel, Boston, 133
    at Park Ridge at Valley Forge,
        PA, 270
Water conservation
    at The Copley Square Hotel,
        Boston, 135
    at Johns Brook Lodge, NY, 187
    at The Keeper's House, ME, 22
    at The Lenox Hotel, 131, 133
    at Park Ridge at Valley Forge,
        PA, 270
    at Rose Island Lighthouse,
        RI, 153
    at Shelburne Farms, VT, 73
    at White Mountain Hostel,
        NH, 59
Water pollution control, at
        Shelburne Farms, VT, 73.
    See also Water conservation
Waterfalls, in Finger Lakes District,
        NY, 207, 208
Waterfalls of New Hampshire, 68
Webb, Lila Vanderbilt, and
        William Seward, 73
Weber, Ken, 166
Web sites, as book feature, 7
Weisel Hostel, PA, 263
Wells National Estuarine Research
        Reserve, ME, 39, 49, 51
West Mountain Inn, Arlington,
        VT, 91-97
    conservation programs, 93
    Creative Cuisine Program, 94
    furnishings including local
        artwork and pottery , 93
    herb garden, 94
    llamas, 92, 93
wildlife events, 91
Whale watching
    in Cape May area, 301
    in Chesapeake Bay area, 337
    in Maine, 48

INDEX TO GREEN DINING

INDEX TO PROVISIONS
Organic Produce and Natural Foods

CHELSEA GREEN

Sustainable living has many facets. Chelsea Green's celebration of the sustainable arts has led us to publish trend-setting books about organic gardening, solar electricity and renewable energy, innovative building techniques, regenerative forestry, local and bioregional democracy, and whole foods. The company's published works, while intensely practical, are also entertaining and inspirational, demonstrating that an ecological approach to life is consistent with producing beautiful, eloquent, and useful books, videos, and audio cassettes.

For more information about Chelsea Green, or to request a free catalog, call toll-free (800) 639-4099, or write to us at P.O. Box 428, White River Junction, Vermont 05001. Visit our Web site at www.chelseagreen.com.

Chelsea Green's titles include:

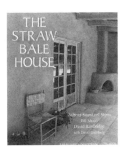  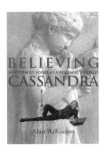

The Straw Bale House
The New Independent Home
Independent Builder:
    Designing & Building a
    House Your own Way
The Rammed Earth House
The Passive Solar House
The Sauna
Wind Power for Home &
    Business
Wind Energy Basics
A Shelter Sketchbook
Mortgage-Free!
Hammer. Nail. Wood.
The Earth-Sheltered House
Solar Living Sourcebook
Stone Circles

Four-Season Harvest
The Apple Grower
The Flower Farmer
Passport to Gardening:
    A Sourcebook for the
    21st-Century
The New Organic Grower
Solar Gardening
Straight-Ahead Organic
The Contrary Farmer
The Contrary Farmer's
    Invitation to Gardening
Good Spirits
Whole Foods Companion
Simple Food for the
    Good Life
Keeping Food Fresh

Believing Cassandra:
    An Optimist Looks at a
    Pessimist's World
Gaviotas
Who Owns the Sun?
Global Spin:
    The Corporate Assault
    on Environmentalism
Hemp Horizons
Renewables are Ready
Beyond the Limits
Loving and Leaving the
    Good Life
The Man Who Planted Trees
The Northern Forest
Genetic Engineering, Food
    and our Environment

THE AUTHOR

Dennis Dahlin is a landscape architect and environmental consultant specializing in earth-friendly planning and design. His professional background spans twenty-five years of environmental writing, research, and design in the United States, Europe, and Latin America. Along with authoring many articles and technical publications, he has served as contributing writer for The Energy Primer.

Design credits include a solar home that has been featured in national magazines, an award-winning restoration plan for a Victorian garden, and numerous other projects.

He is past president of a Habitat for Humanity affiliate, and he currently serves on the board of El Porvenir, a nonprofit organization working with villagers on water projects and appropriate technology in Central America. After living in the Midwest, Northeast, and Pacific Northwest, he now resides in a Northern California cohousing community, taking time now and then to continue his quest for the perfect canoe trip.